Richard and Marilyn Preston
4923 Shetlan
Tampa, FL. 33615
813-886-4628

It is *completely false* that churches must sacrifice quality to get quantity, must artificially choose between evangelism and discipleship, or cannot have depth and growth at the same time. *That's nonsense!* In fact, quality attracts quantity, and genuinely transformed people always cause many more to come to Christ! Few prove this fact better than the ministry of my dear friend Andy Stanley, who has grown North Point Community Church *on purpose* and *with passion.* No Christian leader can afford to miss this book.

—Rick Warren, pastor, Saddleback Church;
author, *The Purpose Driven Life*

All of us admire what Andy has achieved at North Point, but few of us appreciate the price he had to pay along the way. *Deep and Wide* pulls back the curtain for all of us to see what is required behind the scenes to build a prevailing church. I was both challenged and inspired by the book.

—Bill Hybels, founding and senior pastor
of Willow Creek Community Church

Couldn't be prouder of my son, Andy. And I couldn't be more excited about the content of this book. I wish a resource like this existed when I was starting out in the ministry.

—Dr. Charles Stanley, founder of In Touch Ministries

The most common question I get from pastors is, "How do I get the people in my church to be open to change?" From now on, my answer will be, "Read *Deep and Wide* by Andy Stanley. Thanks, Andy. Great book!

—Craig Groeschel, pastor of LifeChurch.tv and author of
It: How Churches and Leaders Get It and Keep It

Andy Stanley is on the front lines of a major shift in how both Christians and non-Christians experience "church" in America. In *Deep and Wide*, Andy opens up his playbook for how North Point Community Church grew into one of the nation's most effective churches, openly shares their victories and failures, and shows you how to take your own church deeper in the Word and wider in appeal. This is a peek behind the curtain that you do not want to miss!

—Dave Ramsey, *New York Times* bestselling author
and nationally syndicated radio show host

No one has given me more practical handles for establishing a focused vision than Andy Stanley. *Deep and Wide* is a rich resource to help all of us stay intentional about the main thing—building a church that reaches people who are far from God.

—Steven Furtick, lead pastor, Elevation Church

Deep and Wide should come with a warning label. You will never view your local church the same way again!

—Perry Noble, senior pastor of NewSpring Church

Deep and Wide, out of its sheer honesty and candor, may well drive you to experience what I experienced: behind the scenes of churches we find the reality of sin, the difficulty of human relationships, and the sheer magnitude of God's marvelous grace in using sinners like you and me to display the marvels of Jesus Christ to our world.

—Scot McKnight, author of *The King Jesus Gospel* and *The Jesus Creed*

Throughout these pages you get a sense that Andy has been writing this book most of his life. That's because he has. This book invites you behind the scenes into Andy's personal journey to build a team and church that take the Great Commission seriously.

—Reggie Joiner, founder and CEO, Orange

Liz and I center our week around attending Buckhead Church. The experience is energizing, carries beyond Sunday, and connects the profound with the practical, the inspiration with the action. Andy and his team have created something powerful that is worth studying and understanding.

—Frank Blake, chairman and CEO, The Home Depot

In *Deep and Wide*, Andy shows a transparency that is refreshing and a generosity of spirit that compels him to want to share everything he's learned with everyone who wants to know. What you'll find is not a clever or crafty plan, rather a falling into greatness born out of clarity of purpose and willingness to change. Trust me, there's something to be learned by every leader, pastor, and church planter from the extraordinary and history-shaping journey Andy is on!

—Louie Giglio, friend of Andy's for a long, long time

My family and I love North Point Community Church. Once you've read *Deep and Wide*, you'll understand why.

—Jeff Foxworthy, comedian and actor

Creating Churches Unchurched People
Love to Attend

DEEP

WIDE

ANDY STANLEY

ZONDERVAN.com/
AUTHORTRACKER
follow your favorite authors

ZONDERVAN

Deep and Wide
Copyright © 2012 by Andy Stanley

This title is also available as a Zondervan ebook. Visit www.zondervan.com/ebooks.

This title is also available in a Zondervan audio edition. Visit www.zondervan.fm.

Requests for information should be addressed to:

Zondervan, *Grand Rapids, Michigan* 49530

Library of Congress Cataloging-in-Publication Data
  Stanley, Andy.
    Deep and wide : creating churches unchurched people love to attend / Andy
  Stanley.
      p. cm.
    ISBN 978-0-310-49484-3 (hardcover)
    1. Hospitality—Religious aspects—Christianity. 2. Non-church-affiliated
  people. 3. Church marketing. I. Title. II. Title: Deep and wide.
  BV4647.H67S73 2012
  253—dc23   2012013282

Cover design: *Ron Huizinga*
Interior design: *Matthew Van Zomeren*

Printed in the United States of America

13 14 15 16 17 18 19 /DCI/ 25 24 23 22 21 20 19 18 17 16 15 14 13 12 11 10 9 8

Deep and Wide
is dedicated to the 708 charter members
of North Point Community Church
(see Appendix E for names).

Who would have thought?
Thank you!

Andy

CONTENTS

Acknowledgments

Books are often credited to individual authors, but no book is the product of individual effort. This book is certainly no exception. *Deep and Wide* reflects the work, creativity, and generosity of thousands of men, women, and children who took a chance on a dream and made it come true. At the point of the spear is a group of dear friends who literally risked their careers to create the content of this book. I'll be forever grateful to Julie Arnold, Rick Holliday, Reggie Joiner, Lane Jones, Bill Willits, and Kevin Ragsdale for leaving perfectly good jobs with predictable paychecks to embrace an idea that had no guaranteed outcome.

On the production side, this project would have never gotten off the ground without the tireless efforts of my agent, Suzy Gray. Suzy, thank you for riding herd on the details. Thank you for reading, rereading, and then reading again. Your commitment to quality and clarity is reflected in the finished product. When I wanted to be *done*, you wanted it to be *better*. Thanks to you, it is.

To John Raymond at Zondervan, thank you for the personal interest you expressed in this book early on. It was your passion for this content that convinced us that

Zondervan was, in fact, our best opportunity for getting our message to church leaders around the world. Thank you for partnering with me.

To my assistant of more than thirteen years, Diane Grant, thank you for handling all the stuff I don't even know to thank you for because you decided I didn't need to know! That's what you do best. It's no mystery as to why so many pastors send their assistants to sit at your feet to learn. You were instrumental in creating the margin necessary to the writing and development of this book.

As you are about to discover, this book reflects a personal journey of sorts. A journey I would have never and could have never taken without the support, inspiration, and encouragement of my best friend for life, Sandra. There are no words. So I won't even try. Thank you. I love you with all my heart.

INTRODUCTION

Blessed is the man who gets the opportunity to devote his life to something bigger than himself and who finds himself surrounded by friends who share his passion. In this way, I have been disproportionately blessed.

This is a book about creating churches that unchurched men, women, and children love to attend. Specifically, this is a book about how some friends and I have gone about creating those kinds of churches. This isn't all there is to know on the subject. This is just all *we* know. As leaders, we are never responsible for filling anyone else's cup. Our responsibility is to empty ours. So for the next three hundred-plus pages, I'm going to pour out every drop on the subject of creating churches unchurched people love to attend.

Before we dive into the content, however, there is something you should know about me. I'm not enamored with big. I've always attended and worked in big churches. In elementary school our family attended a large church in Miami, Florida. During middle school and high school, I attended the largest church in Atlanta. During graduate school, I interned at one of the largest churches in Texas. Texas! Besides that, I'm a preacher's kid (PK). It takes a lot to impress us preachers' kids. If you are a PK, you know exactly what I mean.

Preachers' kids who gravitate toward ministry are commodities. I hire all I can. We see church differently than everybody else. We see it all from the inside out. We know that when people say they "felt the Spirit moving," it probably means the room was full and the music was good. We know that what goes on at home is *the* litmus test of a man or woman's walk with God, not how well he or she does once a microphone is strapped on. We know the difference between giftedness and godliness. We know the two can be mutually exclusive. We know that the best performers usually build the biggest churches but not necessarily the healthiest ones. We aren't impressed with moving lights, slick presentations, "God told me," "the Spirit led me," or long prayers. Heck, all the men I've known who impressed everybody with their long, animated, public prayers had moral problems. That's why I pray short prayers. I'm afraid there might be a correlation. Actually, I think Jesus said something about that. So this isn't a book about how to make your church *bigger*. You don't need me for that. If bigger is your goal, just start promising things in Jesus' name. Religious people love that stuff.

This is a book about how to make your church more appealing to the people who are put off by all the shenanigans that give church, big churches in particular, a bad name — people who know there's more to life than this life but who can't imagine that the church holds any clues. And in case you are wondering, yes, I think every church should be a church irreligious people love to attend. Why? Because the church is the local expression of the presence of Jesus. We are his body. And since people who were nothing like Jesus liked Jesus, people who are nothing like Jesus should like us as well. There should be something about us that causes them to gather at the periphery and stare.

I'm often asked if I'm surprised at how big North Point has grown. When it's church leaders who ask, I assure them I'm not. Here's why. When we launched North Point, every other church in Atlanta was competing for the churched people market. We decided to get into the unchurched people market. That's a much larger market and we didn't have any competition at the time. If somebody liked our brand, we were the only option. If somebody wanted to bring an unchurched friend or family member to church, we were the logical destination. We weren't any better than the other churches in town. We were just the only church designed from the ground up to capture the imaginations of unchurched people. Let's face it, if you have the only hot dog stand in town, your hot dogs don't have to be that good.

As I will discuss in detail later, our ongoing challenge is to make sure we *stay* in the unchurched people market. That's not easy. Now that we're so big, it's not even necessary. Who would know? Who would care? Truth is, only our core would know. But we would all quit if we thought that staying meant spending the rest of our productive lives running a big church rather than making a big difference.

FACT FINDING

As you will discover, we are a bit paranoid about the prospect of unintentionally becoming a church for churched people. So we are constantly looking for ways to discover who's coming, who invited them, who's sticking, and who's not. Like you, we love stories. But anecdotal evidence is hardly evidence. You've been around the local church long enough to know that you can find a story to support just about any idea. Even bad ideas. Especially bad ideas. So while we celebrate stories of life change, we continue to look for ways to gather hard data on whether we really are a church unchurched people in our various communities love to attend.

Fortunately for us, there is a gentleman in our church, Brian Kaznova, who has helped us tremendously in this area. For the past several years, Brian has invested in our organization by designing surveys and then providing objective analysis and recommendations based on the findings. Brian has extensive experience with private corporations consulting on performance and organizational excellence. Several of the companies he's worked with were winners of the Malcolm Baldrige Award.[1] One of the tools Brian created for us is a survey we distribute two or three times a year in our weekend services. Appendix A contains the actual survey card we use as well as a sampling of how the results are tallied. The magic of this particular tool is that it allows us to capture information from both regular attendees and those who have attended five times or less.

According to our survey, 40 percent of the regular attendees in our adult worship environments describe themselves as unchurched before they began attending our church (we define *unchurched* as not having attended a church for five years or longer). On any given weekend, 10 percent of our adult audiences identify themselves as guests (a *guest* being someone who has attended five times or less). Over 40 percent of that group identify themselves as unchurched as well. One of the things we are most interested in is how easy we are making it for our attendees to invite guests. Over 83 percent of our regular attendees marked that they have invited at least one person to church in the past twelve months. The satisfaction level always hovers around the 97 percent range with both regular attendees and guests. According to Brian, our responses are three to four times the numbers necessary to get an accurate read.

Why am I telling you this? Well, I told my publisher that the introduction would include at least two thousand words and I needed some filler. No, I'm telling you this because I want you to know our energy really isn't around big. We genuinely want to be a network of churches that unchurched people find irresistible. We don't grade ourselves on size. We grade ourselves on how attractive we are to our target audience. Now, before you go getting all theological on me and writing us off as a dog-and-pony show, take note:

> We are a church. Our goal isn't to create an *event* unchurched people love to attend. We are creating *churches.*

One last thing about me: I don't consider myself a church planter. As I will describe in chapter two, North Point Community Church launched in the wake of a high-profile divorce and a church split. Not a very scalable model and certainly not something I would recommend. But that's how it all began. Apart from being shoved out of my comfort zone, I'm not sure I would have ever fully engaged in what my heart was telling me I needed to do. Because of that, I have never been tempted to take credit for what we have achieved. I'm often asked how I stay humble. That's a curious question. If in fact I'm humble, it is due in large part to the fact that none of this was my idea. As you are about to discover, most of what has happened, happened in spite of me, not because of me.

BITS AND PIECES

Deep and Wide is organized into five sections. Feel free to skip around. However, if you've ever considered hiring one of your kids, **Section One** is a must read. There I describe growing up as a PK, working for my dad for ten years, and then quitting at the most inopportune time imaginable. This section contains a good bit of detail about my family and my relationship to my dad in particular. So much so, I knew I would have to get his permission to publish it. Instead of sending it to him to read, I drove over to his house, sat at the kitchen table, and read it to him. We laughed. We cried. Then we cried some more. As you will see, the fact that he would even allow me to tell our story makes him the hero.

In **Section Two** I give the biblical justification for our approach to church. From day one, I've had critics. I'm fine with that. All my critics are religious people. (It may be the only thing I have in common with Jesus.) We are unapologetically attractional. In our search for common ground with unchurched people, we've discovered that, like us, they are consumers. So we leverage their consumer instincts. By the way, if your church has heating and air conditioning, you do too. When you read the Gospels, it's hard to overlook the fact that Jesus *attracted* large crowds everywhere he went. He was constantly playing to the consumer instincts of his crowds. Let's face it: It wasn't the content of his messages that appealed to the masses. Most of the time they didn't even understand what he was talking about. Heck, *we're* not always sure what he was talking about. People flocked to Jesus because he *fed* them, *healed* them, *comforted* them, and *promised* them things. Besides, what's the opposite of attractional? Missional? I don't think so.

Section Three is the deep part. In this section I reveal our secret sauce. And it has nothing to do with stage sets and jump backs. I explain and illustrate our spiritual formation model. In the old days we would call it a discipleship model. Everything we do programmatically points people to or engages people with five faith-building dynamics. We program with the assumption that growing faith, which translates into obedience, is the catalyst for personal growth. And personal growth will eventually result in personal maturity. From day one we've rejected the classroom model as well as the sequential-curriculum approach to spiritual development. While we value learning as a component of spiritual maturity, we believe there are four other components that are equally necessary.

If you are involved with service programming for any age group in your church, **Section Four**, the wide part, was written with you in mind. Here I outline the three essential ingredients for irresistible environments. In addition, I explain in detail what we refer to as our "Rules of Engagement." This is the first time we've put these in print. This is the template we adhere to whenever we create environments where unchurched people will be present. Then, for the communicators out there, I've written an entire chapter on how to preach with unchurched people in the house. Here I outline what I've learned through the years about engaging dual audiences with the same message.

Section Five, *Becoming Deep and Wide*, contains three chapters on leading a local church through change. I hope something I've written will inspire, or perhaps provoke, you to look for ways to increase the engagement level between your church and the unchurched in your community. If that's the result of our time together, I will be thrilled; but you will be left with the daunting task of convincing your congregants to join you on your mission. So it seemed appropriate to leave you with what I've learned about instituting change in the institution that resists change like no other.

Oh yeah, about the title. All the good ones were taken. Seriously, I'm sure that somewhere in the world there is an actual "fountain flowing deep and wide." But that has nothing to do with why I chose this title. By the time you finish the book, I hope you will be as convinced as I am that healthy local churches can be, and should be, both *deep* and *wide*. It's not *either/or*. It's *both/and*. Local churches should be characterized by deep roots *and* wide reaches. Churches should be theologically sound *and* culturally relevant. We should be bold in our proclamation *and* winsome in our approach. In the Gospels we find in Jesus the embodiment of both. As his body, we should be as well. Here's one approach to doing just that.

Enjoy!

MY STORY

Starting Up and Starting Over

chapter one

NOT ALL
THAT DEEP

My earliest memory of church was my dad baptizing me when I was six. I still remember what he said: "A pastor has no greater privilege than to baptize his own children."

He was right.

I've baptized all three of mine.

As a preacher's kid, there was never a time in my life that I was not involved in church. And unlike a lot of PKs, I don't remember ever being forced to go. I liked it. Church was always the center of my social life. It's where I made lifelong friends, several of whom I'm still connected with today.

My parents began their ministry together in 1957 in the Smoky Mountains of North Carolina. After graduating from seminary, my dad accepted a call to pastor Fruitland Baptist Church. In addition to pastoring the church, he was invited to teach at the Fruitland Baptist Bible Institute, located directly across the parking lot from the church. FBBI was established in 1946 to assist local pastors who lacked the opportunity or means for theological training. So there he was, all of twenty-four years old, teaching men almost twice his age who had been pastoring for years but who lacked formal training. And he loved it.

Fortunately for me, there was no hospital in Fruitland. Equally fortunate was the fact that my mom did not want to deliver me at home. So technically I'm not from Fruitland. I was born right around the corner in Hendersonville.

From Fruitland we moved to Fairborn, Ohio, where my sister was born. Then my dad accepted a call to First Baptist Church of Miami, Florida. We lived in Miami seven years before transitioning to First Baptist Church of Bartow, forty miles east of Tampa, Florida. We were there only fifteen months when a friend called and asked my dad to pray about coming to First Baptist Church of Atlanta as the senior associate pastor. He wasn't the least bit interested. We loved Bartow. But he assured Felix that he would pray about it, hoping Felix wouldn't call back. But he did. And he kept calling. And apparently so did God.

In 1969, our family moved to Atlanta. It was a rough transition. Miami and Bartow were paradise by comparison. The church in Atlanta wasn't healthy. But, of course, nobody tells you that in an interview process. Maybe they didn't know. The other thing they didn't bother to tell him was that no one knew where the key to his desk was.

Two years after we moved to Atlanta, the deacons asked the senior pastor to step down. Which he did. Then they made the mistake of asking my dad to fill the pulpit while they put together a pastor search committee to begin looking for a replacement. As you may know, my dad knows a thing or two about preaching. It wasn't long before the church began to grow. This was a bit disturbing to the power brokers. They didn't feel like my dad was qualified to be senior pastor because of his age, education, and his irritating propensity to preach about sin, repentance, and personal salvation. Imagine such a thing. It wasn't long before they decided my dad would need to step down. But that was going to be tricky. The church was experiencing new life. The new members class was full. The baptistery was being used every Sunday night. Offerings were increasing.

Clearly, he was not the man for the job.

In spite of all the good things going on, they put pressure on him to resign. It was subtle at first. They explained how difficult it would be for the church to find the "right" man as long as he was around. Promises were made. Severance was assured. Favorable letters would be written. They assumed he would go quietly, like the pastors before him. But my dad was cut from a different cloth than the other guys. As I'll explain in more detail in chapter two, he grew up in an atmosphere where the only predictable and unchanging component was the sovereignty of God. Discovering and doing God's will was everything. Everything. It was that interminable drive that brought order to the chaos of his childhood. So he was not about to let a group of deacons rewrite his life script. He believed then, as he does today, that decisions should be made on your knees. Not in a deacons' meeting. So after each encounter with the power brokers, he would respond by saying, "Let me go home and pray about it."

They had no category for such a thing. In time, the tone of those meetings changed. I can remember him comparing deacons' meetings to the lions' den. As he tells it, "In those days, when I would look around at circumstances, everything said, 'Go.' But on my knees, I sensed God saying, 'You came here out of obedience to me. I'll let you know when it's time to leave.'"

When it became apparent that he wasn't going to take his cue from the board of deacons, things got really ugly. What began as subtle hints turned into not-so-subtle threats. He was told that if he didn't resign he would never work in a Southern Baptist church again. We received nasty anonymous letters at home. In my little book, *Louder Than Words*,[2] I recount the details of the night a board member actually punched my father in the face during a business meeting. That "turn the other cheek" thing took on a whole new meaning. But sitting in the third row as an eighth-grade boy who idolized his father, I wanted to kill the guy.

As my parents agonized over whether to stay, what they could not appreciate was the impact their example was having on their children. These events took place over forty years ago, but I can remember them like it was yesterday. I can remember our family gathering around our glossy pecan coffee table in the den to pray for direction. I can see the face of the man who hit my dad. I remember where I was standing and what I was thinking. I remember hating the men who wanted to hurt my father. But what impacted me most was my parents' courage—their willingness to do the right thing even when it was hard, even when it cost them, even when they didn't know the full extent of the cost.

At thirteen, I saw firsthand that the local church was a big deal. It was worth fighting for. It was worth risk, sacrifice, and even physical pain. I saw my dad turn the other cheek, but he never turned tail and ran. He did the right thing. He obeyed God and God honored it. What I could not have known at the time, however, was that twenty-four years later, it would be the confidence I saw in him then that would give me the confidence I needed to make the most difficult decision of my life.

Church Wars

My dad's transition from *associate* to *senior* pastor happened during a church business meeting called for the express purpose of forcing him to resign. My parents knew going into the meeting that they might come out unemployed and unemployable. Due to the hostile nature of the gathering, they gave me strict instructions to stay in my father's office until the meeting was over.

Fortunately for me, I had a friend who worked overtime that night to ensure I had a blow-by-blow description of everything taking place in the sanctuary. You know him as Louie Giglio. Back then everybody called him Butch. Louie snuck into the empty baptistery to listen, and then would sneak back to my father's office to report what was going on. The meeting lasted over three hours. There were close to two thousand people in attendance. Person after person came forward with stories of how my father's presence had hurt the church and how his continued involvement would impede the process of finding a new and qualified senior pastor.

In the end, a vote was taken to determine whether my father would be allowed to remain in his position as associate pastor. An overwhelming majority voted to keep him. And then something happened that took the opposition completely by surprise. Someone made a motion to elect my father senior pastor. The chairman of the deacons, who was officiating the meeting, rushed to the microphone and moved that the meeting be adjourned immediately! One of his friends seconded the motion. But unfortunately for them, a gentleman by the name of Henry Robert III was in the audience that night. Henry is the grandson of the late General Henry M. Robert, who wrote *Robert's Rules of Order*. As you may know, *Robert's Rules of Order* is the "playbook" for parliamentary procedure, the final word in how to conduct an official meeting of just about any type. Since it had been decided ahead of time that all official church business would be conducted according to this standard, Henry felt compelled to come forward and inform the chairman of the deacons that he could not adjourn the meeting while a motion was still under consideration.

Well, things became a bit chaotic at First Baptist Church that night. But in the end, they decided to follow the rules, allow for the motion, and vote. The chairman of the deacons called for a private ballot. Someone else moved that the vote be taken by a public show of hands. So they had to vote on how to take the vote. You've got to love that. By this time, the power brokers saw the handwriting on the wall. Actually, they saw the hands waving in the air. When the meeting ended, my dad was senior pastor of First Baptist Church of Atlanta. But by the time my parents made it back to my father's office to give me the good news, it was old news. Thanks to Louie.

Waitin' for the Call

The church continued to grow rapidly. Meanwhile I finished high school and enrolled at Georgia State University where I (eventually) received a degree in journalism. It was during the first semester of my junior year in college that I decided to pursue vocational ministry. All my life I had heard about being "called" into ministry. Several of my friends felt God's "call" on their lives. They would go forward after church on Sunday nights and pray with my dad. Then, at the conclusion of the service, he would introduce them to the congregation and announce that God had called them into the ministry. People would clap and come by and congratulate them after the closing song. Many of those guys still serve as pastors, missionaries, parachurch ministry leaders, and seminary professors.

But as for me, I never felt "the call." I sure tried to feel it. But for whatever reason, it just never happened for me.

So one afternoon as my dad and I were driving somewhere, I asked him, "Dad, does a person have to be 'called' into ministry, or can he just volunteer?" He thought for a minute. "I guess it's okay to just volunteer." So I told him that I would like to volunteer. He seemed pleased. And that was that. For a long time I didn't tell anyone. I didn't want the added pressure. And I knew it might limit my options relationally, if you know what I mean.

After college, I headed straight to Dallas Theological Seminary (DTS) where I received my Master of Theology (ThM) degree. I loved seminary. I was at DTS during the years of Charles Ryrie, Dwight Pentecost, Howard Hendricks, and Norm Geisler. I remember my dad attending an evening class with me. In the middle of a lecture by Dr. Ryrie, he turned to me and said, "You have no idea how lucky you are to sit under this kind of teaching." During the break, Dr. Ryrie asked my dad if he would like to address the class. I still remember his answer, "Absolutely not! I'm learning too much."

While finishing my final semester at DTS, I applied to Baylor University to pursue a PhD in religion. I was denied. Ouch. And while the rejection certainly resurfaced unhealed wounds from a particular middle school dance, I didn't have time to wallow in my sorrow. If I wasn't going back to school, I needed to get a job. As it turned out, the director of student ministry who had been serving at my dad's church had resigned six months earlier. When the education director heard I was looking for meaningful employment, he called and asked if I would be interested in filling in while they searched for a permanent replacement. In spite of the fact that the whole serve-until-we-find-the-real-guy thing had turned out to be a nightmare for my dad, I accepted. After all, as my friend and mentor Charlie Renfroe is fond of saying, "Everybody needs to eat and live indoors."

What began as a summer job turned into a ten-year gig. I'm not sure when they stopped looking for that "other guy." All I know is that I fell in love with student ministry. I could not imagine doing anything else. Along with my normal responsibilities, I had the opportunity to preach when my dad was away. Honestly, I don't know how the people at First Baptist Church of Atlanta took me seriously. The building still bore the scars of my adolescence. But folks were gracious. They always had nice things to say. In exchange, I would let 'em out on time.

It was during my student ministry days that I met Sandra. She was a student at Georgia Tech. We were introduced at a campus Bible study on the Tech campus. How appropriate. Actually, I don't remember meeting Sandra that night. I was filling in for the regular teacher. The faculty sponsor, a friend of mine, had invited me to fill the open slot. The day after the study, he called me and asked if I remembered meeting a girl named Sandra Walker. I told him that I remembered meeting two girls. Both blonde. He assured me that one of them was Sandra. Then he insisted that I call her and ask her out. I thought that was tacky. So I declined. Gary hounded me. Finally I relented and called the number he had given me. By the time I finally called, Sandra had changed dorms. Not to be deterred, Gary tracked down her new number. I called. We went out. And we've been going out ever since. We were married on August 6, 1988.

FUTURE TALK

During my student ministry days, people would often ask what I saw in my future; how long did I plan to work with "young people"? My favorite was, "Andy, when are you going to get your own church?" My response to those questions was always the same. "God has given my father an extraordinary platform. I'm here to serve him and help him finish well." And that was the truth. I had no ambition beyond what I was doing. I loved my job. I loved my church. And once my dad began televising my sermons, I was able to preach to more people on a single Sunday than I would preach to in twenty years at the average church. Why would I go anywhere else? Where else would I possibly want to go?

RELOCATING

In 1987, faced with limited space and aging facilities, First Baptist Atlanta voted to relocate from downtown Atlanta to the suburbs.

While seeking a buyer for our downtown property, the church purchased an Avon Products packing facility north of town. Along with the fifty acres of land, there was about four hundred thousand feet of warehouse space. Within a year of making the decision to move, a European group signed a contract to purchase the downtown property. Realizing that even with a buyer it would be a couple of years before the church could build on the new site and relocate, the deacons asked me if I would be willing to begin holding services in a portion of our newly acquired warehouse complex. Their rationale was that it would relieve crowding downtown as well as establish a presence on our future site.

At the meeting when I was asked to take on this new responsibility, the chairman of the deacons kept apologizing for how scaled down everything would be. There wouldn't be a choir or an orchestra. He wanted to know if I would be okay using a band until we could develop space more suited to a traditional worship environment. It was important to them that I understood what I was getting myself into. As one gentleman put it, "It probably won't feel much like church." And, of course, all I could think of was Brer Rabbit. "Please don't throw me in the briar patch!" So I kept a straight face and told them I was willing to take one for the team.

It's important to keep in mind that there were no multi-site churches in those days. A few churches were experimenting with the idea of a second campus, but even that was novel. This was new territory. We had no idea what we were doing, but we could not have been more excited. There were seven of us assigned to the start-up team. Included in that original group were Julie Arnold, Lane Jones, Rick Holliday, Bill Willits, and Reggie Joiner. It was an all-star team. But we didn't know it at the time. Why they chose us, I'll never know. My guess is we were considered nonessential personnel at the downtown location. So they sent us to the badlands to establish an outpost. We were giddy.

My dad and his team took a tremendous chance empowering us the way they did. They put their reputations in our hands. To their credit, they funded the project without micromanaging it. They told us to reach our new community and then gave us complete freedom to dream, design, and create. So we did. And while we didn't know exactly what we were doing, we knew what we didn't want to do. We didn't want to re-create environments designed for church people. We wanted to create a church that unchurched people would love to attend. We didn't know if that was possible. Actually, we were told it had been tried and that it *wasn't* possible in the over-churched South. But we believed it was worth a shot. So we set out to capture the imaginations and, ultimately, the hearts of unchurched people in that community.

The section of warehouse we commandeered for our worship center accommodated eight hundred people. There were no hallways or lobbies. You walked into the worship center from outside. We built a small stage flanked by green painters' scaffolding to support our PA speakers. The floor was concrete and maintained whatever the temperature was outside. The children's area (area, not classrooms) was another renovated warehouse space accessed through another set of doors from the outside. The children's area had fans, no air conditioning.

The environment was raw, to say the least. And the entire complex was butt ugly.

We opened Easter Sunday 1992 with about seven hundred people, most of whom were from the downtown church. Once they realized that "warehouse worship" was going to be a total departure from what they were accustomed to, about half of them elected not to come back. But they were quickly replaced by people from the community. A lot of people. By the third week, we were turning people away. We were turning away so many cars that a committee from another church in the area asked us if they could stand at the entrances to our parking lots and pass out flyers advertising their church to the people who couldn't get into our services.

We added a second service and began developing overflow space. By the end of the second month, we were closing in on two thousand adults in worship. It was crazy.

While God was using us to transform the way people thought about the local church, a transformation was taking place in our hearts as well. To borrow a phrase from my hero and friend, Bill Hybels, *we were ruined.* There was no going back. This was church as we had never experienced church. Truth is, I was ruined on opening day. After my first message, Sandra and I were walking back to the construction trailer that served as our green room. Just as we reached the rickety wooden stairs, I turned to her with tears in my eyes and said, "That's what I want to do for the rest of my life." (Dang it. I got misty just typing that.)

But it wasn't just me. We all felt that way. It's no surprise that five of us from that original team are still working together. And if Reggie Joiner hadn't gotten so busy helping churches all over the country rethink their children's and student ministry cultures, he might still be with us as well. We were all ruined. We loved the environment. We loved the informality. We loved the freedom it gave us to communicate in creative ways. We loved how disarming our raw warehouse space was for those who considered themselves returners and seekers. The freedom of expression we take for granted now didn't exist then. This was new. And we couldn't get enough of it.

Storm Warning

Meanwhile, things downtown weren't going so well. The sale of the property fell through. The buyer walked away six months before closing and there was no backup contract.

To complicate matters further, the economy took a turn for the worse and property values in Atlanta plummeted. It became painfully obvious that what the church assumed they could get for the property was way out of line with current economic reality. So what began as a two-year transition turned into an indefinite period of waiting. More time meant more opportunity for the two campuses to develop different and contrasting identities. It wasn't intentional. Even with what I know now, I'm not sure it could have been avoided.

Families that had been attending downtown, but who lived south of the city and were not planning to make the transition to the new campus, began looking for new church homes. Instead of waiting for the actual relocation to take place, they went ahead and transitioned to other churches. The first to go were singles and young families with children. Seemingly overnight, the downtown congregation felt older. In contrast, the North campus was attracting singles and young families by the hundreds. Before long, attendance tilted in our direction.

As I mentioned earlier, our worship styles differed dramatically. So we were perceived as having a "cool" factor that the downtown church lacked. Suits, ties, and skirts became increasingly rare. The explosive growth at the North campus created an exhilarating level of excitement and anticipation, whereas the people downtown felt as if they were "stuck down there" until the property sold.

Eventually, people began to compare and contrast. The we/they talk began. Things became competitive. It was old versus new, traditional versus contemporary. We couldn't understand why the mother church was so reluctant to fund all our new initiatives. And the mother church couldn't understand why, with our large attendance, we couldn't pay our own way. But in spite of all that, we managed to function as one church in two locations. This was due in large part to the fact that my father and I refused to allow anyone to get between us. We had no tolerance for father versus son. We knew that as long as we were on the same page, we could hold out until the two congregations came back together on the new property.

But in June of 1993, something happened that would ultimately drive a wedge between us. My mom filed for divorce.

chapter two

FAMILY
MATTERS

To understand what happened next requires that I backtrack just a bit. The first cracks in my parents' marriage appeared when I was in the tenth grade. Up until then, they appeared to have the perfect relationship. I never saw them fight. I don't even remember them disagreeing about anything. The only time I heard my mom raise her voice was when I took piano lessons in the first grade. My dad swears that's the first time he ever heard her raise her voice. Consequently, I didn't let my kids take piano lessons.

I've held every theory as to the root of their problems. It was none of the usual suspects. There was no infidelity. It wasn't financial. My dad has always worked hard, but I've never considered him a workaholic. And my mom has never accused him of any of those things.

They both grew up in what we would now consider highly dysfunctional homes. My dad's father passed away when my dad was seventeen months old. There was no insurance. His mom went to work in a mill. He was a latchkey kid before there was such a thing. They were incredibly poor.

He learned about Santa Claus the Christmas morning he found the orange in his stocking that had been in the fridge the night before.

His mom remarried when he was twelve to ensure that he would have a man in his life. Out of sensitivity to my extended family, I can't go into detail as to what a nightmare that turned out to be. He begged his mom to get a divorce, but she refused. In her mind, a vow was a vow. She would not break it. But it almost broke her. When her husband's health took a turn for the worse, she stepped in and nursed him as if he had been the model husband. I was old enough to understand how one-sided the relationship had been and how utterly selfless she was during his final years. After he died, my dad moved his mother to Atlanta where he did his best to make up for the decades of difficulty she had endured.

My mother's parents divorced when she was in high school. Her father, David, was my favorite grandparent. He knew how to have a good time, which, as it turned out, was part of the problem. When I was nine, I went to stay with him for two weeks during the summer. He bought me an alligator. What's not to love about a grandparent who will buy his grandson a two-foot-long reptile? He was *awesome* before anybody used the term. He kept jars of cash in his refrigerator. He sewed diamonds into the hems of his curtains. He always drove a new gold Cadillac. His standard attire was a champagne-colored suit with cufflinks.

He had a condo in Fort Lauderdale, a house on a canal in West Palm Beach with a yacht parked in back, and a farm in North Carolina.

On the negative side of the ledger sheet, he was married four times. Four marriages. That's a lot now. That was a *whole lot* back then. His fourth wife was a wonderful woman under whose influence he eventually became a Christian. By then, he was in his mid-sixties. Once he said the sinner's prayer, he started making up for lost time. In his final years all he wanted to do was discuss the Scriptures. I can still remember his giant-print brown leather Bible. While he was quick to say he was a Christian, he was never confident about heaven. He would say, "Well, I don't know about heaven. I've done a lot of bad things in my life." We never asked. We could only imagine. And while his late-in-life conversion was comforting, the damage that only a father can inflict had been done.

So a young man, who grew up without a father and for whom compartmentalization became a means of survival, married a woman whose father was distracted, to say the least; and together they set out to change the world. But as you know, the past is only the past for a time. It has a way of clawing its way into our futures. And if you don't recognize it for what it is, the results can be devastating. And my parents were no exception.

In 1992, my mom packed up and moved to my parents' lake house outside of Atlanta. Several months later, I received the call from my dad saying he had been served with papers. And speaking of papers, it was all over the papers. Everybody had an opinion about what my dad should do. But nobody except my sister and I knew the whole story. While most of the congregants at First Baptist Atlanta (FBA) were willing to stand by my dad no matter what, there was a group that insisted he take some time off to work on his marriage. What they didn't know and could not have known was that six months prior to my mom moving to the lake, my parents spent three weeks at a conference center with a highly trained team of counselors and doctors "working on their marriage." And that wasn't the first time. They had seen every type of counselor imaginable. By the time she filed, the marriage had been dead for years. But they were both so adamantly opposed to divorce that neither of them wanted to file. On one occasion I got so frustrated I actually asked if I could hire an attorney and file for their divorce myself!

In addition to the take-some-time-off group, there was an element in the church that thought my dad should resign. It was their conviction that if my mom actually went through with the divorce, he would be disqualified to serve in his current capacity. As cruel as that may sound, you need to understand that until that time, First Baptist Atlanta had never had a divorced staff member or deacon. You couldn't be elected to the deacon board if you had been divorced. So, in the minds of the resign-now crowd, they were simply applying what they had been taught.

But, just as things were starting to heat up, my mom suddenly announced that she was dropping the suit. Everybody rejoiced. It looked like God had answered prayer and the marriage would be saved. My sister, Becky, and I knew better. Four months later, my mom refiled. And the whole thing started up again.

THE DIVIDE

A few weeks after my dad had been served with papers, he called me into his office to read a letter he had received from my mom's attorney. I remember exactly where we were standing. When I finished the letter, I looked at him and said, "Dad, you haven't asked me what I think you should do." He smiled and said, "You know I want to know what you think." Actually, I wasn't sure. After all, he had never asked. I knew the advice and "support" he was getting from the people closest to him. They meant well. They just didn't have all the facts. And they did not fully appreciate the level of opposition that was beginning to build.

My advice was for him to walk into the sanctuary the following Sunday morning and read a letter of resignation. Then, after everybody got over the initial shock, I suggested he tell the congregation that he was willing to continue preaching as long as they wanted him to. I said, "Tell them you don't have any desire to leave FBA and that you would like to continue as their pastor. Give them an opportunity to choose whether they want a pastor that might end up divorced." I assured him that the congregation of FBA was not about to let him go anywhere. They loved him too much. My mom had not attended church for years. I was convinced then, as I am today, that in spite of the pending divorce, if the church had an opportunity to reinstate him as pastor, they would have done so. And whatever controversy there was would have died then and there.

Unfortunately, my dad didn't hear anything I said past the word *resign*. That's understandable. He had been hearing that word for months. And now his son was suggesting the same thing. It looked and sounded as if I was siding with the resign-now crowd. He doesn't remember that conversation. I'll never forget it. From then on, he believed I wanted him to step down. Permanently. Soon his suspicions were confirmed as people began whispering in his ear that I was trying to take over the church. His closest friends and staunchest supporters rallied behind the theory that I was using my parents' divorce as leverage to move my dad out so I could move in. "After all," they would argue, "look what he's doing out at the warehouse. All that success has gone to his head." And perhaps it had. But two things are certain. I did not want to take over the church. And I did not want my dad to leave.

LOYALTY WARS

For the next two years, my dad and I met together with a counselor every week. Sometimes twice a week. In spite of that, he continued to be suspicious. And I just got mad. I was mad that he didn't trust me. I was mad that he wouldn't defend me when people made the most ridiculous accusations. (A lady sent an anonymous letter to the entire membership accusing me of driving a hundred-thousand-dollar sports car.) I was mad at his "friends" for not telling him the truth. I was mad at my mom. I was a mess. But to both our credits, we kept the channel of communication open. Sometimes too open. One night I invited him over to see the kids, thinking that surely we could get along in front of my family. By the time the night was over, we were standing in my driveway yelling at each other like a couple of middle-school girls.

Meanwhile, we were getting up every Sunday in front of our respective congregations acting like everything was fine. By this time, we had renovated another large section of warehouse space at the North campus. Over four thousand adults were showing up every week. So there we were. Father and son. Each with his own big church. Problem was, it was the same church. And he was the pastor. And I had become a lightning rod for the folks that thought he should step down. Before long, all the step-down-to-work-on-your-marriage crowd and the resign-now crowd were attending warehouse worship with me. So, of course, my dad was suspicious. Who wouldn't be?

Eventually, Sandra and I realized that there was really just one good option for us. So we began asking God for permission to leave. Leaving would be complicated. But we knew the longer I stayed, the more divisive things would get. I had no credibility with my dad's supporters and I didn't agree with his detractors. And did I mention I was mad?

Things came to a head in the summer of 1995. Sandra was five months pregnant with Allie when she started having a periodic loss of peripheral vision on her left side. We made an appointment with a neurologist. We were scared. On the morning of August 3, I left the office around 10:30 to meet her at the doctor's office. I knew we would probably be stuck in a waiting room, so on my way out I scanned my bookshelf for something to read. My eyes lit upon a book someone had given me a year earlier: *The Tale of Three Kings*, by Gene Edwards.[3] I had no idea what it was about. I had never cracked the cover. I grabbed it and headed out the door.

There was no one in the waiting room, so I began reading out loud. It was as if the author had been following us around for the previous twenty-four months. I couldn't believe it. I continued to read while the doctor ran tests. The neurologist didn't seem overly worried. He told us we could expect the results in a week to ten days. Twenty minutes later we were sitting at the Silver Spoon Café on Peachtree Street having lunch while I continued to read. As we were finishing our meal, I read a sentence that would change the trajectory of our lives:

> Beginning emptyhanded and alone frightens the best of men. It also speaks volumes of just how sure they are that God is with them.

I stopped reading and looked up at Sandra. We knew. We both knew. It was time to go. We had our release papers. It was so clear. I've never had that kind of clarity before or since. I walked her to her car, kissed her good-bye, and drove back to the office to resign.

RESIGNATION

When I arrived, I called my team together and told them how much I appreciated them, but that the time had come for me to go. They weren't completely surprised. They knew I couldn't sustain the strain and suspicion that had come to characterize our work environment. They were worn out as well. We loved what was happening on Sunday. But the Monday-through-Friday part was destroying us. As inevitable as it might have been, my actual resignation signaled a sudden end to our partnership. More than that, it signaled the end of our partnership with what God was doing north of the city. By his grace we had cracked the code on attracting unchurched people to church. And not only were they coming, they were bringing their unchurched friends. This was unheard of in our part of the country. And now it was over.

I left that meeting and went straight to my dad's study. He was going over mail with his assistant. When he looked up and saw me standing in the doorway, I had a strange feeling he knew why I was there. His assistant collected her things and retreated to the outer office. He was sitting in his big chair behind his big desk, a leftover from the previous administration. It was too big to get out the door, so he decided rather than dismantle it, he would just use it.

I don't remember exactly what I said, but I told him I was resigning, effective immediately, and that I would have a letter in his hands by the end of the day. He stared at me for a minute. I was afraid of what might happen next. He rose slowly, walked around the end of his desk, and embraced me. And we both cried. And cried. And cried. My resignation was far more than a termination of employment. It signaled the death of an unspoken dream. What could have been, and perhaps should have been, wouldn't be. So we just stood there and cried.

The following Sunday I showed up for warehouse worship as usual. Smiled. Shook some hands. Sang. And resigned. It was terrible. Terrible. To this day, I meet people who say, "Andy, my first Sunday at the warehouse church was the Sunday you resigned." It still feels like a knife in my heart. These people had trusted me. Followed me. They had given sacrificially. They served like crazy. We had experienced Acts 2 together. From all outward appearances we were just getting started. And now I was leaving. The hardest part was I couldn't tell them why. I even told them that I couldn't tell them why. I assured them that my marriage was fine. My health was fine. Nobody had fired me. And I hadn't received a better offer. Then I prayed and went home.

Immediately, a group started a campaign to separate the two campuses into two independent churches. A delegation came to see me to ask if I would come back as pastor of the North campus if First Baptist would spin it off as a separate church. The rumor at the time was that I was part of this group from the beginning and that once I knew I couldn't take over the entire church, I was plotting to take the North campus. I thanked the group for their offer and assured them that I had no interest in returning.

NOT ON OUR WATCH

As we all know, there are two sides to every story. So before I go any further, I want to stop and ask you to put yourself in my father's shoes. He's just spent the last eighteen years building a large ministry without any support at home. Then his wife files for divorce, which, in addition to being publically humiliating, creates division in his congregation. On the heels of that, his son, whom he has blessed with every opportunity imaginable, including allowing him to create a church that is dramatically different from his own, tries to force him out and take over! When that doesn't work, his son attempts to rally support for dividing the church and hijacking half the congregation. When that plot is foiled, he resigns, leaving several thousand people without a pastor and without any explanation as to why he left. If you were my dad, would you have ever spoken to me again? Parents have changed their wills over less. For all I know, he did. And who would have blamed him?

It's at this point that I can't give my dad enough credit. His is the generation of good guys and bad guys, cowboys and Indians, you are with me or you are against me. For him, loyalty has always been the supreme value. When you combine that with the filter through which he interpreted my actions, he had every reason to paint me as an ungrateful, disloyal, self-centered prima donna. How could anyone who had been given the opportunities I'd been given treat his father with such scorn? Seeing it as he did, he would have been completely justified to write me off as a lost cause and move on.

But he didn't.

Instead, he invited me to lunch.

A lot.

What's Next

The conversations were stilted, to say the least. We were both so mad and so hurt. But he kept initiating. And I kept showing up. During one of our awkward lunch dates, he said something that pierced the hardness of my heart and opened the door to the relationship we share today. He said, "We both know what usually happens to fathers and sons who go through something like this." Then he paused and looked me right in the eye. "Andy, I don't want us to end up like that." It was all I could do to whisper, "Me neither, Dad."

Two months after my resignation, we were having one of our quiet lunches at a Mexican restaurant, when my dad looked up from his salad and asked, "So what are you going to do now?" It had been difficult for both him and Sandra's dad to get their minds around the fact that I had quit a perfectly good job without having another one lined up. Seeing as we had two small kids and Sandra was pregnant with our third, I can understand their bewilderment. It's not something I recommend. Since resigning, we had visited a church in another state and I had preached in anticipation of a call. And they called. And we declined. Earlier that same week I had been invited by a group to discuss starting a new church in the Atlanta area. It was exciting to think about. But at that point, it was still just an idea.

"Well," I said, "if I could do anything, I would gather up some of the people I worked with at FBA, go north of the city, and start over."

Even as the words were coming out of my mouth, I knew I was in no condition to start anything. And I certainly had no business trying to pastor anybody. I was still seeing my counselor. The drama of the previous two years had dislodged all kinds of stuff that had been stuck to the walls of my soul for years. Just three days prior, I was venting to my counselor about how wrong everybody else was and how right I was. When I finally stopped to breathe, Steve said, "Andy, let me ask you something. How do you think you would have responded if you were one of Jesus' disciples and had heard Peter deny knowing Jesus?" Before I could think, I heard my voice saying, "He would be out!" From the heart the mouth speaketh. There was my heart. Angry. Judgmental. Self-righteous. Steve smiled and asked his second question. "How did Jesus respond?" Realizing it wasn't good form to plead the fifth with your counselor, I answered, "Jesus put him in charge of the entire enterprise."

That was a defining moment for me. I caught a glimpse of something I had never seen, and I hated what I saw. Faced with the pharisaical condition of my heart, I was desperate to change. I realized this was the filter through which I preached, counseled, read the Scriptures, and led. I asked God to strip all of that out of me. Thus began a process that I'm sure continues today.

So as I opened up with my dad that afternoon and dreamed out loud, I had no time frame in mind. He asked what I would like to do if I could do anything, so I told him.

And then he told the world.

The following Sunday evening, unbeknownst to me, he preempted the regular order of worship with a surprise update on my whereabouts and plans. "Some of you have been wondering what Andy is up to these days. Well, we had lunch this week. He is planning to go north of the city and start a church." He paused. "And he has my blessing." The wounds were too fresh for him to mean that. He *wanted* to mean it. Eventually he *would* mean it. But he loved me. And he knew how important it was for me to know he was behind me. So he said it anyway. That night my phone started ringing. The paper in our home fax machine was exhausted by noon the next day. Everybody wanted to know when and where and how they could be involved. I just wanted to take a nap.

On November 19, 1995, we had an organizational meeting about starting a new church. About fifteen hundred people showed up. I didn't feel ready. But that didn't seem to matter. Events had been set in motion. The wheels were turning. Ready or not, we were starting a church. Or so it seemed. In reality, we were really restarting a church.

The group that gathered that night was not a random group of curiosity seekers from the community. This was the core. This was the group that for the past three years had worked to create the most unique and dynamic church experience in the city. They believed. They got it. Like me, they had been ruined by what they had seen and experienced at the warehouse. They knew what could and should be. They didn't need vision; they just needed permission.

So after an emotionally charged worship set, I stepped up to the podium and told them what they already knew.

> Atlanta doesn't need another church. Atlanta needs a different kind of church. Atlanta needs a church where church people are comfortable bringing their unchurched friends, family members, and neighbors. A church where unbelievers can come and hear the life-changing truth that God cares for them and that Jesus Christ died for their sin. We've come together to create a church unchurched people will love to attend.

And so we began.

Again.

The morning after our organizational meeting, I typed out a short declaration in English, changed the font to

Greek for the sake of privacy, printed it, and set it on my
desk where it remains to this very day. It reads:

Λορδ, τηις ωας νοτ μψ ιδεα. Ψου γοτ με ιντο τηισ. Ιμ τρυστινγ
ψου το σεε με τηρουγη ιτ.

Lord, this was not my idea. You got me into this. I'm
trusting you to see me through it.

And that's how North Point Community Church got
started. A high-profile divorce and a church split. For a
while, I actually considered hanging a picture of my parents
in the lobby of North Point. Nobody thought that was
funny but me. I don't consider myself a church planter. I
never intended to start a church. God intended otherwise.

My dad turned eighty this year. It goes without saying
that I stand on his shoulders. Those are two very crowded
shoulders. A couple generations of church leaders stand
there along with me. And we are all very grateful. Me most
of all. With the advantage of hindsight, I've concluded that
my father and I responded to the conflict at FBA the same
way. We both did what we were convinced God wanted us
to do. I was convinced God wanted me to leave. He was
convinced God wanted him to stay. So that's what we did.
That's what we've endeavored to do ever since. If you asked
my dad to summarize his life in a sentence, he would tell
you, "Obey God and leave all the consequences to him."

That's good advice.

Now let's talk church.

OUR STORY

Walking Toward
the Messes

One of the perplexing things we face as church leaders is that most church people don't know *what* the church is or *why* it exists. Granted, that's partly our fault. But with two thousand years of history under our belts, we should be further along. Ask the average person what comes to mind when he or she hears the term *church* and you get all kinds of answers.

- A building
- A weekend event
- The longest hour of the week
- Arguing with my parents on Sunday morning
- Arguing with my kids on Sunday morning

For those outside the church, as well as some on the inside, church is an institution for those with overactive consciences. For some, it's perceived as a social hub. For others, it is merely a distribution center serving the poor in a community. The tragedy is that what comes to mind when the average person thinks of church is such a far cry from what actually took place in the era in which the church was born.

In the beginning, the church was a gloriously messy movement with a laser-focused message and a global mission. It was led by men and women who were fueled not by what they believed, but by what they had seen. That simple fact sets *the church* apart from every other religious movement in the history of the world. After all, it wasn't the teaching of Jesus that sent his followers to the streets. It was his resurrection. The men and women who made up the nucleus of *the church* weren't simply believers in an abstract philosophy or even faithful followers of a great leader; they were eyewitnesses of an event.

I'm convinced that the current confusion over the purpose and mission of *the church* stems from a dearth of knowledge regarding the history of *the church*. Not the history of a particular church, but *the* church. This famine of knowledge explains in part the anemic condition of the local church in many parts of our country and the world. The story of the birth and global expansion of the local church is fascinating and inspiring. More to the point, the birth, survival, and growth of the church is unexplainable and undeniable. *Unexplainable* because, well, there is no viable, natural explanation for why the church survived the first century, much less twenty centuries. Like you, I've read books and articles by secular historians, sociologists, and anthropologists who have attempted to come up with plausible, natural explanations for the birth, survival, and growth of the church movement. They are all very interesting. But they are all unconvincing. I applaud their efforts. Searching for natural causes is an extraordinarily important endeavor for every field of study.[4] But when it comes to the story of the church, natural explanations fall short. Things don't add up. Secular explanations underscore the fact that there is something *un*natural about the story. Some of us would go so far as to say, *super*natural.

From a purely secular perspective, the story of the church goes something like this:

A small band of Jewish dissidents defied a superpower and a religious system that had been in place for a thousand years and, in the end, prevailed. At the center of this grassroots movement, originally referred to as *The Way*, was a Jewish carpenter whose messages centered on a "kingdom" that wasn't directly connected to this world. He spoke mostly in parables that few could understand. He insisted that those who followed him love the Romans and pay those onerous taxes. He alienated the influential and the powerful. He offended practically everybody. His family thought he had lost his mind. After only three years of public ministry, he was arrested, publically humiliated, and executed.

Sounds like the perfect way to start a movement, doesn't it?

But it gets even stranger. After his execution, Jesus' dispirited and desperate followers claimed that he rose from the dead and that they had seen him! Touched him. Eaten with him. Then within weeks of this alleged resurrection, dozens and then hundreds of people within walking distance of where Jesus was buried believed this nonsense and began telling others. Before long, Jerusalem was filled to the brim with followers of *The Way*. When resistance from both Rome and the Jewish authorities broke out, several members of the original group were executed and the followers scattered.

Now if this uprising had been like the dozen or so similar messianic uprisings that occurred during this same slice of history, it would have passed as a mere footnote of history. But this one was different. Everywhere they went, followers of *The Way* insisted that God had done something unique in their generation; he had raised a man from the dead.

In a relatively short amount of time, this Jewish knockoff religion replaced the entire pagan pantheon of gods as the primary belief system of the Roman Empire, the same empire responsible for crucifying its central figure. The same empire that launched several vicious inquisitions with the intent of stamping it out completely.

Doesn't really add up, does it? Not without an actual resurrection anyway.

But the story of *the church* is not just unexplainable, it's undeniable. Today over a third of the world's population claims some kind of faith in Jesus. The Roman Empire is long gone. Ancient Judaism died with the destruction of the Jewish temple in AD 70. But today one third of the world's population claims Jesus as the centerpiece of their religious experience. He taught for three years, and twenty centuries later, he is worshiped on every continent on the planet. That's an amazing story. It's a story every Christian and church attendee should know. And as church leaders, it's a story in which we have the privilege of participating. Actually, it's a story we are responsible for shaping. Like it or not, we are the stewards of the church for our generation. More daunting than that is the fact that we determine what comes to mind for the next generation when they hear the term *church*.

Removing the *Move* from *Movement*

If you know your church history, you are painfully aware that once the church was legalized, it got organized. Excruciatingly organized. What began as unexplainable became institutional. Before long, the church was less movement and more establishment. Two thousand years later, the church is still struggling to regain its original identity, purpose, and passion. Say the word *church* today and very few people think "movement." While much of this appears to have been avoidable, it is certainly understandable.

One of the fundamental realities of organizational life is that systems fossilize with time. The church is no exception. Your church and my church are no exceptions. It takes great effort, vigilant leadership, and at times good, old-fashioned goading to keep a movement moving. A cursory reading of the book of Acts, or any of Paul's epistles, reminds us that even in the era when eyewitnesses to the resurrection were still alive to tell their stories, the church struggled to maintain its focus and mission.

But it's that very struggle, that tension, that constant need for course correction and inspiration that makes our presence and our leadership so important in this generation. The uncertainty and need for change in our current church culture underscore the need for bold leadership. Leadership that is willing to embrace the unchanging mandate prescribed to us in the first century and to proclaim it in such a way that our twenty-first century audiences will understand and receive it. The church needs leaders who are willing to do whatever is necessary to ensure that we hand it off to the next generation in better shape than we found it.

To some extent, we are all attempting to reconnect with or stay connected to the mission, theology, and purpose of the church that Jesus promised. This book is an elucidation of our attempts to do just that. In the chapters that follow, we are going to talk in depth about the nuts and bolts of church life and leadership. Because you're a leader, you won't agree with me on every point. That's fine. You can't help it. But before we part ways on method and approach, it's critical that we find common ground around two important questions:

1. What is the church?
2. Who is it for?

Your answers to these questions *should* shape your approach to church ministry. As we will see, it is often the disconnect between the answers people give to these two questions and the approaches they adopt that creates the tension they experience. So let's dive in to the first question: What is the church?

chapter three

WORDS
MATTER

During Jesus' earthly ministry there was constant debate about his identity. Was he a teacher? A rabbi? A prophet? Was he actually divine or simply endued with divine power? He had authority over nature, but where did his authority come from? Whether it was Nicodemus or the woman at the well, the question was the same: "Who is this guy?" ("And why won't he come right out and tell us?")

Eventually, Jesus decided to deal with the issue directly. He broached the subject with his disciples just outside the beautiful city of Caesarea Philippi. Augustus Caesar had given the city to Herod the Great as a reward for loyalty. Herod then erected a magnificent temple of white stone, where citizens could worship their emperor-god, Augustus. After the death of Herod the Great, his son, Philip, beautified the city and made it his capital. Perhaps with Caesarea looming over his shoulder, eleven hundred feet up the slope of Mount Hermon, Jesus asked the Twelve the very question that men and women had been asking them, "Who do people say that I am?"[5] What's the word on the street?

You will remember that the disciples responded based on what they had heard. Some believed Jesus was John the Baptizer returned from the dead (perhaps sent by God to take vengeance on Herod Antipas, whom John had denounced for marrying the ex-wife of Herod Philip). Others suggested Jesus was the prophet Elijah, whom many Jews believed would return to introduce the Messiah.

Jesus then turned the question to the Twelve. "Who do *you* say that I am?"

Simon Peter answered immediately, "You are the Messiah [the Christ], the Son of the living God."[6] Just as quickly, Jesus responded, "Blessed are you, Simon son of Jonah, for this was not revealed to you by man, but by my Father in heaven. And I tell you that you are Peter, and on this rock *I will build my church*, and the gates of Hades will not overcome it."[7]

For the record, that is my favorite Bible prophecy. Jesus predicted us! Every time we gather with other believers to worship and learn, we are a present-day fulfillment of Jesus' words two thousand years ago. Congratulations!

But I'm getting ahead of myself.

This is the first time the term *church* shows up in our English New Testament. The church is referenced within the context of a prediction. Jesus predicted he would build it and that nothing, including death, would stand in his way. Furthermore, he states that the "cornerstone" of the church would be this inspired statement that Peter made regarding his identity.

For millennia, before the invention of concrete, builders used stones to lay a foundation for a new building. They gathered granite, marble, or limestone from a quarry and chiseled the material into giant, brick-shaped blocks. They then selected one particular stone and designated it the "cornerstone" — *the* reference stone that would determine the placement of every other stone in the foundation. As they laid other stones end-to-end to form the outline of the building's foundation, they made sure each one was level and square with the cornerstone.

In a clever play on words, Jesus used Peter's nickname to connect his declaration to what was to come. The cornerstone or foundation for this new entity called *the church* would be the belief that Jesus is the Christ, the Son of the living God. Two millennia later, that is still the unifying factor within the church. Truth is, belief in Jesus as the Son of God is about the only thing all churches hold in common. As Jesus predicted, Peter's declaration became the common ground and a compass point for everything that was to follow.

But something else of extraordinary significance was communicated during this exchange. Something that the English translation of the Bible misses. Specifically, the meaning of the term translated *church*. As you may know, the Greek term translated *church* throughout the New Testament is *ekklesia*.[8] What you may not know is that it was not a religious term. It could refer to citizens called to *gather* for civic purposes. It was used to refer to soldiers called out to *gather* for military purposes. An *ekklesia* was simply a gathering or an assembly of people called out for a specific purpose. *Ekklesia* never referred to a specific place, only a specific gathering.

Jesus' audience may have been familiar with this term from another context as well. The Septuagint, the Greek translation of the Old Testament, describes the ancient Israelites as an *ekklesia*. Interestingly, when the Hebrew people were scattered around the world, they were still known collectively as an *ekklesia*, an "assembly, gathering, community, congregation." While dispersed, the people of Israel gathered in close-knit communities and established synagogues. Each community of God's people called its synagogue — the local gathering of God's people — an *ekklesia*, understanding it to be a local, literal gathering of people who were also members of the broad, spiritual gathering known as Israel. In both secular and sacred literature, *ekklesia* always referred to a gathering of people united by a common identity and purpose.

So, when Jesus used the term, his disciples understood him to say, "I am going to build my own assembly of people and the foundation for this new assembly will be ME!"

Now, if you are following all of this — and I realize I'm getting a bit technical — there are a couple of questions you should be asking yourself now. No, not, "How long is this chapter anyway?" The questions you should be asking is, "If the Greek word means *gathering*, why don't our English Bibles just say 'gathering'? Where did the word *church* come from?"

I'm glad you asked. The answers to those questions are more important than I could ever emphasize. The answers explain, in part, why the movement sparked by Jesus' resurrection became institutionalized and, eventually, culturally marginalized. They explain why most people think of church as a building or a location. But to answer them, we will need to exit the biblical narrative and jump ahead about two hundred and fifty years.

Here's what happened.

From Assembly to Assembly Hall

In AD 313, Constantine, soon to be emperor of Rome, legalized Christianity in the Roman Empire. Actually, he legalized freedom of religion in general. Before this edict, Christianity had been outlawed because Christians insisted that Jesus, not the emperor, was their king. Furthermore, they refused to accept any emperor as divine. Consequently, the church suffered localized but intense persecution for the first three hundred years of its existence. This was especially true during the reigns of emperors Nero, Domitian, and Diocletian. Even during periods of reprieve, Christians were barred from positions of authority, ostracized by their communities, charged with random crimes, and stripped of property. Gathering was difficult and dangerous. But with the arrival of Constantine, things began to change.

In the beginning, few rulers paid attention to the edict. As Constantine's power grew, however, tolerance for Christianity grew as well. Then something really big happened. Constantine declared himself a Christian. Imagine the shock waves that ran though the empire. A Christian emperor. After generations of failed attempts to stamp out this Jewish knockoff religion centered around a Galilean carpenter, the emperor himself had joined the cult. Unbelievable. Suddenly, it became fashionable to be Christian.

Before Constantine's rise to power, Christian worship was relatively informal. Believers met in homes, enjoying what they called "love feasts," the ancient equivalent of a potluck banquet. After a meal, they sang hymns, read Scripture, discussed theology, and shared communion. In rare cases, a gathering of Christians in a tolerant city might dedicate a special room or small building for their meetings, but these were nothing more than ordinary buildings decorated with simple murals. After Constantine's conversion, powerful people brought their former notions of worship with them as they professed belief in Christ and began influencing Christian communities. Christian worship began to incorporate elements of imperial protocol, including incense, ornate clothing, processionals, choirs, and pageantry. Worship became formal and hierarchical, relegating the congregation to mere spectators.

Before the rise of Constantine, it was not unusual for believers to commemorate the anniversary of a martyr's death by sharing communion near his or her grave. As Christianity became the religion of the Roman elite, they used their influence to take this practice to a new level. They began erecting buildings dedicated to worship on the sites identified with a martyr's death. When they could not build on a martyr's grave, they exhumed the bones, transported them to a place of worship, and placed them under the communion table at the front of the sanctuary.

Within a decade, the *ekklesia* ceased to be a movement. It was no longer an expanding group of people sharing a unique identity and purpose. It had become a location. The Romans called each of these gathering places a *basilica*, the Latin word used to denote a public building or official meeting place. Gothic (or Germanic) cultures, also influenced by Christianity, used the word *kirika*, which became *kirche* in modern German.[9] The word meant "house of the lord," and was used to refer to any ritual gathering place, Christian or pagan.

This Germanic term became the one used most often to refer to the *ekklesia* of Jesus, and from it we get the word *church*. Whereas the majority of your English Bible is a word-for-word *translation* of the Greek text, not so in this case. The word *church* is not a *translation* from the Greek. It is a *substitution* for the Greek. And a bad one at that. The German term *kirche* and the Greek term *ekklesia* refer to two very different ideas. A *kirche* is a location. An *ekklesia* is a purposeful gathering of people. You can lock the doors of a *kirche*. Not so with the *ekklesia* of Jesus.

This shift in vocabulary signaled a dramatic shift in emphasis and direction. The church was no longer a grassroots movement built upon the simple understanding of who Jesus is. The church became synonymous with a location. This created a new and unexpected dynamic for the church. Whoever controlled the church building now controlled the church. Worse yet, in the fourth century and beyond, whoever controlled the church building, controlled the Scriptures. By the Middle Ages in Europe, the Bible was literally chained to the pulpit! This led to an even greater tragedy. Those who controlled the church property and controlled the Scriptures eventually controlled the people. And ultimately the government.

What began as a movement, dedicated to carrying the truth of Jesus Christ to every corner of the world, had become an insider-focused, hierarchical, ritualized institution that bore little resemblance to its origins. This shift led to an era of church history that can only be described as horrific. The atrocities carried out in the name of the church would be considered terrorism by modern standards. Cruelty wore a cross around its neck. Hypocrisy draped itself in priestly robes. Torture and murder were justified as rites of purification. The church grew rich and powerful. Kings were beholden. The people lived in fear of excommunication. While it's amazing that the church survived the persecution of the first century, it may be more amazing that it survived the institutionalization and corruption of the centuries that followed.

But it did survive.

Jesus promised it would.

As it turned out, the *kirche* of man could not contain the *ekklesia* of Jesus.

REFORMERS TO THE RESCUE

In 1453, the Ottoman Empire conquered Constantinople. At the time, Constantinople was the capital of the Roman Empire, the seat of both political and religious power. What was seen as a tragic turn of events for the empire turned out to be a blessing in disguise for the true church. As the threat of an Ottoman invasion materialized, Christian scholars fled westward to Europe, carrying with them ancient Hebrew and Greek manuscripts of the Bible. These manuscripts found a welcome audience among reformers in the West, men influenced by John Huss, who were of the conviction that the Bible, not the pope, was to be the church's final authority. Furthermore, they believed that a pope—or any church official—who did not obey the Bible should not be obeyed. During this period, church officials were the only ones who had access to Bibles, which were a Latin translation called the Vulgate, originally created more than a thousand years earlier! These were either locked up in libraries or, as I mentioned earlier, chained to pulpits.

As Greek and Hebrew manuscripts found their way into the hands of church reformers, it was decided that they should be translated into a language that the common people could read. In 1522, William Tyndale determined to translate the Bible into English. When a fellow clergyman challenged Tyndale, suggesting people "might be better without the law of God than the law of the Pope," he replied, "If God spares my life, before many years pass I will make it possible for a boy behind the plow to know more Scripture than you do."[10]

Finding no support in England, he traveled to Germany, where he completed his translation from the Greek rather than the Latin texts. In 1526, Tyndale began smuggling printed copies of this English Bible into his homeland.

Making the Bible available to his countrymen made Tyndale an outlaw in England. Government and church officials plotted to arrest him and try him for heresy. After ten years of searching and scheming, their efforts were rewarded when an acquaintance betrayed him to a band of soldiers hired by church officials. A tribunal of the Holy Roman Empire condemned him as a heretic and turned him over to civil authorities, who bound him to a beam, strangled him with a rope, burned his body, and then scattered his remains.

Think about that. "Church" officials executed a man for translating and distributing the words of Jesus in a language that adults and children could actually read and understand. Can you imagine trying to explain that to first-century Christians? Is there any way to reconcile their actions with Jesus' command to make disciples of all nations? We don't have a category for that type of thinking or behavior. Through our modern filter we can't help but ask, "Why did their hatred for him burn so hot? Why were they so vehemently opposed to people having their own copies of the Scriptures?" In a word, *control*. Church officials knew that once average people had access to the Scriptures, they would discover that the church of the sixteenth century was nothing like the church described in the New Testament. Readers of Tyndale's translation of the New Testament would be shocked by something else they found as well. Actually, they were shocked by something they didn't find in his Bible. The word *church*.

Tyndale had the audacity to actually translate the term *ekklesia* rather than superimpose the German term *kirche*. Instead of *church* he used the term *congregation*. If that wasn't offensive enough, the Greek text led him to use *elder* instead of *priest*, and *repent* instead of *do penance*.[11] Throughout the New Testament, he correctly reflected the Bible's original emphasis on church as a movement rather than a location, on people rather than a building, and on the message of the gospel rather than traditions, liturgy, and hierarchy.

Thanks to the courage of men like Tyndale, Huss, Luther, and others, the *ekklesia* of Jesus became a movement once again. The Protestant Reformation breathed new life into what had become a tightly controlled institution. The gospel was unchained from the pulpit and made accessible to the common man and woman.

It is unfortunate that Tyndale's bold but accurate translation of the term *ekklesia* didn't have more influence with Bible translators and publishers. By the time of the reformers, the German term *church* had become so deeply entrenched in Christian culture and conversation that there was no going back. So while much of Tyndale's translation made its way into the modern and postmodern world, the term *ekklesia* remains a casualty of translation tradition. But fortunately, the *ekklesia* of Jesus is not!

From the first century through the twenty-first century there has always been a remnant, a group who refused to substitute *kirche* for the *ekklesia* of Jesus. There have always been and will always be church leaders who refuse to define church in terms of location alone. There will always be leaders who view the church as a movement with a divinely inspired mission and mandate. And chances are if you've read this far, you may very well be one of those unusual individuals.

What does all this mean for those of us called to lead and shape the twenty-first-century *ekklesia* of God? It means we need to look around our *kirches* and ask some unsettling questions. Questions like:

- Are we *moving* or simply *meeting*?
- Are we making a measurable difference in our local communities or simply conducting services?
- Are we organized around a mission or are we organized around an antiquated ministry model inherited from a previous generation?
- Are we allocating resources as if Jesus is the hope of the world or are the squeaky wheels of church culture driving our budgeting decisions?
- Are we *ekklesia* or have we settled for *kirche*?

Pretty unsettling, huh? Kick off your next staff or elders meeting with a couple of those questions and watch where the conversation goes. As uncomfortable as they are, questions like these reorient us to what Jesus intended when he announced the formation of his new gathering.

As his disciples took turns answering Jesus' question regarding his identity, they had no idea that they were at the precipice of a new era. They had no way of knowing how significant that conversation would turn out to be. They certainly had no idea how significant their role would be in the events that were about to unfold. They were still thinking *kingdom*. Their vision was no bigger than the borders of Israel. But Jesus had something else in mind. The church. His unique *ekklesia*. It was the church that would take his message beyond the borders of Israel. In an astonishingly short span of time, it would be the church that ensured his message reached beyond the borders of the Roman Empire. But in the midst of the explosive, unexplainable growth and expansion, the *ekklesia* of Jesus would find itself wrestling with a question we continue to wrestle with today. Namely, who is the *ekklesia* for? Who gets to participate? What are the requirements for membership? How good do people have to be? How good must they continue to be once they're in?

Is the church for church people?

If so, what exactly does that mean?

If not?

Well, keep reading.

chapter four

Just As
I Ain't

I grew up attending churches designed for church people. No one said it, but the assumption was that church was for church people. The unspoken message to the outside world was, "Once you start believing and behaving like us, you are welcome to join us."

The corollary of being a church for churched people was that we had a tendency to be *against* everything unchurched people were *for*. We were against just about everything at one time or another. We were against certain genres of music, alcohol, the lottery, the equal rights amendment, gay people, and Democrats. Seemed like we were always looking for something or someone to boycott. As strange as all that sounds now, it didn't seem strange at all back then. Funny how time does that. But our dilemma then is a dilemma the church has struggled with throughout its history. *Who is the church for? Who gets to be part of the Jesus gathering?* While it's easy to shake our heads in disgust at the narrow-mindedness of a previous generation, this is an issue every generation is forced to wrestle with at some level and often around some unexpected issue. This generation is no exception.

My first major encounter with both the importance and complexity of this question took place in 1987 while I was working for my dad at our downtown location. For some reason that nobody can remember, our church got crossways with the gay community in Atlanta. This was back when nobody really talked about that kind of thing in church. So I'm not sure what created all the hoopla. But for whatever reason, the organizers of the Gay Pride Day march, which always took place on a Sunday, decided to adjust their schedule so the parade would be passing in front of our church around noon — the approximate time we would be dismissing our congregation from our eleven o'clock worship service.

Well, when our church leaders got word of this, they went on the defensive. They decided to let church out early and send everybody out the back so that by the time the parade was in front of our church, all us good church people would be on our way back to the 'burbs! What happened instead was that they let us out in time to line the streets to watch the parade. After all, the best way to ensure that people look at something is to tell them not to look. So there we were, gawking at the show as it slowly made its way down Peachtree Street.

Two circumstances associated with this event made it a defining moment for me. The first thing was what took place directly across the street from our church. St. Mark United Methodist Church had their members standing along the street handing out cups of water to parade participants. While some handed out water, others held up posters that read, *Everybody Welcomed! Come Worship with Us! God Is*

Love! The contrast could not have been more pronounced. It was embarrassing.

The other thing that impacted me about that weekend was our Sunday evening service. I was scheduled to preach the evening service before we knew anything about the parade. When I found out about the controversy, I asked my dad if he was planning to address the subject of homosexuality in his morning sermon. He was not. So I asked him if it would be alright if I did. I still remember the concerned look on his face. "What are you going to say?" he asked. I said, "I don't know, but since it is going to be on everyone's mind, it seems like somebody should say something!" He agreed.

And he agreed it should be me.

So there I was, a whopping twenty-eight years old, putting together the first sermon I had ever heard, much less preached, on the most controversial topic of our generation.

On the morning of the parade, my dad announced to the church that I would be preaching the evening service on the topic of homosexuality. In our church you never heard sermons on any kind of sexuality. So you can imagine the response.

The evening service started at 6:30. By 5:45 the sanctuary was full. We had a lot of "guests."

As I prepared my outline, the issue I found myself wrestling with was not, "What does the Bible have to say about homosexuality?" That's easy. The same thing it says about greedy people, people who drink too much, and "wrongdoers."[12] Wrongdoers? Hmmm. The real issue was the same issue Christians have wrestled with since the beginning. Who is the church for? Who gets to participate? How good do you have to be? Which sins, if any, disqualify a person? Can the church *welcome* sinners? What about unrepentant sinners? How much baggage does a person have to leave at the door before being admitted? Can someone participate in church if he or she is still working things out? Should we sneak out the back or serve water and hold up posters?

Ironically, the answers to those questions were contained in the pages of my Broadman Hymnal. More specifically, in the lyrics of the song we sang at the close of just about every worship service: "Just As I Am." We loved the first, second, and fifth verses. I don't remember singing verses three and four. Or as our music director would say, "The third and fourth *stanzas.*"

> Just as I am, though tossed about
> with many a conflict, many a doubt,
> fightings and fears within, without,
> O Lamb of God, I come, I come.

> Just as I am, poor, wretched, blind;
> sight, riches, healing of the mind,
> yea, all I need in thee to find,
> O Lamb of God, I come, I come.[13]

Sounds more like *come worship with us* than *sneak out the back*, doesn't it?

GRACE AND TRUTH

As I mentioned earlier, the tension around *who is the church for* is not new. The first-century church wrestled with this question as well. There's a lot to learn from the way they managed that tension. Perhaps the most important lesson is to acknowledge that this is in fact a *tension to manage* and not a *problem to solve* or really even a *question to answer*. When you slow down long enough in your reading of Paul's epistles to consider the kinds of issues the early church wrestled with, you begin to realize just how messy the whole thing really was. When we choose to engage with culture at the level the apostle Paul was forced to engage, it gets messy for us as well. It's the messy middle ground that makes some of us uncomfortable. Actually, I think it makes all of us uncomfortable to some extent. There is something in us that would like a definitive answer on every nuance of every issue. But based on my experience, I would argue that when we attempt to eliminate all the gray, all the messy middle ground, we end up with a poor caricature of what Christ originally intended when he announced his *ekklesia*. Actually, we end up with multiple caricatures. And then we argue with each other over whose caricature is the true church. We stand on opposite sides of the street responding in completely opposite ways to the same group of people.

I grew up around people who believed the church was for saved people who acted like saved people. I'm all too familiar with that church brand. The catch was that they were the ones who decided what *act like a saved person* meant. They got to determine which sins saved people could commit and which ones were evidence of being unsaved. Oddly enough, the lists changed every few years. Worse, the lists never coincided with any of the sin lists in the New Testament. For a long time, divorce was on the list. But that one began mysteriously disappearing in the 1970s. Interracial marriage was on there for a while as well. Greed was never included. Nor was slander or gossip. So those who were actually "tossed about with many a conflict, many a doubt, fightings and fears within, without" didn't feel free to talk about their fightings and fears in those churches. Instead, they covered everything up. Which, of course, made everything worse. Covering up may keep a person in the good graces of the church, but it only fuels the power of whatever sin one is covering up. Churches designed for saved people are full of hypocrites. You pretty much have to be a hypocrite to participate. Transparency and honesty are dangerous in a church created for church people. Consequently, the casualty in a church for church people is *grace*. It's hard to extend grace to people who don't seem to need it. And it's hard to admit you need it when you aren't sure you will receive it.

On the other end of the church spectrum are those who declare that the church is for everyone, regardless of belief or behavior. These are the churches that value openness, tolerance, and acceptance above what more conservative churches would consider orthodoxy and orthopraxy. Growing up, we called these *liberal* churches. The problem with this approach is similar to the problem with the more conservative view. You have to pick and choose which parts of the New Testament to embrace. The casualty in liberal churches is *truth*. *Truth* has such an absolute tone about it. Our culture has grown increasingly uneasy with the idea of absolute truth. If there is a right way of doing things, then there's a wrong way as well. Nobody wants to be wrong. So along with *truth*, *sin* becomes a casualty as well. But the New Testament is clear. We are not *mistakers* in need of *correction*. We are sinners in need of a Savior. We need more than a second chance. We need a second birth.

Not surprisingly, Jesus modeled the way forward. He left us with a remarkable approach for navigating the aforementioned tension. As an eyewitness of all Jesus said and did, the apostle John summarized Jesus' approach this way:

> The Word became flesh and made his dwelling among us. We have seen his glory, the glory of the one and only Son, who came from the Father, *full of grace and truth*. (John 1:14, emphasis added)

Three verses later he repeats this same idea.

> For the law was given through Moses; *grace and truth* came through Jesus Christ. (John 1:17, emphasis added)

I love that. "Full of grace and truth." Not the balance between, but the full embodiment of. Jesus did not come to strike a balance between grace and truth. He brought the full measure of both. John had seen this firsthand. He had watched Jesus apply the full measure of grace and truth to each individual they encountered. He was in the crowd when Jesus said to a woman caught in adultery, "I don't condemn you, now leave your life of sin."[14] Translated: "You're a sinner. What you did is a sin. It was wrong. But I don't condemn you. I'm not going to give you what you deserve. I'm extending to you exactly what you don't deserve: grace." Jesus didn't try to balance grace and truth. He didn't water down the law. He didn't put a condition on grace. He gave her a full dose of both.

In Jesus, we get as clear and as close a look as we will ever get of what grace and truth look like in an otherwise graceless world that has turned its back on truth. In Jesus, there was no conflict between grace and truth. It's that artificial conflict that sends churches toward unhealthy as well as unhelpful extremes. It is our misunderstanding of the grace Jesus modeled and taught that leaves us feeling as if grace allows people to "get by" with things. It is often our misapplication of truth that leaves people feeling condemned and isolated. But in Jesus, we discover that it doesn't have to be that way. Grace doesn't dumb down sin to make it more palatable. Grace doesn't have to. The purpose of truth isn't to isolate people from God or from his people. As we follow Jesus through the Gospels, we find him acknowledging the full implications of sin and yet not condemning sinners.

The only group he consistently condemned were graceless religious people — those who misused truth to control through guilt, fear, and condemnation.

It's easy to create an *all-truth* church model. It may be even easier to create an *all-grace* model. But Jesus didn't leave either option on the table.

If his gathering was to reflect his approach to ministry, it would be characterized by a full dose of truth along with a full dose of grace. This is challenging for us. There is tension with law and grace, justice and grace, truth and grace.

Where they meet, it gets messy. Real messy. But to let go of either, to attempt to build a church model around either, is to abandon what Jesus had in mind when he announced the formation of his gathering. Policies and white papers don't work well in a church that commits to embrace the mess created by grace and truth. It's virtually impossible to be consistent or fair when grace and truth become driving forces in a local congregation.

In my experience, *consistency* and *fairness* virtually vanish from the discussion once a church determines to embrace grace and truth. Read the Gospels and you will have a difficult time finding even one example of Jesus being fair. He chose twelve apostles from among hundreds of disciples. He gave preferential treatment to three of the twelve. He didn't heal everyone. He didn't feed every hungry crowd. He stopped in the middle of a virtual parade and invited himself over to Zacchaeus' house. Why him? He ensured that strangers would live and allowed Lazarus to die. And what about the incident at the pool of Bethesda? John tells us that Jesus singled out one man among "a great number of disabled people ... the blind, the lame, the paralyzed."[15] I don't mean to be crass, but you can't help but imagine him tiptoeing through the crowd saying, "Pardon me, excuse me, pardon me, excuse me." Then he finally reaches the one lucky guy. I say lucky. He had been there for thirty-eight years. Jesus leans down and whispers, "Do you want to get well?" Whenever I read this, my mind goes back to my all-time favorite book in high school, *Mad* magazine's *Snappy Answers to Stupid Questions.* Does he want to get well? Seriously? This must have actually happened. No one would fabricate that question and put it in Jesus' mouth. The man assures Jesus that he does. Jesus heals him. And only him. Then tiptoes back through the crowds of sick people, followed by the healed man carrying his mat. Can you imagine? Talk about unfair. How about this one: He tells the fellow known as the rich young ruler that in order to gain eternal life, he has to sell everything and join his entourage. Then, a few months later he whispers to the criminal crucified next to him that on that very day they will meet in paradise! Seriously? One guy has to dedicate the rest of his life to Jesus; the other guy gets in with a minute left on the clock? I could go on and on. Jesus' seeming inconsistency drove religious leaders crazy. When you read the New Testament, it may drive you crazy as well. At times, it must have driven the apostle John crazy. It's John who describes Jesus' healing of a blind stranger and then two chapters later tells us that he intentionally allowed Lazarus to die. With the advantage of hindsight and a few years of maturity under his belt, he chalked it all up to Jesus' uncompromising commitment to grace and truth. I get the feeling that somewhere in the midst of Jesus' seeming lack of fairness and consistency is a clue for how the local church was meant to operate.

I've worked in churches that tried to be fair. Eventually, fairness became an excuse for nonengagement. The quest for consistency became an excuse not to help. Before long, church leaders were hiding behind, "If we do it for one, we will have to do it for everyone." To which I can hear Jesus shouting, "No you don't! I didn't!" If we're not careful, we will end up doing for *none* because we can't do for *everyone*. The better approach is to do for one what you wish you could do for everyone, knowing that *everyone* is not going to be treated the same way. I've seen churches attempt to be consistent. But I've seen a commitment to consistency get in the way of ministry. I've seen people with financial needs turned away, not because there wasn't enough money to help, but because a line item had been depleted. That's a tough one, isn't it?

THE GLORIOUS MESS

Churches that are heavy on truth and light on grace face challenges unique to that approach. Truth-lite churches have their own set of problems to contend with.

Churches committed to embodying grace and truth will be forced to navigate yet a third sea of complexity. But speaking from personal experience, I'll choose door number three every time. The grace-and-truth approach is messy. It's gloriously messy. We have decided to be fine with that. One of our pastors, John Hambrick, has a saying that we've adopted organization-wide. He says, "We walk toward the messes." In other words, we don't feel compelled to sort everything or everyone out ahead of time. We are not going to spend countless hours creating policies for every eventuality.

Instead we've chosen to wade in hip-deep and sort things out one relationship, one conversation, at a time.

Our decision to cling to both grace and truth impacts the way we do just about everything. And that is important for you to keep in mind as you study our model. Do we get it right every time? No. You can't get it right every time regardless of your model. And that's not an excuse. That's the reality of ministry.

I bet you knew that.

We are inconsistent and at times unfair. Not on purpose. We just find that clinging to grace and truth creates tension. Tension we believe that should not be resolved, but managed. Do we have guidelines for benevolence and things of that nature? Of course. But they are guidelines. Not hard-and-fast rules. We have virtually no policies and lots and lots of conversations. There are several questions we decided ahead of time not to answer via email. But these are questions someone from our staff is always happy to sit down and discuss in person. There are a couple of questions we refuse to answer at all. We learned that from Jesus.[16]

Other examples of our attempt to be a grace-and-truth church: We put people into leadership roles too early, on purpose. We operate under the assumption that adults learn on a need-to-know basis. The sooner they discover what they don't know, the sooner they will be interested in learning what they need to know. We have virtually no formal leadership training. We have new believers attempting to lead beyond their maturity. We think that's a good thing. At times, it creates problems. We like those kinds of problems. We encourage our teenagers to lead small groups with kids just two or three years younger than they are. We encourage nonbelievers to sign up for short-term mission trips. But we don't let 'em lead. They don't always understand that. We don't always explain it to their satisfaction. It would be easier not to let 'em go at all. Once again, we opt for messy over easy.

We let nonbelievers serve in as many roles as possible. Sometimes too many. But we don't let 'em serve everywhere. They accuse us of being inconsistent. We agree. We allow people to serve in the parking lot that we won't allow to volunteer in children's ministries. That's confusing. We allow musicians to play on stage who we would not allow to lead worship. We allow people who are not ordained to baptize. We let women baptize. I'm not comfortable with that. I let 'em do it anyway.

We confront sin. We do church discipline. It always takes people by surprise. On occasion, we ask people not to attend a particular campus. On some occasions, we ask people not to attend any of them. They assure us there are individuals with worse sins whom we've not asked to leave. We agree and ask 'em to leave anyway. For a time.

I give people permission to filter out the "Jesus" parts of my messages. Consequently, Jewish attendees often bring friends. They refer to me as a good motivational speaker. I'm fine with that. A Muslim attendee tweeted that he hums through the Jesus parts of my messages. I retweeted him. I preach hard against greed and sexual sin. I tell the men in our church to erase songs from their playlists that refer to women as *bitches* or *whores*. I told 'em that on Mother's Day. Once every few years, I preach on Jesus' view of divorce and remarriage. It's extreme. Nobody agrees with my interpretation of the text. Including most of our staff. I remind all the remarried people that they committed adultery when they remarried. People get upset. Then they purchase the CD to give their kids when they are old enough to get married. But we allow remarried couples to lead at every level in the organization.

We do virtually no charity work directly through our churches. Instead we find the "superstars" in our communities and support them with financial resources and volunteers. We encourage our people to give directly to those organizations. This builds incredible goodwill in our communities. We support non-Christian charities led by non-Christians. Giving church money to non-church related charities seems strange to some people. But we're okay with that. At the same time, we are usually in the top two or three churches in the country to support Operation Christmas Child.

Our doctrinal statement is conservative. Our approach to ministry is not. You have to allow us to video record a three-minute version of your story to be shown on Sunday morning in order to be baptized. No video, no baptism. We don't have any verses to support that. It keeps the baptism numbers low. But baptism is central to our worship and arguably our most powerful evangelism tool.

You can join our church online without talking to a real person. We don't have guest parking. We have reserved parking for parents with preschoolers. I don't have a reserved parking spot. And I don't have a bathroom attached to my office. Not sure what that has to do with grace and truth. Just thought you should know.

We save seats in the front for people who arrive late. It bugs the people who get there early when they can't get the best seats. Doesn't seem fair. It's not. We are okay with that.

I try to read all the critical email and letters. I don't learn much from people who agree with me. I call the most critical people. They are always surprised. Most of the time, I understand their concerns. Heck, a lot of the time I share their concerns! I remind 'em we are still learning. I assure them that not only are we inconsistent and unfair, but that we will continue to be, and that we would love for them to join us. They usually do.

These are just a few examples of our attempts to extend grace while carpet bombing our community with truth. We believe the church is most appealing when the message of grace is most apparent. We are equally as convinced that God's grace is only as visible as God's truth is clear. It is pointless to tell me I'm forgiven if I'm not sure why I need forgiveness in the first place. That's the beauty of grace and truth. They complement. They are both necessary. They are not part of a continuum. They are not opposite ends of a pole. They are the two essential ingredients. Without massive doses of both, you won't have a healthy gathering.

Now, if the idea of embracing the mess is uncomfortable for you, remember this: Either you were a mess, are a mess, or are one dumb decision away from becoming a mess. And when you were your messiest version of you, you weren't looking for a policy, were you? You needed somebody to take you *just as you were*. That's what Jesus did for me. That's what Jesus did and will do for you. That being the case, it seems to me that's what we should be about as the local church.

At this point, you may have more questions than answers. I understand that. So here's something that should encourage you. The book of Acts, along with Paul's epistles, reflects the real-world drama associated with local churches built on a foundation of grace and truth. If you opt for a grace-and-truth approach for your local church, the New Testament is going to open up to you in ways you never imagined. Paul's epistles in particular reflect the challenges any local church will face when the uncompromising truth of God is presented within a community characterized by grace. Not to be outdone, Luke provides us with a ringside seat at the very first church business meeting. The reason for the meeting was an incident that took place in Antioch. Seems there had been a head-on collision between God's grace and God's truth. Nobody knew exactly how to handle this one. So they brought it to the experts.

chapter five

DEFYING GRAVITY

Fortunately, we aren't the first generation of church leaders to wrestle with the tension that grace and truth pose for the church. The first-century church was forced to confront this early on. The approach they adopted is, well, it's almost incomprehensible. It's a tad unsettling to my conservative roots. But at the same time, those on the liberal end of things may feel a bit reined in by it. I've never heard anyone preach on this particular first-century development. I can understand why. The apostles' conclusion on this matter left so much open to interpretation that Paul spent a great deal of his spare time acting as referee among church people. As many times as I've taught through the book of Acts, I still don't think I fully appreciate the lengths the early church went to in order to keep both grace and truth front and center. They were comfortable with a bit of ambiguity and inconsistency. We should be as well.

The defining moment in this regard for the early church is recorded by Luke in Acts 15. The incident is commonly referred to as the Jerusalem Council. Some twenty years after the resurrection, the church found itself wrestling with questions of participation and salvation. Specifically, what is required for salvation and thus involvement in the church.

As we walk through this historical event, here's something important to keep in mind. If you want to know what people mean by what they say, watch what they do. Actions don't only speak louder than words; actions should be used to interpret words. Paul's epistles are full of practical admonitions regarding the behavior of a believer. But everything he taught should be defined within the context of what takes place in Acts 15.

REACHING JEWS AND GENTILES

According to Luke, the church launched big. On opening day, thousands of Jews and converts to Judaism embraced Jesus as Messiah. These early followers of Christ did not consider themselves *converts* to something new. This new activity of God was simply a fulfillment of what had been promised through Abraham and the prophets. Becoming a follower of Jesus was simply the next step.

As you know, the energy and activity that marked opening day wasn't contained within the borders of Jerusalem. Before long, evangelists left the city to take the message of Jesus' death and resurrection to surrounding villages and towns. Eventually the message overflowed into non-Jewish regions. Gentiles heard and believed. And once they believed, they wanted to join the Jesus gathering. A gathering that was made up primarily of Jews. Many of the Jewish Christians were not quite ready for that. Jesus was *their* Messiah. And they had been waiting a long time for this. Most of his teaching revolved around the "kingdom of

God," and every good Jew knew that was synonymous with the "kingdom of Israel."

If that wasn't confusing enough, a few of Jesus' original apostles became intentional with their Gentile evangelistic efforts. They traveled to predominantly Gentile areas of the region and proclaimed the resurrection of Jesus. Just about everywhere they went, Gentiles believed. These new believers formed new Jesus gatherings. But these gatherings were made up predominantly of Gentiles. Whereas the Jews in the Jesus gatherings did not consider themselves *converts,* the Gentile believers did. They viewed themselves as converts from paganism. The question was: *What exactly were they converting to?* In their minds, they were leaving their pagan beliefs to become followers of Jesus. They didn't view their conversions as conversions to Judaism. And that was a problem for Jewish believers. How could someone become a follower of the Jewish Messiah without becoming Jewish?

Good question.

It's easy to understand why first-century Jewish Jesus followers felt a bit uneasy with this sudden influx of non-Jewish outsiders. Actually, it was worse than uneasy. *Offended* is a better description of what they felt. Whereas Gentile believers abandoned their pagan beliefs, they did not abandon their pagan behaviors. Gentile believers brought their Gentile customs, habits, and values right along with them, many of which were highly offensive to the Jews. Some of their practices were considered sacrilegious. Especially their eating habits. To make matters worse, most of the early Christians, being Jewish, met at local synagogues. Suddenly there were handfuls of Gentiles showing up and wanting to participate. But they knew nothing about the Sabbath, ceremonial cleansing, or any of the traditions that made Saturday a day set apart.

It was messy.

The logical solution was to require Gentile Christians to become Jewish. Just give 'em a list. Now, if becoming a convert to Judaism was as simple as being schooled in the Jewish scriptures and Hebrew theology, it probably would not have been a big deal. Unfortunately for the men, it meant more than that. Much more. Becoming Jewish would require surgery. If you think membership standards in your church are high, think again. The most ardent supporters of the Jewish-first movement taught the following: "Unless you are circumcised, according to the custom taught by Moses, you cannot be saved" (Acts 15:1). Bottom line, the new members classes were full of women and children—while the men waited in the car.

But circumcision was only the beginning.

In addition to circumcision, Gentile believers would be required to submit to the entire law of Moses. Keeping the law was difficult for the average Jew. Thus the sacrificial system. The sacrificial system assumed Jewish people would break their own laws. For an adult Gentile, whose lifestyle had been shaped predominantly by Greek and Roman values and traditions, adapting to Jewish law would be virtually impossible. Learning the law would take years. Reorganizing their entire lives around it would take, well, a lifetime.

As this new standard for membership to the Jesus gathering was beginning to be propagated in select areas, the church continued to flourish just about everywhere the message of Jesus was being preached. This was especially true in the Gentile city of Antioch, located about three hundred miles north of Jerusalem. The apostle Paul had settled there with Barnabas. Together they taught, and many non-Jewish people responded to the offer of salvation.

As you are probably aware, it was in Antioch that the term *Christian* was first used to describe followers of Jesus.[17]

Soon reports began to filter into Jerusalem that Gentiles in Antioch were becoming Christians with no consideration for Jewish tradition. In response, the Jewish Christians appointed a committee and sent them to Antioch to set things straight. Which, of course, only made things worse.

To resolve the conflict, the church leaders in Antioch appointed Barnabas, Paul, and a few others as envoys to Jerusalem, where they would get clarification from the apostles. As you know, there was no formal hierarchal structure in the early years. Local churches operated as autonomous congregations. However, as churches sprang up across the Roman Empire, they looked to the apostles for leadership. After all, these men had spent years listening to and watching Jesus. If anyone would know what to do with this influx of Gentiles, they would.

When the group from Antioch arrived in Jerusalem, they received a warm reception. Barnabas and Paul reported on the extraordinary growth of the church, specifically highlighting the large number of Gentiles who were embracing the message of Christ. When they finished their report, their opponents stood and declared, "The Gentiles must be circumcised and required to keep the law of Moses."[18] According to Luke, some who argued with Paul and Barnabas were actually Pharisees who had become believers. As ardent followers of the law, they just couldn't give it up.

SALVATION OFFERED TO EVERYONE

After a lengthy debate, Peter addressed the group. He began by reminding them of his own experience with Gentiles and

the gospel. God had made it abundantly clear to Peter that
salvation was to be offered to everyone on the same terms:
faith in Christ. Peter reasoned, "He did not discriminate
between us and them [Gentiles], for he purified their hearts
by faith." Then he asked his audience a thought-provoking
as well as convicting question, "Now then, why do you try
to test God by putting on the necks of Gentiles a yoke that
neither we nor our ancestors have been able to bear?"[19]
Translated: "My Jewish friends, who are we kidding? *We*
don't even keep the law all that well. Why burden the
Gentiles with it?" That was a pretty compelling argument.
Peter continued, "No! We believe it is through the *grace* of
our Lord Jesus that we are saved, just as they are."[20]

When Peter sat down, all eyes turned to James. James,
the brother of Jesus, was the most influential church leader
in Jerusalem. In my opinion, James may be our most
convincing proof for the deity of Christ. Think about it. If
you have a brother, what would he have to do to convince
you that he is the Son of God? The fact that James embraced
his brother as Messiah and Lord says a lot.

Like the Pharisees in the room, James came to faith late.
Apparently he was convinced of Jesus' identity after the
resurrection. But unlike the Pharisees, he believed non-
Jewish believers should be allowed into the community of
faith without first converting to Judaism. After quoting a
short passage from the prophet Amos, he concluded his
remarks as follows:

> It is my judgment, therefore, that we should not make it
> difficult for the Gentiles who are turning to God. (Acts 15:19)

I love that statement. Years ago I printed it and hung it in
my study. I look at it every day. I believe James' statement
should be the benchmark by which all decisions are made

in the local church. In other words, churches shouldn't do anything that makes it unnecessarily difficult for people who are turning to God.

Peter and James understood the Jews' attachments to their traditions. After all, most of their rites and rituals were instituted by God and had been a part of their religious and national identity for more than a thousand years. But church leaders also had to acknowledge this new thing God was doing among the Gentiles. They had to make room. Create some new categories. Adjust. But it is how far they adjusted that is staggering. This is the part I've never heard anyone talk about in church. Keep in mind that this entire discussion began around how Jewish a non-Jew had to become to participate in the church. At stake was circumcision along with not ten, but over six hundred commandments plus commentary. Here's the response the Jerusalem Council sent to the Gentile believers in Antioch, Syria, and Cilicia:

> The apostles and elders, your brothers, To the Gentile believers in Antioch, Syria and Cilicia: Greetings. We have heard that some went out from us without our authorization and disturbed you, troubling your minds by what they said. So we all agreed to choose some men and send them to you with our dear friends Barnabas and Paul—men who have risked their lives for the name of our Lord Jesus Christ. Therefore we are sending Judas and Silas to confirm by word of mouth what we are writing. (Acts 15:23–27)

Here's the shocking part:

> It seemed good to the Holy Spirit and to us not to burden you with anything beyond the following requirements: (v. 28)

Here we go:

> You are to abstain from food sacrificed to idols, from blood, from the meat of strangled animals and from sexual immorality. You will do well to avoid these things. Farewell. (v. 29)

Did you follow that? The Jerusalem Council effectively reduced church participation down to two things: Be careful what you eat around your Jewish brothers and don't be immoral. That's it.

Talk about a short new members class.

When the delegation from Jerusalem arrived in Antioch, the letter was read to the entire congregation. As you might imagine, it was well received. Especially by the men. No one had to become Jewish to become a Christian. Gentiles could simply place their faith in a risen Messiah and be adopted into the family of God along with their Jewish brothers and sisters. It was that simple.

But, unfortunately, it didn't stay that way. It never stays that way. If you have even a cursory knowledge of church history, you know there has always been what amounts to an invisible force, something akin to a gravitational pull, drawing the church back in the direction of graceless religion and legalism. It shows up in every generation with a variety of labels, styles, and faces. It has disguised itself as orthodoxy, holiness, morality, and conservatism, among others. But when all is said and done, the message is the same: *The church is for church people.* The church is for those who will sign on to a brand and abide by a custom set of rules.

It's this drift toward churchy, graceless, lifeless church that makes what you do so important. As a church leader, you are mission critical.

It is your responsibility to lead the church in the direction that Jesus originally intended. As a leader, your task is to protect the missional integrity of the Jesus gathering to which you have been called. It is your responsibility to see to it that the church under your care continues to function as a gathering of people in process; a place where the curious, the unconvinced, the skeptical, the used-to-believe, and the broken, as well as the committed, informed, and sold-out come together around Peter's declaration that Jesus is the Christ, the Son of the living God.

Keeping Church for the Unchurched

As committed as our team is to creating churches for unchurched people, we still have to fight the pull toward becoming a church for church people. Honestly, I don't understand why every church wouldn't determine to become a church unchurched people loved to attend.

Nothing brings this conviction into sharper focus for me than baptism. As I mentioned in chapter four, to be baptized in our churches, candidates have to allow us to record a three-to-four minute video describing their faith journeys. We show these videos in our worship services just before individuals are baptized. Week after week, I sit and listen to people of all ages share their stories of how they connected with their heavenly Father as a result of getting connected to church.[21] I'm sure you have stories of your own. I don't share these by way of comparison. It's just that stories like these are the bull's-eye on the target for us. It's why we exist.

I'll never forget Allen's story. He grew up with a single mom who worked three jobs to keep the family afloat. He stopped attending church as soon as he could. When his mother contracted cancer and died, he became very angry with God. His words were, "I couldn't understand how he could let her work so hard and never have anything for herself and die at the age of forty-one. For the next

twenty years I lived a very destructive life." It was Allen's
wife who eventually persuaded him to attend North Point.
He described it this way, "I sat in rows here at North Point
for over six years just to make her happy. Then suddenly
the messages started making sense." Allen still had a lot of
questions, so he joined a Starting Point[22] group as well as
a couple's group. "Eventually all my dots connected and
I truly got it for the first time." Allen said that when he
accepted Christ as his Savior, he cried the entire day.

Then there was my friend Nancy. Nancy began attending
because we hired her husband to play in one of our
bands. Her story began like this: "I grew up in a Jewish
household, the granddaughter of an orthodox cantor. I was
bas mitzvahed at thirteen. My ex-husband was invited to
play in the North Point band and thus my journey began.
At first, I considered Andy's preaching to be motivational
speaking. Yet slowly my heart began to open to the message
of the New Testament. It was in the sermon series *The Star,
the Cross, and the Crescent* that I realized that Jesus was
my Savior." Nancy went on to thank the people God had
brought into her life to facilitate her journey to faith. Then
she concluded by saying, "Today I proudly and profoundly
would like to say that I am Jewish, Jesus Christ is the
Messiah, and he is my personal Lord and Savior."

A few weeks earlier, a thirty-year-old woman began her
baptism story this way: "I had always been told that because I
was gay, God hated me and I was going to hell." She went on
to explain how she turned to alcohol at the age of fifteen to
deal with her rejection. She continued, "I was a miserable lost
person trying to find something to fill my emptiness." But
God brought someone into Jessie's life who challenged her
to get sober and begin attending church. After fifteen years

of avoiding church, she said, "When I came to this church, I immediately felt at home." I have to tell you, that statement was emotional for me. I imagined Jessie as a teenager carrying the secret of same-sex attraction compounded by the lie that she would never be acceptable to God, and then fifteen years later walking into one of our churches and feeling "immediately at home." I don't have words.

The turning point for Jessie came during a message preached by one of our associate pastors Rodney Anderson. She said, "During a message I heard Rodney say, 'There's a monumental difference in believing in God and believing God.' That hit home. I had always believed in God but I had not believed God." She went on to describe the transformation she experienced as a result of embracing God's forgiveness, love, and grace. She concluded with this, "I have now filled my emptiness with the love of Jesus."

That's what happens when you decide to follow the apostle James' advice. That's what happens when you decide that under no circumstance will you do anything that makes it difficult for those who are turning to God. I could go on and on. And in case you visit us someday, you should know that in our churches, when someone comes up out of the water, we cheer. We celebrate. It's not uncommon for friends to bring posters with the name of the person they've come to see baptized written in big bold letters. People throw confetti and ring bells. It's awesome. We take seriously Jesus' words that "there will be more rejoicing in heaven over one sinner who repents than over ninety-nine righteous persons who do not need to repent" (Luke 15:7). We figure if heaven is celebrating, we should join in.

Pardon my naïveté or arrogance, but I think celebrations like the ones I just described should be the norm in every gathering that calls itself a church. From time to time I get notes from attendees thanking me for creating a church to which they can invite their neighbors and unchurched family members. As appreciative as I am, it still strikes me as odd that someone would have to thank a pastor for creating a church that is doing the very thing the church was created to do in the first place. Why should that be the exception and not the rule?

It's a shame that so many churches are married to a designed-by-Christians-for-Christians-only culture. A culture in which they talk about the Great Commission, sing songs about the Great Commission, but refuse to reorganize their churches around the Great Commission. These are often the same churches where members talk about grace, sing about how "amazing" it is, but create graceless cultures where only those who play by the rules feel welcomed.

So we have our work cut out for us. But what an incredible work it is. We are privileged to be stewards of the church of our generation. God has seen fit to bless us with the responsibility to ensure that the twenty-first century church is a place where all kinds of people with all kinds of stuff can gather in Jesus' name and find restoration, acceptance, and grace.

Music comes and goes a lot more quickly than it used to. We sang "Just As I Am" for decades. Currently, the song we sing that captures that same sense of transparency, restoration, and hope is Gungor's song "Beautiful Things": [23]

> All around
> Hope is springing up from this old ground
> Out of chaos life is being found in You
> You make beautiful things
> You make beautiful things out of the dust
> You make beautiful things
> You make beautiful things out of us.

There it is. Another reference to the glorious mess from which God brings life. The church. So church leaders, let's get out there and do what Jesus died to make possible. Let's heed brother James' advice. Let's rid our churches of anything that makes it difficult for those who are turning to God. Let's proclaim God's liberating truth. Let's create communities characterized by grace. Let's get comfortable with the tension, the inconsistency, and the messiness that ensues.

Let's be the church.

GOING DEEP

Rethinking Spiritual Formation

For two thousand years, church leaders have taken their marching orders from the one imperative Jesus left with his followers the afternoon he made his farewell address and returned to the Father: *Make disciples.* While I've never heard anyone dispute the importance of that command, there has certainly been a lot of discussion around what it means and how to pull it off. In this section, I'm going to share our view on what it means to create Jesus followers. Or as we sometimes refer to it, this is our *spiritual formation model.* For that reason, this may be the most important section of the book.

If North Point has a secret sauce, this is it. And it has *nothing* to do with style. This is our take on how individuals mature in their faith. This is an important part of our story because it addresses a question we are constantly asked: *In a church committed to making it easy for unchurched people to feel connected, what do you do to ensure that new believers, as well as seasoned believers, continue to mature in their faith?* The shorter version of the question is: *What does North Point's discipleship model look like?*

I've been asked that question enough to know that most people who ask it are looking for a program, a curriculum, or a series of classes. We have rejected that approach to spiritual formation from the very beginning. We don't believe classes create mature believers. Classes create smart believers. That's different. We have a menu of class options for those who want further theological education. But as you know, theological education and spiritual maturity can be mutually exclusive. They don't have to be. But they can be. So we have never approached spiritual formation as a cognitive exercise.

We have a much more holistic approach. And whether you recognize it or not, your church does as well. I'm hoping through the next three chapters to help you recognize and embrace the way God has chosen to mature people in the faith. But to do that, I've got to go back and tell you a bit more of my story.

chapter six

MY BIG
DISCOVERY

One of the things Dr. Howard Hendricks instilled in me during seminary is that I should always have a group. Specifically, I should always be able to point to a group of men and say, "That's the group I'm currently pouring my life into." As I stated in the introduction, I don't feel like it's my responsibility to fill anybody's cup. But I am responsible to empty mine. So I've always had a handpicked group of guys that I'm investing in. It was in one of those groups that I made a discovery that shaped my view of spiritual formation.

In 1987, my group was comprised of college students who felt like God might be calling them into full-time ministry. We met on Tuesday mornings at 6:30 for about an hour and a half. One of the things I asked each group member to do was develop a chart that reflected his spiritual history beginning with salvation. Keep in mind, these guys were in their early twenties, so it's not like they had a whole lot of life to chart. Specifically, I wanted to see the highs and lows and I wanted them to include the things that contributed to both. As best I can remember, my goal was to get a snapshot of where each of these guys was coming from.

There were five college students in that original group. While the details of their stories were different, there was a good deal of similarity as well. A year and a half later, I asked a second group to do the same exercise. The stories were different, but the dynamics that led to their spiritual growth were similar. After repeating this exercise several more times, I observed five things that surfaced in just about everyone's story.

1995

Fast-forward to the fall of 1995 and I'm sitting in a friend's basement with the original North Point staff hashing out the mission and strategy statement for our newly formed church. It was within the context of this lengthy discussion that the subject of spiritual formation first surfaced. We began wrestling with questions such as: *What should our discipleship model look like? What is our goal for the people who choose to partner with us in ministry? What does a mature believer look like? What role does the church have in developing Christ followers?* More than anything, we wanted to create a model that would *actually* facilitate spiritual maturity. We had enough church staff experience to know that in most churches *spiritual formation* was not the driving force behind programming (or budgeting, for that matter). We wanted to be the exception. We wanted everything we did to focus on building mature followers of Christ. And we knew that if we weren't intentional, spiritual formation would get lost in the plethora of activities that tends to gobble up valuable time and resources.

The mission statement we had settled on was (and still is) *to lead people into a growing relationship with Jesus Christ.* But we felt like that needed further definition. If someone is in a growing relationship with Christ, what specifically is growing? Her hair? His beard? To make a long series of conversations short, we determined that *faith* is what grows in a growing relationship. Specifically, a person's confidence in God. Confidence that God is who he says he is and that he will do what he has promised to do.

Faith, or trust, is at the center of every healthy relationship. As trust goes, so goes the relationship. A break in trust signals a break in the relationship. Sin was introduced to the world through a choice not to trust. In the Garden of Eden, humanity's relationship with God was broken when Eve and Adam quit trusting. God has been on a quest ever since to reengage with mankind in a relationship characterized by trust. The entire Old Testament is the story of God saying, "Trust me." It's no coincidence that God didn't give Israel the law until they first learned to trust him and follow him. With that as a backdrop, we shouldn't be surprised to discover that at the epicenter of Jesus' message was the word *believe.* Just as humankind's relationship with God was destroyed through a lack of faith, so it would be restored through an expression of the same. At its core, Christianity is an invitation to reenter a relationship of trust with the Father. At the cross, sin was forgiven and we were invited to trust. It makes perfect sense that salvation comes by faith, not obedience. Intimate relationships are not built on obedience. They are built on trust. Walking by faith, again, is simply living as if God is who he says he is and that he will do everything he has promised to do. As a person's confidence in God grows, he or she matures.

As we continued our discussion, we talked about the Christians we knew who appeared to have the strongest relationships with Christ. In every case, these were men and women with big faith — extraordinary confidence in God in spite of what life threw at them. These were the people whose faith amazed us. I was convinced then, as I am now, that God is most honored through living, active, death-defying, out-of-the-box faith. During one of these discussions, someone on our team pointed out that the only time Jesus was ever "amazed" was when he saw expressions of great faith and little faith.[24] Big faith was a big deal to Jesus. When people *acted* on what they believed about him, he was impressed. We are as well. Isn't it true that we love the stories about people in our church who trust God against all odds? We revel in the accounts of teenagers who decide to live out their values at school because they *believe* God's promises. What about those hospital visits when you walk in praying for the right thing to say, and you are greeted by a family whose faith in God is staggering? They are confident. No fear. I don't know about you, but there have been plenty of times when I have driven home from a hospital visit wondering why they let me be the pastor. As I write, I'm reminded of a couple in our small group that has two children with severe vision impairment. I've heard Chris and Dave share their story on three occasions. Each time I am moved to tears when I hear Chris talk about their confidence in God through a series of difficult conversations with doctors and two very difficult pregnancies. Maggie and Luke suffer from different conditions, both of which have left them legally blind.

As our team continued to wrestle with the relationship of faith and spiritual maturity, we all agreed that we were way more inspired by the people who have the kind of faith that endures a *no* from God than those who claim their faith arm-twisted a *yes* out of him. Big faith is a sign of big maturity. We concluded that the best discipleship or spiritual formation model would be one designed around *growing people's faith.* The model most of us had grown up with was designed around *increasing people's knowledge.* The models we were exposed to were primarily teaching models. We wanted to go beyond that.

But how?

If our mission was to lead people into a growing relationship with Christ — a growing relationship equated to growing faith — then we needed to know what grows people's faith. So the conversation quickly turned to these questions: *What fuels the development of faith? What are the ingredients that, when stirred together, result in greater confidence in the person and promises of God?* That's when I introduced my findings to our team.

ESSENTIAL INGREDIENTS

I shared my experiences with my various men's groups. Then I explained the five things that showed up in everybody's faith story. One by one, the members of our team acknowledged how each of these five dynamics had played a role in their spiritual formations as well. It was a defining moment for our team. We decided that if this was how God grew people's faith, we should create a ministry model that continually pointed people back to these five dynamics. If these were the essential ingredients to big faith, we should build our entire model around them. So that's exactly what we did.

Early in our discussion someone suggested we name these things. As you will see, they aren't steps or principles. I often refer to them as *dynamics*. But that can mean a lot of things. I think it was Reggie Joiner who suggested the term *catalysts*. So from that point forward, we've referred to these as the *five faith catalysts*. During our weekend services, I sometimes refer to them as *five things God uses to grow your faith*.[25]

As you might expect, you won't find this list anywhere in the Scriptures. Remember, this list is the result of what we've *observed*. We've made no effort to make the list complete or balanced. These five things are what surface on their own when people tell their faith stories. Since those early days, we've tested our theory on numerous occasions. For several years, Reggie Joiner incorporated the five faith catalysts into his leadership training for student pastors. In one exercise he would write each of the five on a three-by-five card, turn them over so no one could read them, and then attach them from left to right across the top of a planning board. Then he would ask his audience to think through the things that contributed most to their spiritual development, good and bad, and begin calling them out. He would write down whatever came to their minds on cards and tack them under one of the five catalyst cards across the top of the board. When everyone had finished sharing, he would turn the cards over to reveal the five catalysts. Time after time, summer after summer, everything these leaders threw out as major factors in their spiritual development fit at least one of the five.

As I've stated throughout this book, I'm not expecting you to do what we do. But we are absolutely convinced that these five things reflect the way faith is developed. We've presented this idea to church leaders from every church background imaginable. Each time we do, we walk away even more convinced that these five things represent the common ground for faith development. I'm convinced this is how God works in spite of how we organize and program our churches. But imagine what would happen if we actually organized and programmed in concert with the way God works? We believe that what we've seen over the past seventeen years is a direct result of our efforts to do just that. So for the remainder of this section, I'll walk you through the five faith catalysts, along with examples of how we've allowed them to shape our programming as well as our model.

In case you have to leave early, I'll go ahead and give you all five upfront. Yes, they all start with the letter "P." No, I'm not a fan of lists that all begin with the same letter. This is one of those rare cases in the history of list making when someone didn't have to force a word to fit the motif.

The Five Faith Catalysts:
- Practical Teaching
- Private Disciplines
- Personal Ministry
- Providential Relationships
- Pivotal Circumstances

chapter seven

PLAYING
MY PART

The first three catalysts we'll look at require us to play our part. *Practical teaching*, *private disciplines*, and *personal ministry* encompass the activities of a growing faith. If you think of a relationship with God as consisting of things he does and things we do, these are on us.

CATALYST #1: PRACTICAL TEACHING

When individuals describe their faith journeys, they always reference the first time they were exposed to practical Bible teaching. For some, this happened at a college Bible study. For others, it was in a home. For many women in our country, it was Beth Moore who served as an introduction to this type of teaching. For most, it was when they heard the Bible presented in practical terms for the first time in a local church. When people tell their stories, it becomes evident that this was not their first *exposure* to the Bible. It represents the first time they *understood* what was being taught from the Bible. It was the first time they actually knew what to do with what was being taught. Most Christians can tell you where they were and who was speaking the first time someone made the Bible come alive for them.

It's unfortunate that someone can grow up hearing sermons and Sunday school lessons, yet never be captivated by the Scriptures. But, unfortunately, that seems to be the rule rather than the exception. And this is not a twentieth- or twenty-first century problem.

When Jesus finished what we commonly refer to as the Sermon on the Mount, Matthew records the crowd's response.

> When Jesus had finished saying these things, the crowds were amazed at his teaching, because he taught as one who had authority, and not as their teachers of the law. (Matthew 7:28–29)

All teaching and preaching is not the same. The first-century teachers of the law were teaching from the same script Jesus would refer to throughout his earthly ministry. But there was something different about his presentation. He spoke with authority. Apparently he had a passion the other teachers lacked. More specifically, he wasn't satisfied to simply say what was true. He wanted his audience to *act* on what they heard. As you may recall, he closed that particular message with a specific call to action along with an emotionally charged promise and warning:

> Therefore everyone who hears these words of mine and puts them into practice is like a wise man who built his house on the rock.... But everyone who hears these words of mine and does not put them into practice is like a foolish man who built his house on sand. (Matthew 7:24, 26)

Jesus taught for a response. He taught for life change. He didn't come to simply dispense information. We rarely find him chastising people for their lack of knowledge. It was almost always their lack of faith evidenced by a lack of application. "You of little faith, why are you so afraid?" he asked the disciples in the midst of a terrifying ordeal on the water (Matthew 8:26). Jesus wasn't after mental assent to facts. Jesus was after active, living, do-the-right-thing faith. And when he taught, he taught with that in mind.

Remember the first time you were challenged at that level? Remember how interesting the Bible suddenly became? You sat on the edge of your chair. The time flew by. You took notes. You wanted to know what kind of Bible the teacher or preacher was using so you could get one like it. You couldn't wait to come back for another round. Yeah, you remember. Something came alive inside of you. Then you did something really crazy. You went out and applied some of what you had heard. And God honored your active faith. Your faith intersected with his faithfulness and your confidence in God got bigger. Practical teaching that moves people to action is one of the primary things God uses to grow our faith.

Fortunately for me, I grew up in a church where this was the norm. I would sit week after week and listen to my dad teach the application of Scripture to my everyday life. Often I was sitting in the back of the balcony and there were a few Sundays as a teenager that I was sitting at the Varsity. For those of you not familiar with Atlanta, the Varsity is the world's largest drive-in restaurant. It also has rooms where you can watch TV and eat hot dogs. It was ahead of its time. The Varsity is about five blocks from where First Baptist Church of Atlanta used to be. Back in the '70s, my dad was on live TV on Sunday mornings. So Louie Giglio and I would sneak out of Sunday school and head down to the

Varsity for "church." Church consisted of Louie, an assorted number of winos sleeping off their Saturday night, and me. I'd climb up on a chair and switch the channel to my dad's program (the winos were in no shape to argue). We thought of it as evangelism. We would eat and watch TV and then on the way home I could talk about the sermon and my dad would think I had been there. But whether I was watching from the back row of the balcony or the Varsity, my dad showed me that teaching the Word of God wasn't about *knowing* stuff; it was about *doing* stuff. And the impact of that exploded my faith, as well as the faith of thousands of other people.

That being the case, our messages and lesson preparations are not complete until we know what we want our audiences to *do* with what they are about to hear. To grow our congregants' faith, we must preach and teach for life change.

Here's something else you should know. Unchurched, unbelieving people are attracted to communicators who have *here's what to do next* tacked on the end of their messages. This is true even when they don't agree with or understand the premise of what we are talking about. Either way, they like it when we give 'em something to do. Here's why.

And this is very important.

People are far more interested in what works than what's true. I hate to burst your bubble, but virtually nobody in your church is on a truth quest. Including your spouse. They are on happiness quests. As long as you are dishing out truth with no *here's the difference it will make* tacked on the end, you will be perceived as irrelevant by most of the people in your church, student ministry, or home Bible study. You may be spot-on theologically, like the teachers of the law in Jesus' day, but you will not be perceived as one who teaches with authority. Worse, nobody is going to want to listen to you.

Now, that may be discouraging. Especially the fact that you are one of the few who is actually on a quest for truth. And, yes, it is unfortunate that people aren't more like you in that regard. But that's the way it is. It's pointless to resist. If you try, you will end up with a little congregation of truth seekers who consider themselves superior to all the other Christians in the community. But at the end of the day, you won't make an iota of a difference in this world. And your kids ... more than likely your kids, are going to confuse your church with *the* church, and once they are out of your house, they probably won't visit the church house. Then one day they will show up in a church like mine and want to get baptized again because they won't be sure the first one took. And I'll be happy to pastor your kids. But I would rather you face the reality of the world we live in and adjust your sails. Culture is like the wind. You can't stop it. You shouldn't spit in it. But, if like a good sailor you will adjust your sails, you can harness the winds of culture to take your audience where they need to go. If people are more interested in being happy, then play to that. Jesus did.

You've studied the Sermon on the Mount. Surely you know that the term Jesus uses over and over in the opening lines of what was perhaps his earliest sermon can be (some say should be) translated *happy*.[26] But even if you are more comfortable with the term *blessed*, think about what Jesus does at the beginning of his message. Who doesn't want to be blessed? Favored? Fortunate? He plays to their human nature, their desire for happiness. Their *I-wanna-be-blessed* quest. And then, one by one, he challenges their most basic assumptions about ... well, about everything! Even the way they prayed.[27] Jesus' instructions to his first-century audience were so specific. So extreme. We are still wrestling with them today. Wrestling with. That means we don't actually do them, we just talk about 'em a lot.

BACK AT THE CHURCH

This first faith catalyst explains why we do several things in our churches. It underscores why we are so adamant about our content being *helpful*, not simply *true*. Jesus wasn't content with saying true things. We shouldn't be either. Truth without handles is static. Truth with next steps grows people's faith. This faith catalyst is why we create topical sermons or message series instead of simply teaching through books of the Bible. On those rare occasions when I do teach through a book of the Bible, we look for a practical angle that ties the series together.

We close every message and every series in every age group with a specific call to action. Sometimes we assign homework. Jeff Henderson, one of our lead pastors, did a series recently entitled *Climate Change*. His big idea was that everybody has a climate. When people see you coming, they know what to forecast. At the end of week one, his assignment was for everybody to ask three people this question: "What's it like to be on the other side of me?" Ouch. After my first two conversations, I was ready to resign. It was a painful application. But extremely helpful. Helpful for believers and nonbelievers alike.

Our children's ministry creates an activity for the entire family around the virtue or principle they are discussing that month. Middle school and high school communicators close their talks each week by previewing three or four application-oriented questions kids will discuss with their small group leaders. All of this is our way of driving our communicators toward action-oriented teaching. We are constantly asking our preachers and teachers:

- What do you want them to know?
- What do you want them to do?
- What can we do to create next steps?

All of this with the goal of growing people's faith.

CATALYST #2: PRIVATE DISCIPLINES

A second theme that surfaces when people tell their faith stories revolves around the development of a *private devotional life*. Somewhere along the way, Christians begin to pray. Alone. They begin exploring the Bible on their own. They memorize their first Scripture verse. It's not uncommon to hear people speak of getting up a little earlier in the morning to spend time with God. Personal spiritual disciplines introduce a sense of intimacy and accountability to our faith walks. Private spiritual disciplines tune our hearts to the heart of God and underscore personal accountability to our heavenly Father.

There is a direct correlation between a person's private devotional life and his or her personal faith. And regardless of how long you've been in ministry, this is something you can't afford to lose sight of. When God speaks to us personally through his Word or answers a specific prayer, our faith is strengthened. This is why private disciplines is a faith catalyst. One of the most impactful things I heard my dad say growing up was, "The most important thing in your life is your personal relationship with Jesus Christ."

That's direct. And I have found it to be absolutely correct. As my personal devotional life goes, so goes my faith, my confidence in God. And I don't know if this is true for everybody, but as my confidence in God goes, so goes my personal confidence.

When it came to maintaining a private devotional life, first-century Jews were at somewhat of a disadvantage. They didn't have copies of the Old Testament they could cart around in their backpacks and purses. So that element of their devotional lives was limited to prayer and recitation. But during the Sermon on the Mount, Jesus threw in a couple of additional components: giving and fasting.[28] These "acts of righteousness," as he refers to them, were to be done in secret. They comprised the private, intimate side of faith for first-century Jews. Jesus underscores that idea when he states:

> "But when you pray, go into your room, close the door and pray to your Father, who is unseen. Then your Father, who sees what is done in secret ..."

Don't run by that too quickly. Jesus says your heavenly Father *sees* what is done in secret. I've been a Christian since I was six, and that's still a pretty staggering thought. God *sees* me pray, give, and fast. But Jesus doesn't stop there.

> "Then your Father, who sees what is done in secret, will reward you." (Matthew 6:6)

God responds to our private acts of righteousness. Jesus uses the term *reward* to describe his response. Ever had an answer to prayer? What happened to your faith? Remember the last time someone in your church or student ministry rushed up to you and poured out a story of answered prayer? That person's faith got bigger, didn't it?

The same thing transpires when individuals begin giving for the first time. Percentage giving is an invitation for God to get involved in our personal finances. The percentage isn't the issue. I tell new believers to pick a percentage and start there. The point is to learn to trust God financially. When people experience God's faithfulness in the realm of their personal finances, their faith expands. Money loses its grip. They are no longer possessed by their possessions.

CLOSET CHRISTIAN

The secret side of the Christian experience is a really big deal to me. I'm not sure I would be doing what I'm doing today if it weren't for something God whispered to me during a quiet time in college. I've shared this story in a prior book. So I'll spare you the details. Bottom line, when I was a junior in college, I was in my closet praying. Literally, in my closet praying. Since I "wrestle with" so much of what Jesus taught, this seemed like a reasonable trade-off.

So during college I created a prayer closet under the stairs in the basement of my parents' house. One morning, as I was praying, I told God how committed I was and how I would do anything and go anywhere and marry anybody. Okay, go anywhere and do anything. I just wanted to be used. Right in the middle of my sign-me-up-for-anything diatribe, a thought popped into my mind that was so strong it was like a voice. The thought went something like this: *You cheated on two exams your freshman year and* ... The "and" related to a prank that went terribly wrong and resulted in a terrifying evening for a family I knew — still makes my stomach churn to think about it. Bottom line, I had never owned up to it. Honestly, I was afraid I might be arrested.

Besides, I was in high school when the incident took place. These memories were so shocking I literally stopped praying and looked around the closet. Sure that it was the devil trying to distract me, I closed my eyes and went right back to it. But all I could think about were those two dishonest grades and the family that I had sinned against.

Gee, I hope my kids don't read this ... like my kids would actually read one of my books.

For the next several months ... yes months ... every time I got on my knees to pray, I couldn't pray. I've never heard God's voice. But the message was unmistakably clear. *Before we go forward, we have to go back.* Overactive conscience? Nope. I've never struggled with that. It got to the point where I felt that my potential for future ministry hung in the balance of how I would respond to that not-so-still, not-so-quiet voice screaming in my head. So I retook both college freshman classes during my junior year. There was no point confessing. There was nobody to confess to. I retook the classes and paid for them myself. And eventually I drove over to the office of the man whose family I had terrorized and confessed. Hardest thing I've ever done. All because of a quiet time. Some reward, huh?

Actually, the entire episode did wonders for my faith. God saw me praying. He loved me enough not to lead me forward until I first went back. That's a lot of love.

I bet you have your own story, don't you? I bet you've heard that not-so-still, not-so-quiet voice as well. And as disturbing as it was, acting on what God told you did wonders for your faith, didn't it? Wouldn't it be great if all the teenagers, college students, and single and married adults in your congregation had devotional lives that put them in a position to hear from God? Imagine what would happen in our churches. If that level of personal discipline and focus is to become the rule rather than the exception, we must weave this value into the fabric of everything we do organizationally. Here are some ways we've attempted to do just that.

BACK AT THE CHURCH

From the beginning we have looked for ways to coax, bribe, bait, and equip everybody from kindergarten up to engage in some kind of private devotional exercise. I'm constantly telling people during the weekend services to go home and read their Bibles. The practical application for many of our messages is to go home and begin praying a specific prayer. Often, we will print the prayer on a card and hand it out at the end of a message or series. Occasionally, I will select four to eight passages that go along with a series and we will create memory verse cards to hand out to our congregants. Not an inexpensive endeavor. We encourage people to read ahead for the next week.

As mentioned earlier, one of our most important ministries, Starting Point, introduces seekers and returners to the importance of self-study and prayer. In that environment, attendees are given simple guides for reading the Bible on their own. In addition, they are given Bibles along with the curriculum.

On the giving side of things, we are very upfront with the importance of what I refer to as *priority, progressive, percentage* giving. Priority as in: give first, save second, and live on the rest. Percentage as in: choose a percentage and give it consistently. Progressive is a challenge to up the amount by a percentage every year. While I'm a big believer in tithing, people who have never given away a percentage of their incomes are not going to begin with 10 percent. Sure, some will. But if you are going to teach people to tithe, you may have to start with some baby steps.

On the family side, parents of elementary-age kids are given a *Parent Card* every month. This card is a simple guide to help parents lead their children in a daily devotion. Every year our middle school and high school divisions create a curriculum or weekend event around the importance of private spiritual disciplines. Recently, our high school ministry created an entire weekend experience around the theme *To Hear God Speak ... Hide and Seek.* We build a gadget-free *quiet time* into the daily schedule of all our student camps. Each student is given a devotional to read and is required to sit alone for thirty minutes to read, reflect, and pray. One of the most emotional and memorable moments of my summer is standing on a hotel balcony and seeing eight or nine hundred high school students spread out along the beach reading their Bibles, scribbling notes, and praying. It gives me hope for our nation and our world. For many of those kids, that exercise jump-starts their devotional lives.

Now, before we move on to the third catalyst, there's an important facet of this one I don't want you to miss. The sooner we can get unbelievers reading their Bibles and praying, the better. You don't need to be shy about pushing them to do so. But for it to work, you've got to put the cookies on the bottom shelf. *The way you talk about the Bible on the weekend will determine their interest in the Bible during the week.* You've got to make it accessible. You've got to *give them permission to read it before they believe it.* As I mentioned during the discussion of the first catalyst, if you present the Scriptures in helpful terms, you've just removed an obstacle.

This is another reason we print prayers and hand them out. People who don't normally pray often don't know where to begin. It may be second nature for you. It's terrifying for some of them. Terrifying. They need printed prayers to prime the pump. Now, I've been around long enough to know that somebody out there in reader world is thinking: *But does God hear the prayers of unbelievers?* I'm inclined to think God hears whatever he wants to hear. Based on what Luke tells us in Acts 10 about Cornelius, the Roman centurion, we know God hears sincere prayers. Heck, Cornelius got a visit from an angel. I've never had one of those and I have a master's in theology. So I wouldn't worry too much about encouraging the seekers, skeptics, and Roman centurions in your church to start praying.

Here are a few other things to ponder:

- In your model, at what age do you begin teaching the importance of private spiritual disciplines?
- How and how often is this value reinforced with your students?
- What devotional and personal Bible study resources do you make available, and how accessible are they?
- How difficult is it for people in your church to get a Bible?
- When is the last time you did a weekend message on spiritual disciplines?
- How could you use the weekend to reinforce this value on a regular basis?
- What could you do to prioritize this in the mix of everything else you are doing?
- Are spiritual disciplines a priority in *your* life?

CATALYST #3: PERSONAL MINISTRY

The third faith catalyst is *personal ministry*. When people describe their faith journeys, they always talk about the first time they engaged in some kind of personal ministry. For some, it was a short-term mission trip. For others, it was leading a children's small group. It's not uncommon to hear stories of people being thrust into ministry environments almost against their wills.

When people describe their first ministry experiences, they use phrases like: *"I was so afraid." "I felt so inadequate." "I felt so unprepared." "I hoped they didn't ask me any hard questions." "I've never been so dependent on God."* And then they talk about the rush that followed when they realized God had used them; given them the words to say; allowed them to leverage their pasts to help someone move forward. Few things stretch and thus grow our faith like stepping into a ministry environment for which we feel unprepared.

The Bible is full of illustrations of God calling and prodding people into service in spite of their overwhelming sense of inadequacy. And in every instance their faith in God got bigger. This was the case with Moses, Joshua, Gideon, all the way up through Saul of Tarsus. Then, of course, there were the disciples. Jesus was constantly stretching their faith by pushing them into impossible situations. Perhaps the most famous was the afternoon they insisted he send the crowds back into the nearby villages to find something to eat. Remember Jesus' response?

> "They do not need to go away. You give them something to eat." (Matthew 14:16)

Suddenly the disciples found themselves staring down the barrel of their own inadequacy. They were right where Jesus wanted them. It was a test of their faith. He knew exactly what he was doing and what he was planning to do.[28]

If you've been in ministry for even a short amount of time, you know a little bit of what the disciples felt. Unlike us, however, they couldn't pretend that they didn't hear correctly. What do you do when Jesus is actually standing there telling you to do something you know you can't do? Apparently you do what we do. You make excuses and tell him things he already knows.

> "We have here only five loaves of bread and two fish," they answered. (Matthew 14:17)

Some things never change. I'm not smart enough. I'm not educated enough. I'm not resourced enough. Get somebody else! Yeah, some things never change, including Jesus' response.

> "Bring them here to me," he said. (v. 18)

In other words, "Just bring me what you do have and I'll work with that. Bring me your limited education, your lack of experience, along with your fear and insecurity, and watch what I can do." Isn't that your story? It's certainly mine. To some degree, it's the story of every volunteer in your church. And the results are similar as well. If we, or the people in our churches, ever get to the place where we are willing to make what we have available to God, amazing things will happen. And after the dust settles, everybody's faith will be bigger. Our confidence will increase. We will experience Emmanuel—God with us. The disciples sure did. Stepping into ministry positions us to experience God's power through us. It stretches us; scares us. It takes us to the end of our adequacy. Ministry forces us to be consciously dependent on God, and thus our faith is strengthened.

One of the reasons I love our church is that I've gotten to
see this catalyst play out in the lives of my kids. Part of our
strategy for volunteering is to get our high school students
involved in serving. All three of my kids were leading small
groups as soon as they were old enough. Sandra and I are
constantly amazed at their commitment to the kids in their
groups. If it had just been our oldest, I would be tempted
to chalk it up to birth order and personality. But all three
plugged in early and have remained committed through a
four-year cycle.

There's one incident in particular that stands out to
me. It took place early one Sunday morning when I was
planning to skip church and sleep in. Yep, I do that from
time to time. But on this particular Sunday morning, I
had a good excuse. To begin with, I wasn't scheduled to
preach. No surprise there. But what made my justification
ironclad were the events of the previous evening. We had
invited my mom over for dinner. As she was getting her
things together to leave, she had a seizure. This was the
first time something like this had happened. Her mother
had had a series of strokes before she died, and we were
afraid that this might be the case with my mom. We called
the paramedics. They arrived just as she was waking up. For
precaution's sake, they suggested that I let them take her
to the hospital. I agreed. So off we went. The ER doctors
quickly diagnosed her condition but decided to keep her
overnight for observation.

Sandra and I didn't get home until two in the morning.
There was no way we were going to church. And if I wasn't
going, I sure wasn't expecting my kids to go. They were
seventeen, fifteen, and fourteen at the time. We went to
bed expecting to sleep late. Guilt-free. So you can imagine

how surprised we were to be awakened at eight by three showered and ready-for-church teenagers who popped in to tell us they were headed out. Don't judge me too harshly for this, but all I could think to say was, "Really? Why?" Their response: "We don't want to miss our groups."

All I could think of was the series of illnesses I rotated through Sunday after Sunday in an effort to convince my parents I was too sick to go to church. My kids were going without me. And I'm the preacher. As the clatter of their footsteps faded down the hall, I turned to Sandra and said, "We may have just witnessed a miracle."

BACK AT THE CHURCH

Since personal ministry is an integral component to spiritual growth, we are committed to involving as many people as possible, as young as possible, as soon as possible. Sometimes too young and too soon! But we intentionally err on the side of too fast rather than too slow. We don't wait until people feel "prepared" or "fully equipped." Seriously, when is anyone ever completely prepared for ministry? Truth is, the "I'm ready, I got this, hand me the reins" people scare me. I like the "I'm not ready; if God doesn't show up, this will be a disaster" folks. If you wait to engage people in ministry until they feel like they're ready, or you feel like they're ready, you will wait a long time. Too long. A little fear is a good thing. Keeps people teachable, flexible, and dependent.

One reason we are able to get people involved quickly is our approach to leadership development. Our entire leadership development model revolves around apprenticing rather than traditional classroom training. As I mentioned in chapter 4, the reason we adopted this model is our conviction that, for the most part, adults learn on a need-to-know basis. Experience has taught us that the sooner we can get people into ministry environments, the better. Even if they are not fully trained. Once they are actually in the environments, several things happen. First, they are confronted with what they don't know but need to know and they become extraordinarily teachable. Unlike classroom training, nobody falls asleep in an apprenticing environment. The second thing that happens is that they usually recognize immediately if they've chosen an appropriate place to serve. But perhaps the most important thing that happens, happens in their hearts. When individuals step into a ministry environment, what was once a category of people becomes people with names, faces, and stories. When people express an interest in our middle school ministry, we invite them to sit in on a middle school small group as soon as possible. This is true for every area of involvement. If you capture someone's heart, you will eventually get his hands and feet as well. Putting people in ministry environments is the quickest way to capture their hearts. So we move quickly.

Because ministry involvement is such a significant faith builder, we involve unbelievers in ministry whenever possible. We have guidelines. But we push the envelope in this regard. Before you judge me, every church has unbelievers involved in their ministries. The difference is, we do it on purpose, and in most cases we know who they are. Most churches do it by accident! Heck, I've worked at churches where I'm pretty sure some of the staff weren't Christians. We're careful. We don't let professing unbelievers teach or lead worship. But we invite them to join our Guest Services teams, participate in service projects, serve as audio and video engineers, play in bands, create sets, build sets, edit, produce, act, and anything else we can think of. Several years ago, Sandra and I took a group to Kenya to tour several Compassion International sites. I invited my Jewish doctor and his daughter to come along. They knew they were going to be stuck with a bunch of Christians for a couple of weeks. And yes, there were a few awkward moments. But, all in all, it was a fantastic trip. I'm glad we invited them. They're glad they went.

We almost always involve unbelievers in our small groups. And we give them opportunities to lead the discussion. One of my most memorable small group experiences was the night John led. The first night we were together as a group, John announced that the only reason he was attending was to make his wife happy. Week two, he raised his hand as we were getting started and said something along the lines of, "Last week as we were finishing up, somebody prayed. Don't expect me to ever do that." We assured him that prayer would always be voluntary. But as the weeks progressed, God started softening John's heart. In week eight I handed John the leader's guide for the curriculum we were studying and asked him if he would lead the discussion the following week. He looked at me like I was crazy. Then he smiled and said, "Sure, I'll lead" as if he was calling my bluff. But I was serious.

The following week John showed up thoroughly prepared. But the moment that made the entire night unforgettable was when he said, "Alright, the leader's guide says we are supposed to open with prayer, and it says we are supposed to get on our knees. So let's get on our knees and I'll say the prayer." I couldn't believe what I was hearing. There was not a dry eye in the group as John prayed his first *out loud* prayer. Whew. It was simple. Heartfelt. Unforgettable. And John would be the first to tell you that he was not a Christian that night. That came later. But he was not about to let any of us out-lead him. And the process of preparing to lead our discussion that night was a faith-expanding experience for John. Heck, hearing him pray was a faith-expanding experience for our entire group! Was it risky handing an unbeliever the leader's guide and asking him to *lead* our Bible study? Maybe. Was it worth it? Absolutely.

Ministry makes people's faith bigger. If you want to increase someone's confidence in God, put him in a ministry position before he feels fully equipped. With all that as a backdrop, here are a few things to consider before we look at the final two faith catalysts.

- How easy is it for new people and nonmembers to get involved in ministry in your model?
- Does your approach to *equipping* and *training* keep people out of ministry environments longer than necessary?
- Are there steps you could shorten or eliminate altogether?
- Are there areas where nonbelievers could be encouraged to serve?

chapter eight

FROM OUT OF NOWHERE

The final two faith catalysts are *providential relationships* and *pivotal circumstances*. I group these two together because, unlike the other three, they are dynamics we have very little control over. We choose to place ourselves under practical teaching. We choose to participate in private spiritual disciplines. And we choose whether or not to serve in ministry. But there is a sense in which these final two faith catalysts choose us. Yet every faith story I've heard included both of these components.

CATALYST #4: PROVIDENTIAL RELATIONSHIPS

When people tell their faith stories, they always talk about the individuals they believe God put in their paths. You hear things like: *"Then I met this couple." "Then I ran into an old friend from college." "A guy at work invited me to church." "A lady I barely knew said she had heard about my circumstances and asked how she could help." "One afternoon my boss called me into his office."* I've never heard a faith story without a relational component. There's always mention of *that guy, that couple, that neighbor I barely knew.*

We call these *providential relationships* because when people tell their stories, they are convinced God providentially brought these individuals or couples into their lives. Encounters that initially appeared accidental or random are eventually viewed as divine appointments. As you're reading this, I bet you can think of that person, couple, or perhaps group God brought along at just the right time. And if you are like most people, this is not a one-time occurrence. At every critical juncture in our faith journeys, there are individuals whose paths intersect with ours. In some cases, long-term relationships are formed. On other occasions, the relationships are only for a short time. But in either case, there is no doubt in our minds that the encounters were providential.

Two things make a relationship providential: when we *hear* from God through someone and when we *see* God in someone. When either of those things happens, our faith gets bigger. Isn't it true that when we see God's faithfulness in someone else's life, it is easier to trust him with ours? That's the power of a divinely ordained relationship.

Whenever I talk about providential relationships, I can't help but think about Dan Dehaan. I was fifteen when I met Dan. He was in his late twenties. After our first encounter, I decided I wanted to be like Dan when I grew up. Dan taught our church camp every summer. He was the communicator that made the Scriptures come alive for me. I still remember a message he gave in the summer of 1975 about the dangers of drifting. Beyond summer camp, Dan took a personal interest in Louie Giglio and me. He took us camping. Rafting. Had us over to his house. Dan taught us how to have a quiet time. Sometimes when I'm watching Louie preach, I see traces of Dan.

Along the way there have been other men God dropped into my life at just the right time: Robert Rohm, Charlie Renfroe, Steve Youngerberg. When I look back on those relationships, as well as others, there's no better word than *providential* to describe their significance.

Back at the Church

So right about now you're thinking, *Hmm. How do you program that?*

You don't.

You can create practical Bible teaching, but you can't create a providential relationship.

Our team spent a lot of time discussing the church's role in this important faith catalyst. Here's what we concluded. While it's beyond our ability to manufacture any type of relationship, much less one characterized as providential, what we can do is create environments that are conducive to the development of these types of relationships. So we determined to do just that. I'm not exaggerating when I say that may be the most significant decision we've made as a team. We determined to create a model that was relationship-centric. We began looking for ways to get people connected more quickly and to keep them connected longer. This had significant implications for the way we approached family ministry and adult groups.

In *Creating Community*,[30] Bill Willits provides a full description of our adult group model. What's relevant to our discussion here is that the value we placed on providential relationships was what drove us to build our model around closed rather than open groups. We decided not to leverage adult groups as a growth engine, but rather to do everything in our power to create authentic community. So our adult Community Groups are designed to stay together for two years. We were told this wouldn't work. But then, we were told a lot of things wouldn't work in those days. Our entire ministry model is designed to move people into groups. We believe circles are better than rows. And we know anecdotally that within the context of our adult groups, men and women who may otherwise have never met are being used in significant ways in each other's lives. At least 90 percent of the adults we baptize thank specific individuals in their small groups for the roles they played in their coming to faith and their decisions to be baptized. They may not use the term *providential* to describe these relationships, but when they tell their faith stories, it's obvious that they were.

On the family ministry side of the aisle, our commitment to create environments conducive to providential relationships caused us to make several strategic decisions. The most significant was our decision to keep group leaders with their small groups as long as possible. The longer a group leader was with a group of kids, the more likely it was that a relationship would develop — and thus the greater chance of God using a group leader in a significant way in the life of one of the kids in his or her group. So when adults volunteer to lead a group of first graders, they stay with that group of children (and their parents) all the way through fifth grade. Not only does this create the potential for long-term relationships, it creates a degree of accountability that goes way beyond the weekend experience. It's not unusual for group leaders to stay with their groups as they transition into our middle school ministry. That provides them with eight years of influence during what is arguably the most important time for a child developmentally, spiritually, and relationally.

We've seen this pay huge dividends in our middle school and high school environments. You know as well as I do that to be assigned to a group of eleventh- or twelfth-grade boys or girls as their group leader would be a tough assignment. By the time you finally gain a little trust, the school year is over and they are gone. But imagine being a small group leader for eleventh-grade boys or girls whom you've been with since they were in eighth or ninth grade? That would make a big difference relationally, wouldn't it? And it does. Year after year. We have large student ministries at all of our churches. As an outsider you might be tempted to think it's the music and the energy in the room that draws the kids. But the kids, my kids, will tell you that it's their group leaders who make the environment special. The middle school and high school kids at our churches wouldn't use the term *providential* to describe their relationships with their leaders. But when you hear their stories, when you watch their baptism videos, when you hear parents talk about the difference the leaders have made in the lives of their students, there's no doubt about it. These are providential relationships. When those kids are adults and they describe their faith journeys, you can rest assured their high school small group leaders will be part of their stories.

We don't have new members classes. For those who are exploring or returning to faith, we created Starting Point. We market Starting Point as a *conversation* rather than a *class*. We limit group size to twelve. We don't mind asking people to wait. Whereas the content is very valuable, the relationships formed in that intimate setting are of equal or greater value. Similarly, we do not offer premarital counseling. Instead we have a program called 2 to 1 Premarital Mentoring. Engaged couples are assigned to married couples and typically meet together eight times to go through a series of lessons. The relational nature of these sessions makes it more mentoring than counseling. Once a couple is married, they can always call their 2 to 1 mentors if they have questions or unexpected challenges.

Perhaps our most aggressive (some would say unorthodox) initiative in this regard is the effort we make to transition unchurched and unbelieving people into groups and onto service teams. We want people who are considering faith or who have questions about faith to be surrounded by people of faith. The more Christians they come into contact with, the more likely it is that one of those individuals will be the one who makes that off-the-cuff comment that opens the door to a conversation that leads to a defining moment. Again, we can't create a providential relationship. But we can certainly create some contact points.

Now, I'm sure there's somebody out there in reader world who's thinking, *Hey, Andy, you don't have the only church where cool stuff like that happens. We see the same type of thing in our church!*

Of course you do. That's my point. This is how God works. The question is: *Are you working with God?* Is the kind of thing I've described happening *because* of your ministry model or *in spite* of it? It's *going* to happen. God uses providential relationships to grab people's attention and blow up their faith. My responsibility, and yours, is to do whatever we can to facilitate and make room for those relationships to develop. The writer of Hebrews nailed it when he (or she?) wrote:

> And let us consider how we may spur one another on toward love and good deeds, not giving up meeting together, as some are in the habit of doing, but encouraging one another — and all the more as you see the Day approaching. (Hebrews 10:24–25)

I love the first phrase: "And let us *consider* how." In other words, let's give this some thought. Let's not just assume it's going to happen. Let's facilitate it. Let's get in each other's lives and "spur" one another on. So, here's a little spurring. Does your ministry model connect people quickly and keep them connected? Does your model have easy, obvious steps into community? Is it easy for nonbelievers to find their places? Are you classing people to death? What can you do programmatically to create more relational connection opportunities in your ministry model?

Catalyst #5: Pivotal Circumstances

The fifth and final faith catalyst is *pivotal circumstances.* When people describe their faith journeys, they always include events that could be described as "defining moments." Some of these are good: being awarded a scholarship, discovering a new opportunity, getting married, having a baby, receiving a promotion or a job transfer. But just as often, these defining moments involve pain and disappointment: the death of a friend or family member, divorce, prolonged illness, a job transfer, betrayal by a friend. As you know, when it comes to faith, circumstances cut both ways. A positive event can adversely affect faith or strengthen it. Adverse circumstances can damage an individual's faith or deepen it. People lose faith when life gets too easy, but people lose faith in the face of tragedy as well. Either way, life has the potential to impact faith for good or bad.

The challenge with this catalyst is that there's no way to program a pivotal circumstance. We don't see 'em coming. We don't schedule them. And we never know how they will impact our faith until we are in the middle of them. So this one is a bit tricky. But as you know from your own story, big, emotionally charged, unexpected life events are major factors in the development or erosion of our confidence in God. Consequently, we decided this was too big to ignore in spite of the fact that *pivotal circumstances* are in a category of their own. So we spent a good bit of time discussing what makes the difference as to which way a pivotal circumstance pushes a person in relation to his or her faith. As we shared our personal bouts with life's surprises and the effect those events had on our faith, we arrived at the following conclusion: It wasn't really the event itself that grew or eroded our faith; it was our *interpretation* of the event that determined which way we went. The conclusions we draw about God in the midst of our pivotal circumstances drive us toward or away from him.

One of the richest men in America, a man who has influenced every one of our lives through his development of international media distribution, grew up wanting to be a missionary. While he was young, his sister contracted leukemia. As he tells the story, he and his family prayed and prayed. He was told that if they had enough faith, she would survive. When she didn't, he determined that if there was a God he certainly couldn't be trusted. He walked away from faith and never looked back. He *interpreted* his sister's death as evidence of God's weakness, inattentiveness, or nonexistence. But, like me, you know people who have walked that same path and have come out on the other end with greater faith in God. The difference? Interpretation.

The Power of a Picture

Steve Jobs experienced a similar crisis of faith. On the cover of the July 12, 1968, edition of *Life* magazine was a disturbing picture of two children from the war-torn region of Biafra. Biafra was a secessionist state in Nigeria that maintained its independence for only two and a half years before being integrated back into Nigeria. More than one million people died either from civil war or famine during that time. At thirteen, Steve found it impossible to reconcile that picture with the lessons he was being taught at his local Lutheran church.

Whereas the average thirteen-year-old boy would have shrugged it off and gone on with his thirteen-year-old life, Steve wanted answers. His biographer, Walter Isaacson, describes what happened next:

> Steve took it (the magazine) to Sunday school and confronted the church's pastor. "If I raise my finger, will God know which one I'm going to raise even before I do it?" The pastor answered, "Yes, God knows everything." Jobs then pulled out the *Life* cover and asked, 'Well, does God know about this and what's going to happen to those children?"[31]

The answer he received was less than acceptable. According to Isaacson, after that conversation, Steve never went back to church. But it wasn't the picture on the cover that undermined Steve's faith. It was his *interpretation* of the picture that drove him away. The conclusions he drew were what made his Sunday-school God and hungry children irreconcilable.

Here's why I say that.

When my kids were ten, twelve, and fourteen, Sandra and I held their hands and led them down the muddy, sewage-saturated paths of the Mathare Valley slum in Nairobi, Kenya. The slum is approximately three square miles in size and serves as the home of over half a million people, most of whom live in six-by-eight-foot shanties made of rusted tin and mud. There is no electricity or running water. There is a smattering of public toilets that residents have to pay to use. Those who can't pay use "flying toilets," plastic bags that are used to collect excrement and then thrown into the Nairobi River (which is the source of the residents' water supply). The children look just like the ones on the cover of *Life* magazine that created such consternation in young Steve Jobs. But my kids didn't lose faith. Neither did the other kids whose families accompanied us on our "tour." On the contrary, they came home motivated to do something about what they saw.

You've probably walked through areas where poverty has robbed children of their futures. But what you saw didn't kick the legs out from underneath your faith either. You responded like my kids did. You came home grateful for what you had and motivated to do something about what you saw. You knew God hated it as much or more than you did. And you believe, like I do, that sin, sorrow, and death will be swept away one day once and for all! You *interpreted* what you saw differently. How a person interprets his or her circumstances makes all the difference.

Determining Factors

Once we recognized the relationship between events and the interpretation of those events, we spent some time wrestling with this question: *What determines how we interpret events and circumstances?* We landed on two things:

1. Our worldviews
2. Who we are doing life with at the time

Regarding worldview, if someone is convinced that every "good and perfect gift" comes from God,[32] that everything belongs to God, and that we are simply managers,[33] then when good things happen, those good things won't be distractions to faith. If an individual believes God doesn't keep bad things from happening to good people, but instead uses those things to strengthen faith and draw attention to him,[34] then painful pivotal circumstances will be viewed as opportunities. In the end, they strengthen faith. Even a casual reading of the Old or New Testament would lead one to the conclusion that *God often showcases his power on the stage of human weakness.* But even that statement involves an interpretation of events. An interpretation based on a worldview shaped by the Scriptures. Helping people view the world through the lens of Scripture is critical to providing them with the proper context from which to interpret life.

The second factor that influences how we interpret the pivotal circumstances of life is who has access to us at the time: friends, family, mentors, teachers. The writer of Ecclesiastes says we should have pity on those who fall and have no one to help them get back on their feet.[35] We've all seen what happens when life takes somebody down and there's no one around to help him properly contextualize his circumstances. When our faith is down for the count, we need people who will speak truth to us, friends who will remind us of God's past faithfulness. We need people who will draw our attention outside of the realm of our immediate circumstances, people to put our circumstances in their proper context.

Perhaps the best New Testament example of this dynamic revolves around John the Baptist's arrest and incarceration. John, commissioned by God to announce the arrival of the Messiah, suddenly finds himself in jail with no prospect of release. And unlike other New Testament heroes who found themselves in similar straits, there's no midnight miracle. No angelic visits. No earthquakes. He didn't even receive a care package from his famous cousin—just the stench of Herod's dungeon. Consequently, his faith took a big hit. He began to doubt. So he sent a message to Jesus through friends. More a question than a message, he asked, "Are you the one who is to come, or should we expect someone else?"[36] In other words: *This isn't making any sense. Interpret, please!* Jesus responded by drawing John's attention away from his immediate circumstances to God's broader activity in the world. He said, "Go back and report to John what you hear and see: The blind receive sight, the lame walk, those who have leprosy are cleansed, the deaf hear, the dead are raised, and the good news is proclaimed to the poor."[37] In other words: *Tell John what's going on outside of his misery. Tell him not to let his faith get swallowed up in his immediate surroundings. Point him to the broader context. Doing so will help him rightly interpret what's happening to him.* After Jesus sent John's friends away, he made a remarkable statement to those standing around him, "Blessed is anyone who does not stumble on account of me."[38] The implications of that statement are staggering. Jesus acknowledges that his activity or lack of activity has the potential to undermine our faith. His lack of activity almost undermined John's. And you know how that story ended. Not well. Jesus never came to his rescue. Apparently, he never bothered to visit. Herod eventually executed John. But apparently John died with his faith intact.

Back at the Church

Armed with these observations, we realized how important it was for us to be intentional about helping people develop a biblical worldview. So we determined to provide adults, teenagers, and children with a theological context that would enable them to maintain faith regardless of what came their way.

These observations undergirded our commitment to create a ministry model that was highly relational in nature. While it is always dangerous to be disconnected from other believers, it is especially dangerous when things aren't going well. Here are several things we built into our model that both create opportunities to reiterate a Christian worldview and formalize healthy relational connections:

- **Baptism**
  Baptism videos continually illustrate how God uses pivotal circumstances to bring people to faith. In addition, they illustrate how people have maintained faith in the midst of difficulty. Sometimes, extreme difficulty.
- **2 to 1 Mentoring**
  Our 2 to 1 Premarital Mentoring program provides engaged couples with seasoned married couples who bring needed perspective to the unique challenges associated with being newly married.
- **Small Group Structure**
  Our closed Community Groups model provides relational support as well as proper contextualization for singles and couples who are facing challenges.

- **Family Ministry Group Structure**
  Keeping children and students with the same small
  group leader for several years creates a healthy
  relational dynamic. Children and students are
  particularly susceptible to misinterpreting negative
  events. Having a mature adult in their lives in
  addition to their parents can make all the difference
  when grappling with challenging circumstances.

When we are able to find God in the midst of life's pivotal
circumstances, our faith is strengthened. When we help
people recognize God in the midst of their life circumstances,
their faith is strengthened. Pivotal circumstances test, and
therefore potentially strengthen, our confidence in God. For
that to happen, people need context. A biblical worldview.
And often, they will need someone to help them interpret
what's happening.

AGELESS AND TIMELESS
So there they are: our five faith catalysts.

- Practical Teaching
- Private Disciplines
- Personal Ministry
- Providential Relationships
- Pivotal Circumstances

We're convinced that God uses these dynamics to grow
our faith. We're convinced, as well, that these dynamics
are at work in the lives of every individual at every church,
whether they are aware of them or not. But I can tell you
from experience, something powerful happens in the lives
of church attendees when church leaders are on the lookout

for ways to leverage these five catalysts. We are constantly looking for new ways to structure our organization around them. I want God to be free to work through our model, not in spite of it. Before we leave this topic, however, I want to point out the primary reason we believe this approach to spiritual formation is superior to more traditional approaches.

When addressing the subject of his own spiritual development, the apostle Paul described the process in the following way:

> Not that I have already obtained all this, or have already arrived at my goal, but I press on to take hold of that for which Christ Jesus took hold of me. Brothers and sisters, I do not consider myself yet to have taken hold of it. But one thing I do: Forgetting what is behind and straining toward what is ahead, I press on toward the goal to win the prize for which God has called me heavenward in Christ Jesus. (Philippians 3:12–14)

Even this seasoned follower of Jesus didn't view himself as having "arrived." There was more to learn. More to experience. More to comprehend. He viewed himself as a follower-in-process. He chooses the terms *straining* and *pressing on* to describe his approach to maturity. There's a great deal of energy behind those words. The quest for spiritual maturity was not a passive or casual endeavor for Paul. He makes spiritual formation sound more like an athletic event than a Bible study. And while I'm tempted to smirk and chalk up Paul's extreme language to an effort to make up for his rather embarrassing activist past, he won't let me. Or you either.

> All of us, then, who are mature should take such a view of things. (Philippians 3:15)

"All." That's pretty inclusive. "All" of us should be *straining* and *pressing on*. And you thought after a couple seasons of Bible Study Fellowship, three years volunteering in the church preschool, and a mission trip to Burundi, you could put a check in the spiritually mature box. Apparently not. Apparently, the quest for spiritual maturity is a lifelong endeavor. And if that's the case, then your approach to spiritual formation must be flexible and dynamic enough to support you through every season of life. More to the point, the approach to spiritual formation that you teach and build your ministry model around must be flexible and dynamic enough to support your congregants through every season of life. People of all ages need to know they can trust God with the specific challenges and temptations associated with their specific stage of life. Big faith is a necessity in every chapter. But the expressions of that faith will change with time.

The teenagers in your church need a faith that is strong enough to endure the challenges of adolescence. Your college students need faith that's big enough to enable them to trust God with their futures. The singles in your church face a different set of challenges than either of those groups. The married couples in your church need to know they can trust God with their spouses and children. The seniors in your church need to know they can trust God during a stage of life when losing loved ones is commonplace and every day brings new reminders of their mortality.

This is the beauty and the power of the five faith catalysts approach to maturity. Each of the catalysts looks a bit different at different stages of life. But though the expressions will change, the catalysts themselves carry over year after year, from season to season. This simple framework can be taught to children, students, and adults, providing them with a tool to monitor and pursue spiritual maturity throughout their lives.

For example, our approach to private disciplines may change through the years, but we will always need those disciplines to stay centered in our faith. Nobody matures past his or her need for prayer and meditation. Trusting God with our money feels different at forty than it did at fourteen. But that discipline is a lifetime measure of our confidence in God. Generosity makes our faith bigger in every stage of life.

Each season will bring its own round of pivotal circumstances. Teenage boys get texts from their girlfriends saying they want to just be friends. Husbands get served with divorce papers. Children mourn the loss of a pet. Adults mourn the loss of their parents. While the magnitude of what life brings our way changes, our responses and our ability to rightly interpret those unforeseen changes in the landscape of our lives will always be critical to the health of our faith. The twenty-third Psalm never changes. But its significance certainly does. The "valley of the shadow of death" looks different in each stage of our lives, doesn't it? Blessed is the middle school student whose leaders taught her how to navigate the betrayal of a best friend, for when she is old, she will be better prepared to navigate more substantial losses.

This morning I woke up at 5:10 to tweet my prayer support for a staff member and his wife, who is having a C-section. Baby Hallie is not expected to live more than a few minutes. Perhaps a day.[39] As I read Chris' last blog post before they headed to the hospital, I wept. Not so much for his and Katie's circumstances, but at their confidence in God. Their big faith. That kind of faith is not born from a series of classes or Bible studies. It comes from having experienced God's faithfulness in the past. It's the overflow of the providential relationships that have intersected their lives for years. It is birthed from a devotional life where they've heard God whisper. They would be quick to tell you that their faith is due in part to hearing God's Word preached and taught with handles. So they are *pressing on*. They are *straining toward what is ahead*. And when this trial is behind them, they will redeem it by stepping into a new realm of personal ministry to other couples facing the same challenge. And those couples will consider their interaction with Chris and Katie to be providential. How do I know? Isn't that always the way our heavenly Father works? The names and the faces change. God doesn't.

As I've stated repeatedly throughout this book, my goal isn't for you to do what we do. But part of my goal is to push you to closely examine what you're doing. So in the area of spiritual formation, what's your model? Is it teachable? Is it portable? Most importantly, will it carry people their entire lives? Have you created language that can be passed from children's ministry through your adult ministry? Your organization's spiritual growth model is perfectly designed to produce the results you are currently getting. So if you like what's happening, document your process so you don't accidentally drift from it. But if you secretly wonder whether people are actually changing or simply listening to sermons and attending classes, then I want to urge you to consider adopting the five faith catalysts as a framework. Like you, I don't want to build a church full of people who simply know the Bible. I want to build a church full of men and women of great faith, men and women who are confident that God is who he says he is and that he will do precisely what he has promised to do. I want to be surrounded by people whose lives, and responses to life, cause the community to look up and take notice. It was that kind of faith that sustained and fueled the church through the trials of its first three centuries. And it is that kind of faith that should characterize our churches today.

GOING WIDE

Why They Love to Attend

Several years ago Sandra and I visited friends who had recently transitioned to the West Coast. Don't you love it when friends move to places you actually want to visit? We arrived on a Thursday. Sean informed me he had joined a Friday morning men's group and wondered if I would like to tag along. Seeing as my internal clock was probably going to wake me up at 5 a.m. anyway, I agreed to go.

The study was held at a local church (not the one they were currently attending). If you are like me, the minute you step onto a church campus, you start evaluating as well as looking for ideas to "borrow." While I didn't see much worth borrowing, there was much to evaluate.

The group met in a medium-sized assembly hall with a wall of windows on one side and a bank of classrooms down the other. The first thing I noticed was the smell. The room smelled like … like old. The second thing that caught my attention was the clutter. Stuff was scattered everywhere. Sunday school literature. Bibles. Hymnals. Umbrellas. There was even a llama grazing on Cheerios in the corner. The blinds on the half-dozen windows were all pulled to varying heights. There was a bulletin board with a half-dozen flyers randomly tacked to it. The wall color was bad. The carpet needed replacing. Did I mention the smell? And no, there wasn't really a llama in the corner.

This was an adult Sunday school assembly space. Grown-ups met in this room. For Bible study. After being in the environment for less than a minute, I knew one thing for certain: The people who meet in this room on Sundays have met here for so long they don't see it anymore. The room is invisible to them. It's not that they enjoy clutter. They don't see it. But a newcomer would notice it immediately. I certainly did. The real tragedy from my perspective was that this adult ministry environment taught a series of lessons the Sunday school department wasn't aware of.

> Lesson #1: We aren't expecting guests.
> Lesson #2: What we are doing here is not all that important.
> Lesson #3: We expect somebody to clean up after us.
> Lesson #4: We don't take pride in our church.

Think I'm being too harsh? Hoping I don't visit your church anytime soon? If so, then this may be the most important section in the book for you to digest, and then teach your team. But before we jump into the content, one more story.

For the first three and a half years, North Point met on Sunday nights in rented facilities. Not fun. But it gave me an opportunity to visit other churches on Sunday mornings. Honestly, I was consistently underwhelmed.

Our most stressful and disappointing experience took place at a church touted for its children's ministry. We arrived about twenty minutes before the service was scheduled to begin. Andrew was with us. He had just turned three. We had to ask twice where to find the children's area. Signage was almost nonexistent. Someone finally pointed us to a door. We peeked in and the only person in the room was a man who looked to be in his late twenties. When he saw us, he came to the door with a big smile on his face. A little too big for me. We told him this was our first visit. He assured us that we were at the right place, and he invited Andrew into the room. That's when I noticed a back door standing open that led to what looked like an outdoor playground. But it was hard to tell exactly where it led. Sandra asked if we needed to fill out any paperwork. He looked a bit confused and said we didn't and that he hoped we enjoyed the service. Then he turned and went over and began talking to Andrew. We just stood there—both thinking the same thing, but neither of us wanting to say it aloud. Ignoring our raging parental instincts, we headed off to big church.

During the second song, Sandra turned to me and asked, "Do you feel okay about Andrew's situation?" I assured her that I did not and that it was all I had been thinking about since we left his classroom. She immediately slid out of our row and headed back to the children's wing. It took every ounce of self-control I had to not follow. A few minutes later she came back and informed me that there was, in fact, another adult in the room along with a dozen or more children.

If you have children, I bet you aren't surprised to know that we never visited that church again. Worse, that's the only thing I remember about our visit. Every time someone mentions the name of that church, I think about that incident. I will be the first to admit that our experience couldn't possibly be the norm. But I still wouldn't go back. That was seventeen years ago. Similar to my previous story, this church taught several lessons they didn't intend to teach.

> Lesson #1: We don't expect new families. We have the same kids every week.
> Lesson #2: If there is an emergency, we don't plan to notify you.
> Lesson #3: Your child's security is not our primary concern.
> Lesson #4: Our volunteers don't understand the way parents think (i.e., our volunteers are untrained).

The one thing those two stories have in common is that neither of my assessments had anything to do with the preaching. If your response to my assessment is, "Andy, you're not being fair. You shouldn't judge a church based on one visit," you would be correct. My assessment isn't fair. And that's my point.

Every Sunday people walk onto your campus and determine whether or not they will return the following week before your preacher opens his mouth. And that's not fair. But it's true. The moral of the story: *Environment matters.* So in this section I'm going to teach you everything we've learned about creating irresistible ministry environments.

Here we go.

chapter nine

CREATING IRRESISTIBLE ENVIRONMENTS

Every ministry environment communicates something. There are no neutral environments. Environments are the messages before the *message*. The messages your environments communicate have the potential to trump your primary message. I do not remember a single thing about the message preached at the church referenced in the illustration on page 154. Not a thing. I was too distracted by the four-point message of the children's environment.

As I am constantly reminding our leaders, *the sermon begins in the parking lot.* By the time I stand up to deliver what is traditionally considered *the message*, everybody in our audience has already received a dozen or more messages. Many have already made up their minds as to whether they will come back the following week. The same is true for your church. The quality, consistency, and personal impact of your ministry environments define your church. To put it another way, your environments determine what comes to mind when people think about your church. This is especially true for first-time attendees. Regardless of the size or denominational affiliation of your church, it is a conglomeration of environments. Whether you refer to them as classes, programs, ministries, or services, at their core they are environments — environments that involve a physical setting combined with some type of presentation.

You Decide

As stewards of a local church or even a department within a church, I think we should determine the messages our environments communicate. We should choose the messages before the message. It's our responsibility to shape the way people view our local churches. We can't leave this to chance. And as much as I love 'em, we can't leave this to the individual whims of our volunteers.

Unless . . .

Unless you are content to have a church for church people. In fact, if you want to be a church for church people, you can skip this chapter. Church people will put up with just about anything as long as you let 'em out on time. Don't believe me? Just visit the average church. It is amazing what church people will put up with, neglect, refuse to spend money on, acquire a taste for, grin and bear, or flat-out ignore. But the moment a church, or even a group of leaders within a church, catches a vision for capturing the hearts and imaginations of those who consider themselves unchurched or dechurched, environments take on new significance.

TIME IN, AWARENESS OF

Before we jump into the details of what makes a great ministry environment, I need to warn you about one thing. The longer you've served where you are and the longer you've done what you are currently doing, the more difficult it will be for you to see your environments with the objectivity needed to make the changes that need to be made. The shorter version: *Time in erodes awareness of.*

The longer you serve in a particular ministry environment, the less aware of it you become. This is why adults, many of whom pay to have their houses cleaned, can walk into the Sunday school assembly room I described in the section introduction and not be distressed by what they see. They don't see it. The mess is invisible to them. *Time in erodes awareness of.*

If there are things in your current ministry environments that are offensive to outsiders, you probably don't know what they are. If you did, you would have already done something.[40] That should bother you. It sure bothers me. So we have systems in place in our churches to ensure that we don't unintentionally make it difficult for those who are coming for the first time or the first time in a long time. In this regard, I'm pretty much worthless. I've been around our church from the beginning. I love everything we do and I love the way we do it. But that doesn't make it right. That just makes it comfortable. Predictable. But perhaps ineffectual. Like most leaders, I go with my intuition at times. But intuition is not enough. Leaders need objective ways to measure effectiveness. As church leaders, we need objective means by which to measure the effectiveness of our ministry environments. Attendance is a measure. But it is only one measure. And attendance can be deceiving.

We all like full rooms. But if you are determined to create churches unchurched people love to attend, it is important that your environments are not only full, but full of the right people.

Simply Irresistible

When we began talking about the kinds of environments we wanted to create, we camped out around the word *relevant*. We wanted to create *relevant environments.* This was a reaction to programming we had been forced to babysit in our previous church assignments. We felt like much of what we inherited programmatically was *irrelevant.* So *relevant* seemed like a giant step forward. As time went by, however, *relevant* didn't seem all that relevant. So we transitioned to the term *irresistible.* Our objective was to create *irresistible* environments.

We began asking questions like:

- What does an irresistible ministry environment for children look like?
- What makes for an irresistible ministry environment for middle school and high school students?
- How can we make our groups' model more irresistible?
- How can we make our worship service more irresistible?
- What could we do to make our weekend gatherings more irresistible for men?
- What would make singles ministry more irresistible?

Our goal was to make our environments so irresistible that even people who didn't buy our theology would want to come back and participate. As a result of God's favor and a whole lot of off-sites and hard work, we've been able to accomplish just that. Our family ministry environments are so magnetic, I warn people in our community not to bring their kids to our church until they're sure they want to attend on a regular basis. When they ask why, I tell them that once their kids "come and see" the environments we've created for them, they'll never be satisfied anywhere else. I assure them that I'm not being arrogant. I just don't want to make their Sunday mornings any harder than they already are.

As you would imagine, the questions listed above surfaced hundreds of ideas. Some good. Some not so much. As our ministry environments began to take shape, we realized we were operating from some shared assumptions that, while intuitive to us, might not be to our volunteers or the next generation of staff. That well-founded concern led us to stop and define on paper what we meant by an *irresistible environment*—not just for a specific area of ministry, but for every area.

The remainder of this chapter is devoted to explaining how we evaluate whether an environment is doing what it was designed to do. I'm going to give you the lens through which we evaluate all of our environments regardless of the target audience. This may not be *the* recipe for creating irresistible environments. But it is ours. You may like it. You may hate it. You may use it as it is or you may adapt it and take credit for it. None of that really matters. What matters is that you provide your ministry leaders with a simple tool with which they can evaluate the effectiveness of *all* your ministry environments—not just the environments they participate in. It's important that your staff and volunteers evaluate through the same filter. They need to know what makes an environment *great* as your organization defines *great*.

Embracing an agreed-upon standard of excellence is how you create a culture. More specifically, it is how you create a culture of excellence. Defining what a great environment looks and feels like ahead of time provides a powerful safeguard for your entire ministry culture. When your leaders understand and own the standard by which environments are evaluated, they become sensitized to the things that don't meet your standards. Regardless of where they serve, they will feel empowered to speak up when they notice something that's not hitting the mark. In time, the *cringe factor* becomes the same for everybody.

For example, after I preach two or three times on the weekends, my assistant and one of our city police officers walk me to my car. Nine times out of ten, the officer that accompanies me is Lieutenant Scott Rose. In addition to walking me to my car, Scott sits through the services just to keep an eye on things. He is often backstage with the team and me between services when we are discussing what worked and what needs some attention.

The primary reason my assistant, Diane, walks with us is to find out which of the two or three versions of my message I want to send to our other churches and which one I would like for them to post online. So as we walk, I evaluate aloud. I usually like the opening of one and the conclusion of another. Sometimes I'll comment on how I wish I had done a better job with an illustration. So Scott had been listening to Diane and me talk through the strengths and weaknesses of my messages for a couple of years when one Sunday afternoon, out of the blue, he chimed in! I can still remember what he said as we walked: "Yeah, you seemed like you were tired in the second service. I think the first message was the strongest; you didn't repeat yourself as much." Diane and I looked at each other and started laughing. I'm not sure Scott even noticed. He was in evaluation mode. He felt right at home jumping in and I'm glad he did. And yes, we took his advice and went with the first message.

If you standardize and quantify *great* for your ministry environments, evaluation becomes a way of life. It won't be limited to a meeting. Your entire organization will operate at higher standards with a lower threshold of tolerance for average.

If this sounds like a lot of unnecessary work, let me remind you of something.

Every one of your ministry environments is being evaluated every week. Based on that evaluation, some people choose not to return. Additionally, every volunteer and staff member is evaluating the success of his or her particular environment against some standard. If you don't define what excellence looks like for your staff and volunteers, they will define it for themselves. And when you don't like what you see, you will only have yourself to blame.

If you don't create an objective standard, evaluation in your church will rest on two legs: attendance and stories. While those are two good things to pay attention to, they are not enough.

THREE ESSENTIAL INGREDIENTS

We've identified three things that are mission critical when it comes to creating great environments. We refer to these as our *three essential ingredients*. This is the litmus test we apply to all our ministry environments, from family ministry to groups to our weekend experiences. This is also the filter through which we evaluate the *irresistibility* of our camps, retreats, and conferences. As you might guess, every ministry environment has environment-specific filters it uses as well. But these three apply to everything we do. We state our essentials in the form of questions. This makes them less static and more portable.

QUESTION #1: IS THE SETTING APPEALING?

Every ministry environment involves a physical setting. It may be a large room or a small room. It may include chairs or circular carpets for seating. It may be a park or a living room. Regardless of the type of setting, it needs to be appealing to the target audience. You know from experience the physical and emotional effects a comfortable, inviting environment can have. You've walked into offices, homes, and vacation spots and immediately felt at home. You've walked into those same environments at other locations and felt just the opposite.

Today I'm working in an Audi dealership while my car is being serviced. When I showed up, they told me it would take two-and-a-half to three hours to service my car. They offered me a free rental car. I declined. This is one of my favorite places to work. Somebody took the time to create an appealing setting for people like me to work in while they wait for their cars. In addition to a well-appointed living room environment, they built a bank of workstations. Each workstation is equipped with a comfortable chair and a power outlet. And, of course, there's free wireless Internet.

I've owned several cars in my life. I've never once visited a dealership where the environment was so appealing that I actually wanted to stay and work. You have your own story. You can think immediately of a setting that is so comfortable to you that you hate to leave—an environment you wished you could visit more often.

The desire to create order from chaos is a vestige of the thumbprint of God on our souls. Some of us do that intuitively with numbers. Others with organizations. And then there are those talented people who can do the same with physical space. God has gifted a subset of us with the ability to take a space and make it comfortable. Attractive. Appealing. I'm not one of those people. But I have made it a habit to make sure there are a bunch of them around me with their eyes on our environments. Why? I want our physical environments to be magnetic. Irresistible.

If this is not your *thing*, you will be tempted to discount its importance. That's a mistake. Unless, of course, you want a church full of people just like you. The problem with that, of course, is that no one will get along. Generally speaking, we aren't attracted to people who are exactly like us. But you probably need to see your counselor about that.

It could be argued that the very first thing God did in time was to create an appealing environment tailored for his prize creation, that portion of creation that would be fashioned in his image, the image of the one who created an irresistible environment. Essentially, that's the story of creation.

In the beginning, the earth was like an unpainted, poorly lit room with all the furniture in boxes in the hallway waiting to be assembled and properly arranged. So God started rearranging the furniture.

> And God said, "Let there be light," and there was light. God saw that the light was good. (Genesis 1:3–4)

"Good." In other words, better. God improved things. Light was better than darkness. He didn't put Adam and Eve in a formless, empty, chaotic darkroom. He created an

appealing environment and then he placed them in it. God
created a garden—an environment perfectly suited for his
prize creation. Now I realize Genesis was not given to us as
an apologetic for the importance of appropriately appointed
children's classrooms. But it's interesting to think about.
God was the original interior designer. He was the original
organizer. It's no wonder that the desire for order and the
appreciation for beauty are in us. This is simply a reflection
of something we find in him.

First Impressions

The physical setting of your ministry environments creates
first impressions. Since we only get one chance to make a
first impression, somebody needs to keep an eye on our
physical environments. As I pointed out in the illustration
on page 153, the physical environment does more than
leave an impression; it sends a message. Sometimes, several
messages. Those messages can overpower *the* message. An
uncomfortable or distracting setting can derail ministry
before it begins.

I have a friend who dropped out of church for thirteen
years after his three-year-old daughter died. When I first
met Lou, I assumed he didn't return because he was mad at
God. Later, he told me it had nothing to do with that. Lou
grew up Catholic. His daughter's funeral was in a Catholic
church. He said that the one time he went back to church
after the funeral, all he could think about was his daughter's
little casket beside the altar down front. He wasn't mad at
God. The physical setting was too painful. I assured Lou
that our worship center didn't have any resemblance to a
Catholic church. I smiled and said, "Lou, we don't even

have an altar." He came. Then he came back. Months later, I had the privilege of baptizing him. Granted, that's an extreme example. But it represents the potential power of a physical setting. An uncomfortable setting makes people *uncomfortable*.

Isn't this why so many of us have gone to such lengths to build and renovate buildings to make them not look like churches? Isn't it true that our departure from traditional church architecture has made it easier for a lot of people who have been away to come back? It has made it easier for some who've never been. Truth is, after attending some of our churches, people say they still feel like they haven't been. And we like it that way. We celebrate that. Don't we all take it as a compliment when we hear someone say, "Sure doesn't look like a church to me"? Or, "There's nothing very churchy about your church." Most of us are already sensitive to the importance of creating the right kind of setting. We know that architecture, design, décor, sound, and light impact the way people size up our ministries. That being the case, let's not do what a previous generation did and assume that what's appealing today will be appealing tomorrow.

My oldest child, Andrew, is twenty. The only church he knows is North Point. Loud music, screens, moving lights, visuals, a stool, and a bar table *are* tradition for him. Will that always be appealing? Of course it will! It's what God has blessed! It's what got us here! This is the North Point way; *walk ye in it*. Touch not God's anointed! Dance with the one who brung you! Sail your vessel 'til the river runs dry; like a bird upon the wind, these waters are my sky![41]

Sorry.

No. It won't always be appealing. But I will be the last to know. I'll be the one defending the church of the tens, or the twenty-tens, or however we are going to say that. I'll be the guardian of what once worked but works no more. That is, unless I've empowered and chosen to listen to the next generation to modify and adapt our environments as we go.

Every physical setting communicates something. There are no neutral settings. *Clean and tidy* communicates that you are expecting someone. We've all had guests drop by unexpectedly when our houses were a mess. If we had known they were coming, we would've *cleaned* and *tidied* things up a bit. In the same way, when our church environments aren't clean, we are communicating something: "We didn't think you were actually going to show up!" We clean for family, but we scrub for guests. *Dirty* says, "You weren't worth cleaning up for." Or worse, "Dirt is invisible to us." I don't care how good the preaching is at your church, if parents get the impression that you are *germ-tolerant*, don't ask about registering their babies. They are first- and last-time visitors.

Sandra's and my experience with babysitters taught us that there are people who see messes and people who don't. The ones who don't, never will. The ones who do, clean up. If you don't see a mess, if you aren't bothered by clutter, you need to make sure there is someone around you who *does* see it and is bothered by it. If you aren't sure, look at the interior of your car. Look around your office. If there are piles of papers, magazines, and "stuff" in the corners and on every flat surface, then you are probably one of those people who doesn't see a mess. If that's the case, this ain't your thing. Don't try to make it your thing. Just empower someone on your team to make sure things look great.

Organized communicates that you take what you do seriously. Organized says: *We are doing something important here.* That's why you will never visit a national bank that gives an appearance of being disorganized. It is important for banks to communicate that all is well and that they've got everything under control. Their success depends upon the perception that people's money is safe with them. Banks understand something that churches often miss. *Being* organized is not enough. You must *appear* to be organized. This is why it is imperative for you to put people in your parking lot, whether you have a parking challenge or not. People in the parking lot directing cars communicates something. It says: *We are expecting you and we are on top of things.* Disorganized is *unappealing.* People are smart. If your church is disorganized in the places they *can* see, they will assume it is even worse behind the scenes. A lot of truth there. That's why you should clean out the interior of your car before a job interview or a first date.

What's true of *organized* is true of *safe* as well. It is not enough for your family ministry environments to *be* safe. They must *appear* safe. Unsafe is *unappealing.* I often refer to our children's environments as the safest places in Fulton County. Yes, children are going to learn about Jesus. But that is not a parent's primary concern, is it? An environment that appears safe communicates that you value their kids the way you value your own. So don't leave the back door to the outdoor playground open when parents are checking their kids in for the first time. And have more than one volunteer in the room. Bet you already do that, don't you? Really? Well, I bet the children's director at the church I referenced at the beginning of this section will read this book and think the same thing! Handbooks and policy manuals are important and necessary. But who's walking around to ensure that all those pieces are actually in place? I know you do background checks. But your guests don't. Safe environments must *appear* safe if the environment is going to be appealing.

Former United States Senator-turned-actor Fred Thompson is quoted as saying, "In politics it is not enough to do good. You must be seen doing good." This is applicable to so many things we do in church world — but if, and only if, you are interested in creating a church unchurched people want to attend.

Church people aren't nearly as picky. Well, they are picky, just not about important things, things like how the facility appears to people who don't go and give there. So yes, perception is everything.

Fair? No.

True? Absolutely.

Design, décor, and attention to detail communicate that you understand your target audience. It assures attendees that you've done your homework, that you took some time to investigate what would make them feel comfortable. If you create an appealing setting for my middle school student, I will have a much easier time believing that you will present content that is relevant to his stage of life. Design, décor, and attention to detail communicate whom you value. When you walk down the halls of our churches, there can be no doubt that we value children. The cool decorations on the walls and in the hallways are not there for the children. Those things are advertisements to parents that children's ministry is a priority.

We experienced the reverse of this firsthand when I was asked to speak at a large church in another city. The church was fifteen years old at the time and had recently built a state-of-the-art worship center. Very impressive. After a quick mic check, Sandra and I asked for a tour, specifically of the children's areas. The pastor's wife was hosting us. She frowned and warned us that the children's space wasn't what we were accustomed to. That was an understatement. The children's wing was clearly an afterthought. All the money went into the adult environments. Not surprisingly, a lot of babies and children were in the adult service. Equally unsurprising, this church is known for their worship, not their family ministry. Their adult-to-children ratio is less than half of ours.

As a church committed to attracting unchurched people, we put our money where our mission is and created living room-style environments for returners and seekers. The only small group spaces in our facility dedicated to adult groups are our Starting Point rooms. Because Starting Point is a conversation rather than a class, we have created a physical setting that is conducive to discussion. The rooms are decorated and furnished like living rooms, not classrooms. Participants are always surprised when they walk in. The setting sends three messages:

1. This environment is important to us.
2. You are important to us.
3. We know some really good decorators!

FRESH EYES

From time to time, we all need a set of fresh eyes on our ministry environments. Again, the longer you live somewhere, the more things tend to disappear in plain sight. Besides, what's appealing today may not be so appealing

tomorrow. Over time every environment begins to look a
bit tired. Dated. Someone in your organization needs to
see the way your guests see. More to the point, he or she
needs to see *what* your guests will see before they see it.
Empower someone to walk through with a critical eye.
What's distracting? What's tired? Where do you need paint?
What needs to be thrown away? Replaced?

Are your settings appealing?

QUESTION #2: IS THE PRESENTATION ENGAGING?

The second ingredient of an irresistible environment in
our world is an *engaging presentation*. So we ask of every
environment: *Was the presentation engaging?* Not, *was it
true?* We assume that. Let's face it: Churches aren't empty
because preachers are lying. Twentysomethings haven't
abandoned the church because pastors have abandoned the
Bible. The church isn't suffering from a lack of truth-talks.
What we are missing is *engaging* presentations. The reason
more people aren't engaged with the local church is ... we
aren't all that engaging!

Would you like more people in your community to
engage with your church? Become more engaging. Make
an uncompromising commitment to engaging presentations
at every level of your organization.

It's a shame that the group that gathers in Jesus' name
does such a poor job communicating on his behalf. This is
especially shameful when we read the Gospels and discover
how engaging Jesus was. How many times did Jesus begin
a presentation with, "The kingdom of heaven is like ..."?
Then he would tell a story. A parable. He took what they

knew and used it to explain what they wondered about. Consider these examples from Matthew 13:

> *"The kingdom of heaven* is like a man who sowed good seed in his field." (v. 24)

> *"The kingdom of heaven* is like a mustard seed, which a man took and planted in his field." (v. 31)

> *"The kingdom of heaven* is like yeast that a woman took and mixed into about sixty pounds of flour until it worked all through the dough." (v. 33)

> *"The kingdom of heaven* is like treasure hidden in a field." (v. 44)

> *"The kingdom of heaven* is like a merchant looking for fine pearls." (v. 45)

> *"The kingdom of* heaven is like a net that was let down into the lake and caught all kinds of fish." (v. 47)

After the Sermon on the Mount, Matthew tells us: "When Jesus had finished saying these things, the crowds were amazed at his teaching, because he taught as one who had authority, and not as their teachers of the law."[42] This immediately followed his story about the wise and foolish builder. You know that one: "And the rains came down and the floods came up, the rains came down ..." Even Jesus wasn't content to say, "Hey, OBEY!" Instead he crafted an engaging story to illustrate what eventually happens to the obedient and the disobedient.

Jesus was not content to simply say what was true. Being right was not enough. Being biblical was not enough. Being exegetically correct was not enough. That was not his purpose in coming. He came to seek and to save that which was lost. And he communicated to that end. Jesus understood what too many of us have either forgotten or were never told in the first place. To seek and to save the lost, you must first capture their attention. That's exactly what he did. As his body, that's what we must do as well. Unless. Unless we are content presenting to church people. Church people are amazing in this regard. They will come back week after week for unengaging, uninspiring, unimaginative presentations. I'm convinced there are church people who think enduring an uninspiring presentation of the Scripture is a necessary discipline in being a follower of Christ. Why else would they do that to themselves? Why else would they do that to their children?

Once again, I agree with Howard Hendricks, who was fond of saying, "It is a sin to bore a child with the Word of God." To present the Scripture to a child or a teenager in an unengaging manner is to teach the very opposite of what is intended:

Lesson #1: The Bible is boring.
Lesson #2: The Bible is irrelevant.
Lesson #3: Church is irrelevant.

Hey kids, come back next week for another exciting episode. And bring a friend! No wonder kids graduate from high school and disappear from church life for years. Or for good!

MISSION CRITICAL

Engaging presentations are central to the success of the church's mission. We are in the presentation business. We are the only entity charged with the responsibility of *presenting* the gospel. Since this responsibility is ours alone, it stands to reason that we need to be good at it. Since people aren't breaking our doors down to hear it, we've got to harness every bit of our creative energies to make our presentations engaging.

To engage is to *secure one's attention*. We decided early on that we wanted our presentations to be outstanding at every level of the organization. We wanted engaging presentations to be the hallmark of what we do. In most instances, *the presentation is what makes information interesting*. It's the presentation that creates and maintains interest. Just about every time you go to a restaurant, you order chicken, beef, or fish (unless, of course, you are a vegetarian). Your favorite restaurant is not the one with the exotic meat selection. It's the one with the best presentation of chicken, beef, or fish. In our world, the best presentation is not the one that focuses on some lost, first-century text (exotic meat). A great presentation is one that makes a well-known text come alive through illustration and fresh application. Face it, David always beats Goliath, and there will always be ten commandments. The only thing that changes is the presentation.

Presentation determines something else as well: attention span. This explains why someone who falls asleep five minutes into a sermon finds himself on the edge of his seat through all three hours of *The Lord of the Rings*. An engaging presentation makes length almost irrelevant. Consider stand-up comedians. They can keep audiences engaged for an hour or more. They have no points. No applications. No helpful content at all. And the time flies.

I know, I know. We aren't in the comedy business. We aren't in the entertainment business. You're right. And if that's your response, chances are you are neither funny nor entertaining. And you're feeling threatened right now. You know your presentations aren't all that engaging. You've been hiding behind, "Well, I'm preaching the Word." Relax. You are all alone. You are reading a book.

I don't even know you. All I'm saying is that in most communication environments, it's the presentation that determines interest, not the content. There are some disinterested people in your community who need to hear the truth you are bringing. There are some disinterested children and students in your community who need to hear the truth your family ministry environments are serving up. If it's going to stick, it's got to be engaging. So for the sake of the people in your community who aren't attending your church (yet), I want to invite you out from behind your wall of excuses for just a few pages. I want you to consider making a few small changes to your approach — changes that may empower you to ramp up and amp up the engagement factor of the presentations throughout your ministry.

Here are some things we've learned along the way.

RETHINKING YOUR APPROACH

Engaging presentations require engaging presenters or an engaging means of presentation. However, engaging presenters are not always good content creators. Likewise, some insightful content creators have no business on a stage with a microphone. In the entertainment world, it's the difference between writers and actors. Yes, I know, we are not in the entertainment business. We've covered that.

But there's an important truth here for the church. If you want to make a great movie, you need great actors and great writers. You don't need great actors who can write. And you don't go looking for great writers who can act.

In church world, however, we have a tendency to expect content creators to be engaging presenters and presenters to be great content creators. Now, there are people who are really good at both. But they are the exceptions, not the rule. To complicate matters even more, in our world there is often a third component to this equation: small group leaders. A great small group leader may not be a strong presenter or content creator, but she may be off the chart when it comes to facilitating a conversation. The challenge is that many of us have inherited, or created, ministry models that require our presenters and group leaders to be proficient in two or three of these disciplines. So we give group leaders a curriculum and expect them to present it well. Or we hire a student pastor and expect him or her to be able to create great content for our students and present it in a way that engages one of the most difficult-to-engage groups on the planet. Then we get frustrated when our highly relational middle school group leaders don't "teach the lesson." And we can't understand why Mr. Stage Personality doesn't have anything deep or insightful to say. In Hollywood terms, we expect great actors to be great writers and editors.

If your system depends on your staff and volunteers being proficient in two or three of these disciplines, you are always going to get mediocre results. The exception will be the superstar staff member who can do it all. And every once in a while, you meet somebody like that. The problem is, everybody on staff will hate him! Well, maybe *hate* is too strong a word. No. They will hate him. But even if they don't, you can't build a successful ministry model around the exception to the rule. You need a system that allows engaging presenters to present, skilled content creators to create content, and relationally savvy group leaders to facilitate groups.

They're Out There

Now here's something I know about your church. Somewhere in your congregation are people who make a living presenting information. They are engaging presenters. They may never volunteer to serve in your children's or student areas. But if you were to provide them with an outline and a microphone, you might be surprised what will happen. You've got a bunch of teachers in your church. The last thing they want to do is sit in circles with eight children for an hour on Sundays. But they know curriculum. They know how to organize content. And some of them would love to present the Bible story in a large group setting as long as they don't have to take ownership of a small group. You also have some folks who aren't afraid of middle school boys, but they don't know jack about the Bible ... yet. They are scared to death you are going to give them Bible lessons to teach. But if they knew their only responsibility was to sit with their kids while a really good presenter did a really good presentation, and then discuss three specific questions from that really good presentation, they would be all over that. You get the point. If you create a system that divides these disciplines, you are going to recruit a different kind of volunteer. But more to the point, you will have a system that frees your engaging presenters to make engaging presentations.

We've gone to great lengths to create a system that frees communicators and content developers to do what they do best. The corollary is we've gone to great lengths to protect our audiences from presenters who aren't engaging. We choose our most engaging presenters, give them great content, and then turn them loose. And we use those presenters in different departments throughout the organization.

The person in our organization who has modeled this from the beginning is our student director, Kevin Ragsdale. Kevin was our seventh hire. He had no experience in student ministry when we hired him. But we hired him to create and administer our student environments. He told us right away that we would never see him upfront. He also said that if we were okay with a student pastor who didn't teach, play the guitar, or create lesson plans, but who would recruit people who did, he was our guy. Now Kevin oversees the five student ministries at our Atlanta-area churches. He still can't play the guitar, and to my knowledge he's never taught a large group Bible study. Kevin is actually a great small group leader. Of the three disciplines referenced above, small group leader is the only one he has any passion around. But Kevin is a brilliant recruiter. He sees potential, develops it, and then hands off the reins. If we had hired to the traditional student pastor model, we never would have hired Kevin in that position.

One of my most enjoyable tasks is to sit with Kevin's content team and brainstorm bottom lines for the presenters who present in our high school master-teacher environment, InsideOut. There are people in the room who have no interest in getting up on a stage in front of students, but they know the Bible and know what needs to be communicated. Kevin recruited several of the presenters who now speak during our weekend services on a regular basis. Even at that level they prepare with a team. They invite men and women who will never step foot onstage with a microphone strapped to their faces, but who know the Scriptures and understand how to create compelling content and illustrations. Those presenters are better because they've made it a habit to include insightful content creators in the process.

Beyond Talking Heads

Engaging presentations are certainly not limited to talking heads. In fact, live preaching or teaching may be one of the least-engaging forms of presentation. As a general rule, if you can present something in any way other than someone standing on a stage and talking, do so! If you can communicate something via video, go video. One way we've applied this is by replacing the dreaded weekend announcements with a video segment we call the 10Before. The best way to understand the 10Before is to see it. If you go to our website and look down at the bottom right hand corner of the landing page, you can actually view the 10Before from this past weekend's service (*www.northpoint.org*).

The 10Before is a short video that welcomes the crowd and orients them to the service. It also contains fun and informative video clips about upcoming opportunities for involvement. It is highly entertaining. Often funny. Our congregants look forward to the 10Before. This means, and please don't let this get out, they look forward to the announcements.

Speaking of announcements. In the churches I grew up in, the education director did the Sunday morning announcements. Wanna know why? Because he was the education director and that's what the education director did. It had absolutely nothing to do with an education director's ability to present in an engaging manner. Some could. Most couldn't. Doing the announcements was part of the role. Now, this next statement is so important I wish I could highlight it for you. Never assign a task that is gift-dependent to a staffing position. Never. Assign responsibility, not tasks. If we had assigned Kevin Ragsdale with the *task* of teaching our students, he would have failed as the student director. Actually, he is smart enough that he never would have taken the job to begin with. We assigned him the *responsibility* of making sure the students were taught well.

Now the astute readers and thinkers in the audience are wondering, "Does that mean a church shouldn't assign the preaching responsibility to the pastor?" Ahhh. Good question. Here's another one: Should a church assign the pastoring role to the pastor? How about this one: Should a church assign the leadership role of the church to the pastor? Public speaking, pastoring, and leading are all a bit gift-dependent, aren't they? And finding one man or one woman who is competent in all three of those disciplines is difficult. Sounds like a recipe for disaster to me. We will come back to that in chapter fourteen.

There's so much more we could talk about under this heading: visuals, interviews, note-taking outlines, pictures. All those things add an element of engagement to a verbal presentation. The bottom line is this: Do what it takes to create a culture characterized by a relentless commitment to engaging presentations at every level of the organization. Your message is too important to do anything less than that. The adults and children in your congregation and your community deserve your best efforts in this regard.

If a presentation of any kind is going to be made in your church, it should be engaging. Set the bar high. Create a culture that has a low tolerance for less-than-engaging presentations. Adjust your system or model so that your best presenters are presenting. Find the theologically astute thinkers in your crowd who might be good at helping with content. Employ the skills of your teachers and educators. Design a system that frees your small group leaders to facilitate rather than present. At every level of your organization ask: *Was the presentation engaging?*

QUESTION #3: IS THE CONTENT HELPFUL?

The third and final component of an irresistible ministry environment in our world is *helpful content*. The question we ask of all our curricula, messages, camp talks, leadership lessons, and small group outlines: *Is the content helpful?* We assume it's true. But is it helpful? By helpful we mean *useful*. Will the audience find it useful? Will it change the way people think? Does it offer a fresh perspective? Will the audience know what to do with what they've heard? Is it actionable?

For content to be helpful, it must accomplish at least one of three things:

1. Help people think biblically.
2. Help people behave biblically.
3. Help people contextualize biblical teaching.

THINK RIGHT

Jesus' trilogy of parables that ended with the story of the prodigal son was given to adjust his audience's thinking about how God viewed sinners. We all have seen what happens when people embrace the truth that God's love is a "regardless" kind of love. For many, that one idea is transformational. They are never the same. They would consider that teaching helpful. Practical? Not directly. But extremely helpful. Helping people think correctly is extraordinarily helpful. Believing correctly is often a precursor to behaving correctly. When teenagers are convinced of the fact that their friends determine the direction and quality of their lives, that is helpful. When a single adult acknowledges the truth that moral purity paves the way to intimacy, that's transformational. We've all seen what happens when resourced people are confronted with and accept the truth that God owns it all and that they are simply managers, stewards. You probably have a story of your own. You can remember where you were the first time you really understood—and whatever it was signified a paradigm shift. It was a defining moment. Nothing had changed, but somehow you changed. And the entire change revolved around a shift in your thinking.

We've heard it, read it, politicians misuse it, many of us have taught it, but still we underestimate the significance of Jesus' words when he said, "Then you will know the truth, and the truth will set you free."[43] The same holds true for the apostle Paul's oft-quoted statement in his letter to the Christians in Rome: "Do not conform to the pattern of this world, but be transformed by the renewing of your mind."[44] In short, renewed minds result in changed lives. Helping people think differently is helpful. It can be life changing. It's for this reason I spend so much time crafting simple statements that have the potential to lodge in the minds and hearts of an audience. But it doesn't stop there. I insist that our communicators and curriculum creators write and communicate to a simple and clearly crafted bottom line. Truth isn't helpful if no one understands or remembers it. But when stated clearly, truth can set us free. Carefully crafted truth statements have the power to change the way a person sees relationships, marriage, morality, parenting, money, poverty, the world! And that's helpful.

Thinking right. Believing right. Seeing the world through God's eyes. Those are catalysts for change. But at the end

of the day, *it's application that makes all the difference.* Both
Jesus and his brother James could not have been any clearer
on this point. We are all familiar with James' declaration that
faith without works is dead.[45] What is sometimes overlooked
is that he defines for us in a preceding verse what he means by
dead. There he declares that faith without works is *useless.*[46]
In other words, it's useless to know something if you don't
know what to do with it. Or more to his point, it's useless
to know it if you have no intention of doing anything with
it. As Howard Hendricks often says, "Biblically speaking, to
hear and not to do is not to hear at all."

Jesus concluded the Sermon on the Mount with a
challenge to apply what he taught. "Therefore everyone
who hears these words of mine and puts them into *practice*
is like a wise man who built his house on the rock."[47] As we
read the parable in its entirety, Jesus' point is unmistakable:
*Glad you could attend today's sermon on the mount. Matthew
will make copies of his notes and distribute them at a later
date. However, if you don't apply what you've heard today,
you might as well have stayed at home. Even though I'm Jesus,
hearing me preach won't help you. But applying what you
heard today will preserve and establish you.*

Knowledge alone makes Christians *haughty.* Application
makes us *holy.* You can use that. If you want a church full
of biblically educated believers, just teach what the Bible
says. If you want to make a difference in your community
and possibly the world, give people handles, next steps,
and specific applications. Challenge them to do something.
As we've all seen, it's not safe to assume that people
automatically know what to do with what they've been
taught. They need specific direction. This is hard. This
requires an extra step in preparation. But this is how you

grow people. So we ask of all our presentations and lessons: *Will the audience know what to do with what was taught?* If not, then we've got more work to do.

INTENTIONAL CONTEXTUALIZING

Reggie Joiner has a saying that gets him into trouble sometimes: "While all Scripture is equally inspired, it's not all equally applicable." Granted, it's a bit jarring the first time you hear or read that. But if you are a parent, you know instinctively that there's a lot of truth packed into that pithy, easy-to-remember statement. I've heard him say it this way as well: "While all Scripture is equally inspired, it's not equally applicable to all age groups." If your content is going to be helpful, you must take the additional step of contextualizing it for your audiences. Content that is perceived as helpful always addresses a felt need. Content that doesn't address a felt need is perceived as irrelevant. Notice I said *perceived*. It may be the most relevant information an audience has ever heard. But if an audience doesn't understand how content interfaces with their lives, it's just not all that interesting. So, helpful content is content presented in a way that is age- and stage-of-life specific.

We all do this intuitively to some degree. Odds are you don't teach the story of David and Bathsheba to your preschoolers. And your student pastor probably hasn't done an extended series on the seven seals of Revelation. But simply *avoiding* content that seems inappropriate to a specific audience isn't helpful. It's considerate, but not helpful. *Avoiding what's inappropriate does nothing to ensure that an audience will hear what's most appropriate.* Avoiding food that's bad for you doesn't ensure that you will eat what's best for you. But for content to be extraordinarily helpful requires more than a defensive posture. It requires some intentionality. It requires narrowing the focus of our content to what is most helpful for a specific audience. So while it's certainly appropriate for your children's ministry to skip the story of David and Bathsheba, it should probably be a recurring component in your adult small group curriculum! While middle school students don't necessarily need an explanation of the seven seals of Revelation, they could do with a consistent dose of Solomon's insight in Proverbs 13:20 regarding the impact their friends have on their lives.

We decided from the beginning that it wasn't enough to avoid what's inappropriate. So we've been intentional in the selection of our content for each of our audiences. We realize our time with each segment of our church population is limited. People move. Today's children are tomorrow's teenagers. Most singles are only single for a stage of their lives. The questions a newlywed couple asks are a bit different than the questions couples with kids are asking. Each age and stage of life introduces a new set of challenges as well as opportunities. For content to be truly helpful, each of these dynamics must be taken into consideration.

In the early days, we asked questions such as: What would be most helpful for preschoolers to know? What would be most helpful for elementary-aged children to know? What is the handful of truths we want middle school and high school students to know before they exit our influence? Which biblical narratives and principles would be most helpful for singles? In light of what the Scriptures teach regarding marriage, what do newlyweds need to know?

What do parents need to know? What should we focus on when meeting with our newly divorced single parents? What do new Christians need to know? Questions like these forced us to narrow our focus and narrow the scope of our teaching.

You may have read or seen our book *The Seven Checkpoints for Student Leaders*.[48] The entire book was written as a result of this exercise. We identified seven principles we wanted students to understand and internalize before they transitioned out of our student ministry. Eighty to 90 percent of all our teaching in middle and high school is related to one of these seven ideas. How do we keep it from feeling repetitious? That goes back to the preceding section. It's all in the ever-changing presentation. Our preschool and children's divisions each have three big ideas that drive their content selection. Our marrieds division narrowed its focus to six primary ideas. Whenever we teach this idea to church leaders, they all ask the same question: "Where can we get a copy of your lists?" I would ask the same thing. But perhaps the better question to ask is, "How quickly can I get my team together to begin a discussion around the content that would be most helpful for the various groups in our church?"

But I should warn you. That's a conversation that may be fraught with peril. *Fraught with peril*. I should be writing novels.

The Whole Truth

As obvious as all this may seem, a commitment to contextualization will put you at odds with a widely accepted approach to Bible teaching and curriculum development. My problem is not with the assumption behind the approach, but with the approach itself. According to this view, which is the view I grew up with, since all Scripture is inspired, it all needs to be taught. To adults anyway. And I wholeheartedly agree. It all needs to be taught — *somewhere*. But not everywhere. Specifically, not in big church. And not in Sunday school or in small groups. And the truth is, nobody in a local church setting actually teaches the entire Bible to anybody. He may survey the Bible. But he doesn't teach it. Here's how I know that to be the case.

There are 1,189 chapters in the Bible. There are over 31,000 verses. You can do the math. If you planned to teach through the entire Bible in a year, you would have to cover over twenty-two chapters a week. That's a survey. If you decided to teach through the Bible in two years, that's over eleven chapters a week. That's a survey. If you taught a chapter a week, that would take nearly twenty-three years. And that's assuming you never missed a weekend service. You get the point. Nobody actually preaches or teaches verse-by-verse through the entire Bible to the same congregation. Everybody picks and chooses and skips and skimps and cuts corners and "runs out of time" and "feels called to a different church." Here's my point: Since we have to pick and choose anyway, why not pick and choose the passages and principles that are most appropriate for specific audiences? Let's not simply avoid the awkward and inappropriate. Let's be intentional about what we teach, where we teach it, and to whom we teach it. Like … like Jesus.

Luke tells us that when Jesus went into a synagogue, it was his custom to stand up and read a text. On one particular occasion he was handed the scroll from the prophet Isaiah.

But he didn't begin reading at the beginning. In fact, he *scrolled* down to the end of the book. Here's Luke's description of what happened:

> He stood up to read, and the scroll of the prophet Isaiah was handed to him. Unrolling it, *he found the place where it is written*: "The Spirit of the Lord is on me, because he has anointed me to proclaim good news to the poor. He has sent me to proclaim freedom for the prisoners and recovery of sight for the blind, to set the oppressed free, to proclaim the year of the Lord's favor." (Luke 4:16–19, emphasis added)

Did you catch that? There was something his audience needed to know, so he went to the specific text that said it best.

Sounds like a great idea to me.

Even at the weekend level, my goal has never been to teach through the entire Bible. My goal is to equip and inspire adults to become followers of Jesus. Our mission statement captures it well: *to lead people into a growing relationship with Jesus Christ.* Like most local church pastors, I minister in a very specific local church context. My responsibility is to present the gospel as irresistibly as I can. Beyond that, my charge is to choose scriptural themes, narratives, principles, applications, and theology that address the specific issues people in my community are wrestling with and to do my best to answer the questions they are asking. Am I responsible to teach the "whole counsel of God," as it is sometimes called? Yes. The entire Bible? Only if you plan to stay at your current church at least twenty-two years without missing a Sunday.

So every year I preach a message or two on marriage, money, parenting, generosity, greed, sexual purity, forgiveness, and decision-making. And yes, I reteach the same texts every other year or so. I figure if we can get the Christians in our country to live out what the Bible teaches on that handful of topics, that would pretty much change everything. Heck, it's simpler than that. If we could just have a twelve-month reprieve on sexual immorality in our country, everything would be different.

I'm not trying to produce Bible scholars. And by the way, teaching through the entire Bible doesn't create Bible scholars anyway. It creates people who *think* they are Bible scholars. And those are some of the meanest, most uncompassionate human beings on the planet. You know who I'm talking about. You've got 'em in your church too. They correct you when you make the slightest error. But they aren't about to serve anywhere. Too busy for that. Not only do they believe in a literal hell, you get the impression they are happy about the fact that people are going there. I'm partial to hungry, ignorant Christians myself. The kind who are content to love Jesus and the people he died for. I'll take the Christian who doesn't know it all but is committed to doing what he or she knows over the Christian who knows it all and that's as far as it goes. Remember the widow who gave everything she had? Jesus liked her more than he liked the Pharisees. She was a doer. Jesus liked doers. I imagine he still does.

Somewhere, Not Everywhere

A few paragraphs ago, I made the point that the entire Bible should be taught somewhere, but not everywhere. Specifically, not in big church. So where's somewhere? In our network we have three avenues for the super-interested to get a more holistic Bible education. We have a leadership track called Theopraxis.[49] It is a series of six-week classes designed to help our volunteer ministry leaders develop a more sophisticated theological and biblical framework. This is not skill training. It is purely biblical and theological in nature. In addition to Theopraxis, we partner with a ministry called Bible Training Centre for Pastors and Leaders.[50] BTCP is a two-year series of courses that is the equivalent of a graduate study in theology, Bible survey, and Bible study methods. This course is taught all over the world. The founder, a good friend, is gracious enough to send his trainers to our churches to conduct these studies. Then for the super-serious, we host the Dallas Theological Seminary extension campus.

The good news is, for the people in our churches who want more in-depth theological training, there is more teaching and training available than they could avail themselves of in a lifetime. For the men or women or students, for that matter, who want to study their way through the entire text, they are living in the right age. Thanks to the Internet, it's all out there in every conceivable size, shape, language, and edition. And I am so grateful for the teachers and scholars who work tirelessly to provide us with such excellent and easily accessible resources. We are certainly a generation without excuse!

But back to the point of this section for just a moment. As you develop the filter through which you evaluate your content, let me suggest four questions to add to your arsenal:

1. Is the content *helpful*?
2. Does this content offer a potentially new and helpful perspective?
3. Does this content provide handles, applications, or next steps?
4. Is the content age- and stage-of-life specific?

THE BIG THREE

So those are the three filters we use to gauge the irresistibility of our environments. We evaluate setting, presentation, and content. Of each ministry environment we ask:

1. Is the setting appealing?
2. Is the presentation engaging?
3. Is the content helpful?

That's our filter. What's yours? Remember, every ministry environment is evaluated every weekend. The only question is, by *what* or *whose* standard? If you want your environments to be great, you've got to define *great*. If you want them to be irresistible, then you must define *irresistible* in transferable, easy-to-understand terms. Every staff member and volunteer in your church is convinced they know what great looks like. They show up on the weekends to work toward some predetermined end. You owe it to them to make the bull's-eye on the target as clear as humanly possible.

Getting there will not be easy. Everybody will have an opinion. If you don't like meetings, you may hate the process. But in the end, it will be worth it. Once you get there, everything will be better. Everything will run smoother. Everybody will be working and evaluating from the same playbook. When guests walk onto your campus for the first time, they will know something significant is going on. They will see the consistency. They will feel safe. For some, they will know immediately that yours is an organization they want to be a part of and that they want their children to take part in. Environment matters. So, take a fresh look at your ministry environments. Make them the best they can possibly be.

chapter ten

Rules of Engagement

Perhaps the most important environment in any church is the weekend worship service. Whether it's Sunday morning or Saturday night, this environment more than any defines your church. Your weekend services determine how people perceive and experience your church. And this makes the team that creates the weekend worship experiences one of, if not *the* most important team in your organization. To a great extent, they determine the reputation of your church in the community. This is one reason I meet every Tuesday morning with the service programming directors from all of our Atlanta-area churches. Nothing is more mission critical than the weekend service.

That being the case, it is imperative that your service programming team be aligned around a common purpose as well as an approach. As in all things, *purpose* should determine *approach*. At the end of the day, it's what we do, not what we purposed to do, that defines our lives and reputations. The same is true for our churches. One of the most common disconnects in church world is the discrepancy between *purpose* and *approach*. Nearly all the senior pastors I've ever talked to would swear (well, maybe not swear), would claim adamantly that they want unchurched people to attend and connect with their churches. But then they turn right around and create weekend services that assume everybody present is a believer and attends every week. That's what I mean by a disconnect between purpose and approach. The approach a church chooses trumps its purpose every time. Unless, of course, the approach and purpose are aligned. But don't deceive yourself. If your stated purpose is at odds with your approach, you will never accomplish what you have purposed to accomplish.

So one of the first things a service programming team must do is clarify the purpose of the weekend experience. In our world we refer to this as "clarifying the win." There is an in-depth explanation of what it means to *clarify the win* in chapter ten of our book *The Seven Practices of Effective Ministry*.[51] The section titled "Four Steps to Clarifying the Win," in my opinion, is worth the price of the entire book. There we argue that every team responsible for any environment within a church should gather the team together and ask a series of questions that will result in a simple statement that clarifies the win for that environment. In Appendix C, we provide a list of "wins" for each of our ministry areas. If the win is unclear, you force your team— both leaders and volunteers—to guess what a win looks like. Everybody will guess differently. As a result, everyone will evaluate differently. And since everyone likes to win, chances are people will consider their areas of ministry successful whether they are or not. This is why it is so excruciatingly difficult to change or eliminate programming in a local church. The most invested will always be convinced it is working. Whatever *it* is. Why? Because according to the way they measure success, it is! If you don't clarify the win for a team, they will do it themselves. And once a group falls in love with a ministry or style of ministry, they will find a way to convince themselves that what they are doing is essential to the success of your church. Whether it is or not.

THE WEEKEND WIN

Here's a question your team should wrestle to the ground: What's the win for your weekend services? What makes you and members of your team feel like, *Wow, this weekend, we killed it!* What is *it*? I know. I know. It's a variety of things. So make a list. Begin the discussion.

What's the win for the weekend?

This is a tough question. Every message series is different. You don't always have control over what guest speakers are going to say. You don't want things to get too predictable. I get all that. But in spite of all the unavoidable variables, your service programming team has something in mind when they sit down to create a weekend experience. They begin with an unwritten set of assumptions that defines success. Somewhere there is consensus around what makes a great weekend a great weekend. That being the case, you owe it to yourself and to your team to discover what everybody's thinking and create some verbiage around it. My hunch is that once you begin poking around and surfacing how members of the team define a weekend win, you will discover both alignment and misalignment. Dig around long enough and you will stumble upon *the* thing that raises the level of energy in the room — the thing that causes everybody to sit up on the edges of their seats. Whatever the common denominator is, you need to find it and put some words around it. Once you do, then all that's left is to decide if what the win *is* is what the win ought to be.

For too many teams, a weekend win is a full room. For the preschool director, the win may be the service letting out on time so the volunteers don't mutiny. For the worship leader, the win may be permission to introduce a new song. *Preferably, one of his or her own!* For the preacher, the win may be a large response at the end of the message — a response so large that the service time is extended, thus creating a problem for the preschool director. Which means next Sunday the preacher will ask for more time to preach, which will require the worship director to cut a song. *Preferably, someone else's.* The win for the education director may be more time for announcements.

I know what you're thinking. *How did he know?* I know because I live in the same world you do. But I'm telling you, once your team agrees on the weekend win, it reduces the unavoidable tension created when everybody chases the win that's right in his or her own eyes.

OUR WINS

We've determined two wins for our weekend services. One immediate and one long-term. Our immediate win is when a regular attendee brings an unchurched friend who enjoys the service so much that he or she returns the following week. If the unchurched friend returns the following Sunday with another unchurched friend in tow, we break out the champagne and hire a band. Seriously, our goal on the weekend is to create a setting so appealing, a presentation so engaging, and content so helpful that unchurched people would not only want to come back the following week, but that they would be both comfortable and motivated to invite a friend. That's what we celebrate. Those are the stories we show up to staff meetings longing to hear. Those are the letters and emails we pass around the office. Those are the stories I circulate among our elders.

Do we celebrate people crossing the line of faith? Yes. Do we celebrate when someone elects to be baptized? Already covered that. And, yes, we love it when the music sends chills up our spines and brings tears to our eyes. We love it when people sign up to volunteer. I'm thrilled when people respond publically to my preaching. We love to get out on time and we applaud the songwriting skills of our worship leaders. Those are all wonderful and important components. But the win—the thing that wakes us up in the morning and keeps us awake at night—is when one of our attendees takes a risk and invites a friend who is far from God, and that friend shows up, is moved, and chooses to return the following weekend. That's the bull's-eye on the target, baby. *It don't get no better than that!* So we plan our weekend services with our inviters and their invitees in mind. Our service programming teams view themselves as partners in evangelism with our members and regular attendees. Does that mean we tailor the content to non-Christians? Nope. We tailor the experience to non-Christians. There's a big difference. And that difference is what this chapter is all about.

I mentioned we had a long-term as well as an immediate win. The long-term win is *life change.* The long-term win is when individuals who attend our services on a regular basis shift their thinking and their behavior in a divine direction. We want our weekend services to be catalysts for personal life change. We want to inspire people to believe differently and behave differently. As is the case with our immediate wins, these are the emails, letters, and tweets we forward, read, copy, and circulate around the office. When significant life change is part of a baptism story, we show the video in our staff gatherings, elders meetings, and, when we get permission, we post 'em on our Facebook pages. Here's an important distinction. Whereas our weekend experience is designed with the unchurched in mind, our message content is designed for life change.

As I've reiterated from the beginning, I'm not suggesting that every church adopt *our win* for the weekend. What I'm urging you to do is discover or define yours. Once you do, then the real fun begins.

Once you've determined your win for the weekend, the next step is to create an approach or template that supports the win. Creating it is one thing; implementing it is something else altogether. As you know, transitioning a church to a new approach to the weekend service has the potential to split a congregation. I experienced this firsthand. At the end of this chapter, I've included some insights on preparing your church for change. But honestly, that is not an area I can speak to with as much authority as others. Our team was successful in transitioning a large group of committed volunteers and leaders to a new weekend model. But that is different than transitioning an established church. But take heart; it can be done. It has been done. God may call you to do it!

Developing Your Template

When I talk to pastors and service programming teams about creating a template for their weekends, I always get the same pushback. And I am sympathetic. The idea of following the same template week after week feels limiting.

Creative types feel nauseated. Theological types immediately raise their hands and ask about the role of the Holy Spirit in worship. Does a template leave room for the work of the Spirit? Doesn't a template put everybody in a box?

Actually, it doesn't. A template doesn't *put* your team in a box. Your team is already in a box. Your team designs the weekend experience within the limits of some type of box whether you follow a template or not. We all have a time box. It may be an hour or two hours. But eventually you run out of time. There's a resource box, more commonly known as line items in your budget. There's a talent box. Then there's the denominational box. There's a style box. In other words, you are already working with limits. Creating and following a template ensures that you get the most out of the limited resources you have available. More importantly, a template ensures that your approach supports your objective. In our case, our template forces us to think like outsiders.

Creativity always has constraints. Once a painter chooses the size of her canvas, she has constrained herself. Filmmakers have about a two-and-a-half-hour time constraint. Playwrights work within constraints. Sculptors have constraints.

Songwriters who hope to get airplay have about a three-and-a-half-minute time constraint. And interestingly enough, just about every hit over the past fifty years has followed a similar template: verse-chorus-verse-chorus-bridge-chorus-chorus. Think about that. Within a three-to-four-minute time frame, there seems to be an endless variety of melodies, themes, chord progressions, and styles. Are there constraints? Yes. Is there room to create within those constraints? Just turn on the radio.

Every time you *create* a weekend experience, you are working within constraints. Just like Picasso. What I want to help you do is find or create the template that will allow you to harness your team's creative ability in a way that supports what you consider the win for the weekend within the constraints you've been given. I want to help you settle on your version of verse-chorus-verse-chorus-bridge-chorus-chorus.

Whether you realize it or not, you already have a template for your weekend experience. You may not know what it is, but you have one. And anybody who has attended your church for six months or more has a pretty good idea of what it is.

Why? Because your worship services follow pretty much the same pattern, a.k.a. template, every week. The songs and message topics change. The dreaded announcements change. The title package changes. The host and worship leader may change. But on any given Sunday, there are songs, a message, announcements, a title package, a worship leader, and a host. You have a template. You have your own version of verse-chorus-etc. The question is: Do you have the right one? Do you have one that supports your win? Is it fine-tuned to help you accomplish what you *say* you are there to accomplish? The first step is to discover the template you are currently following. Pull the team together and put some terminology around your heretofore unwritten, secret-sauce assumptions and approaches to your weekend services. Discovering and creating terminology for what you are currently doing is important for a couple of reasons. To begin with ...

Perfectly Designed

If you like what's happening on the weekends, you owe it to yourself to discover your secret sauce and guard it with your life. *Your current template is perfectly designed to produce the results you are currently getting.* If you love your results, the last thing you want to do is unintentionally drift in a different direction. The only way to ensure that you don't drift is to set your anchor deep. And that will require bringing some objectivity to what may currently be a predominantly intuitive process. On the other hand, if you are dissatisfied with your current results, you need to make some changes. But it is difficult to discuss and change something that has never been identified and defined in the first place. Either way, you need to identify and create descriptive terminology for your current weekend template. Once you do that, you have to ask the most difficult question of all: In light of what we've established as our *win,* is this really the best *approach?* Does your approach facilitate your win?

In the pages that follow, I'm going to walk you through our template. As I stated earlier, we didn't face the challenge of transitioning a local church weekend template. We had the advantage of starting off with an approach that we believed supported the weekend objectives described at the beginning of this chapter. Our template has evolved. There are things we can do now that we couldn't do in the beginning. There are things we did in the beginning that we abandoned along the way. We are constantly tweaking and adjusting as culture shifts. But we are crazy-committed to creating an experience that brings first-timers back and moves people toward maturity.

The North Point Template

Our template is designed to move a diverse group of adults, assuming little or no interest, from wherever they are when they drive onto our property to the *point* of the message. The short version: *Our goal is to host our attendees from the parking lot to the point.* Like your church, our audience runs the gamut from skeptic to saint. And while our immediate goal is to hook the skeptic, our long-term goal applies to everyone in the room. To move an audience, especially a diverse audience, from where they are to where you want them to be requires *common ground.* If you want me to follow you on a journey, you have to come get me. The journey must begin where I am, not where you are or where you think I should be.

This is a really big deal. Where a weekend experience consistently begins will ultimately determine who consistently shows up to take the journey. If the journey begins with the assumption that everybody here knows what we are doing, you will eventually have an audience of people who already know what you are doing. If your journey begins with the assumption that everybody in the audience is a believer, then eventually your audience will be full of believers. Who shows up for Third Day concerts? Primarily people who know and are expecting Third Day music. Where you consistently begin and what you consistently assume determine who consistently shows up. Why? Because your assumptions create the common ground for the journey. Great communicators do this intuitively. Somehow they know where you are and they take you with them to where they want you to be.

So what is the common ground in an audience of diverse backgrounds, ages, stages of life, church experiences, theological sophistication, etc.? What could a group that diverse have in common? Since our immediate win involves individuals who do not necessarily share our worldview, much less our theology, the common ground can't be either. So we back way up and leverage *common experiences and emotions.*

More often than not, we lean hard into a specific emotion. We've learned that tapping into a common emotion is often the best on-ramp to influencing the way an individual views and approaches life. Everyone, from skeptic to saint, knows what it is to hurt, what it is to doubt, and what it is to hope. Everyone loves to laugh. Everyone loves to celebrate a story of redemption. Everybody has doubts and fears. Everybody questions. So we work hard to create a moment early on when everybody in the room is in agreement, shaking their heads in the same direction.

Now, if that bothers you, you have just experienced the very thing we try to do every weekend in all our churches. If you started an imaginary conversation with me about how cheap and unbiblical that approach is, you are experiencing just how powerful this approach is. You are emotionally engaged. You are interested. You are interested because you disagree. Some of my favorite messages are the ones where I open up with a statement that makes everybody uncomfortable. Create tension and you've created interest. Iron out all the tension and you will eliminate interest. Don't ever forget that. But before you dismiss this as a cheap gimmick, you might be interested to know where we got the idea.

THE MASTER TEACHER

One day Jesus looked up and found himself surrounded by an extraordinarily diverse audience: tax gatherers, fishermen, Pharisees, the powerful of Rome, along with the destitute of Palestine. It was the entire spectrum. People who didn't consider themselves as bad as some, but knew they weren't nearly as good as others. As diverse as they were, Jesus recognized they all had something in common. They all shared a common confusion regarding God's attitude toward sinners. So he chose this particular opportunity to address their confusion. But where do you begin a somewhat theological discussion with a group with varying degrees of theological sophistication? Where do you begin a discussion regarding God's view of sinners with a group that includes sinners who don't see themselves as sinners shoulder-to-shoulder with sinners who see themselves as too far gone to ever be redeemed?

How's this for an approach:

> "Suppose one of you has a hundred sheep and loses one of them." (Luke 15:4)

Perfect. A hypothetical situation involving sheep.

Jesus began his discussion by tapping into a common human experience that evoked a common emotion. Loss. Everybody in his audience had lost something along the way. And everybody in his audience knew what *he* would do if he had a hundred sheep and discovered that one had wandered off.

> "Doesn't he leave the ninety-nine in the open country and go after the lost sheep until he finds it?" (v. 4)

At this point, all the heads are nodding. And I can imagine that there are some uncomfortable Pharisees who suddenly find themselves agreeing with tax collectors. Brilliant! Absolutely brilliant. Everybody agrees. Everybody feels the same. Jesus, the master teacher, knew that if his diverse audience were to follow him to somewhere new, he would first have to go to where they were. He would have to find common ground with a group that had little in common. So that's what he did. That's what we must do as well. This isn't a gimmick. This is leaning into the way we were created.

This is about caring so much for other people that you go to where they are before asking them to follow you to where you are convinced they need to be. Jesus continued:

> "And when he finds it, he joyfully puts it on his shoulders and goes home. Then he calls his friends and neighbors together and says, 'Rejoice with me; I have found my lost sheep.'" (vv. 5–6)

Again, all the heads were probably nodding. That's exactly what they would do. That's what people do when they find something they have lost. Especially if it is something of value. Now that they were all in agreement, he would ask them to follow him somewhere new.

> "I tell you that in the same way there will be more rejoicing in heaven over one sinner who repents than over ninety-nine righteous persons who do not need to repent." (v. 7)

That was new. Jesus had just challenged the accepted view of God's attitude toward the sinners and the righteous. But still, he doesn't have them turn to Genesis, chapter two. Instead he said:

> "Or suppose a woman has ten silver coins and loses one. Doesn't she light a lamp, sweep the house and search carefully until she finds it? And when she finds it, she calls her friends and neighbors together and says, 'Rejoice with me; I have found my lost coin.'" (vv. 8–9)

While the Pharisees in the crowd may not have connected with the lost sheep illustration, most could connect with a lost coin, especially one their wives might have lost.

> "In the same way, I tell you, there is rejoicing in the presence of the angels of God over one sinner who repents." (v. 10)

By this time, everybody is starting to catch on. The Pharisees are certainly engaged. "Wait a minute, are you saying that God *feels* the same way about a sinner that I *feel* about a lost coin? Coins are valuable. Sinners are ... sinners." The sinners are engaged. "So God *feels* about me the same way the shepherd felt about the sheep?"

Having engaged his audience with common emotion, Jesus raises the stakes by moving from sheep and coins to the intimate relationship of a father and his son. Surrounded by perhaps dozens, maybe hundreds, of men, many of whom claimed to be sons of Abraham and some of whom wouldn't claim any relationship with God at all, he challenges them to make a shift in their thinking about how God views sinners—how God viewed *them!* But he didn't begin with God. He began with *them.* He began by eliciting an emotion that became the catalyst for what might arguably be his most important message. Did everybody buy it? Nope. Were some offended by what Jesus had to say? Absolutely. Was everybody engaged? Most likely. Did anybody miss his point? It's highly unlikely. His point was so unavoidably clear that this trilogy of parables is one of the most popular passages in the entire Bible.

Rules of Engagement

From the outset we are looking to engage people emotionally. And when I say from the outset, I mean from the parking lot. Our template is designed to create a journey for our attendees. As you can see from the diagram on page 208, it includes three large pieces with several incremental steps within each. At the macro level our goal is to *engage* the audience, *involve* the audience, and finally *challenge* them. The reason we created our template in the shape of a funnel is to remind us that our responsibility every week is to *engage* our entire audience. Not just the church people. In my experience, this is where most churches miss the mark completely. They begin with the assumption that everybody is already interested, engaged, and informed. That's fine for a church designed for church people. It is not fine for churches committed to engaging the hearts and minds of the unchurched. We want everyone from the skeptic to the saint to be engaged from the beginning.

The second step in the journey is to *involve*. This is challenging, but necessary. We've discovered that if we've done a good job of engaging our audience emotionally, it is possible to involve them physically. Finally, we *challenge* them. To challenge people before they're engaged and involved violates the created order of things. Unfortunately, churches and communicators in particular attempt this all the time. If you think in terms of personal relationships, you can immediately understand why it doesn't work. Challenge the behavior or attitude of someone you don't know and see what difference that makes. You may be right. You may make your point. But you won't make a difference. What you will make is an enemy.

If a church or a pastor's goal is simply to speak the truth, then engaging and involving are unnecessary steps. Just sing a couple songs, take the offering, and preach! There's no need to build a relational bridge. But if the goal is to make a difference, to actually shift someone's thinking or behavior, then relational bridge building is a critical step. We resist being influenced by people we don't know or don't trust. We are open to the influence of those whom we trust or whom we perceive have our best interests at heart. Trust requires common ground. Trust requires empathy. All that to say, there is some work we must do before we can expect people to internalize our messages and to live by them. And this is especially true for those who are new to church or those who have had bad experiences with organized religion.

Rules of Engagement

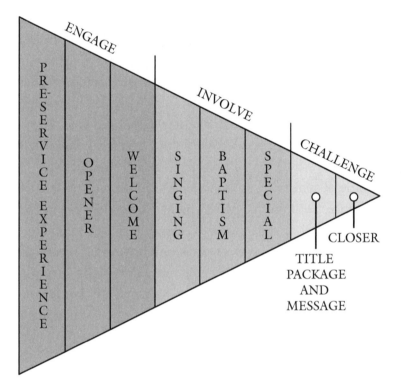

To take our audience on this three-step journey, we employ eight elements in our worship services. Four of the eight are part of every service. The remaining four are used when appropriate.

TEMPLATE ELEMENT #1: PRE-SERVICE EXPERIENCE

The *pre-service experience* encompasses everything our audience encounters from the time they drive onto our campus until the service actually begins. This includes what they experience in the parking lot and the hallways, the check-in procedure for their children, and the process of finding seats in our worship center. It includes the clarity of the signage, the cleanliness of the restrooms, the temperature of the building, and the lighting. As you know, if you offend someone *before* a service, it's going to be next to impossible to engage him *in* the service. So we work hard in pre-service to create as enjoyable an experience as possible.

More specifically, we want people to feel comfortable. Why comfortable? Because anytime we walk into a new environment, especially if our children are involved, there is an element of discomfort. We aren't sure where to go or what to do. Bringing children into an unknown environment surfaces a litany of questions. Men generally want to know how long things will last, what time they will be home. We go out of our way to address these issues as early as possible.

One of the best things we did in this regard was to create a website where people who have never attended, but who are planning to attend, can watch short videos of any of our weekend environments (*www.northpoint.org/new*).

They can see what happens in our toddler rooms, our elementary-age environments, and our middle school and high school environments. And, of course, there is a video synopsis of what takes place in our worship environment. Those bringing children can even register them online so that when they show up at check-in, somebody will actually be expecting them. All of this in the name of making things more comfortable.

In the pre-service experience, *comfortable* takes precedence over *theological.*

That may sound a bit extreme. But if our immediate win is to capture the interest of unchurched people, then at the broadest end of the funnel, we must remove every possible obstacle from the path of the disinterested, suspicious, here-against-my-will, would-rather-be-somewhere-else, unchurched guests. The parking lot, hallways, auditorium, and stage must be obstacle-free zones.

Several years ago I sensed that we were beginning to slip in this area. So I brought the service programming teams from our Atlanta-area churches together for a powwow. I didn't tell them the purpose of our gathering. I took them into one of our auditoriums where I had the stage lights and house lights turned on like we would during a weekend service. I handed them envelopes and pens and had them take seats in different areas of the auditorium. I asked them to just sit still for several minutes and then open the envelopes and follow the instructions on the sheets inside. The instructions went something like this:

> Imagine that this is your first time to our church. You are not a regular church attendee. You aren't anti-church. You just don't see any need for it. Someone invited you and here you are.

Then I had them answer several questions from the standpoint of a newcomer. Questions such as: *When you look at the stage, what comes to mind? What concerns you? What do you wish you knew? What do you hope doesn't happen? What would make you more comfortable right now? What information would you like to see pop up on the screen?*

As you might imagine, we had an incredible debriefing session. For the first time in a long time, we were looking at our room like outsiders rather than insiders. As insiders, we suffer from what Dan and Chip Heath refer to as the "curse of knowledge."[52] We know so much about our church that it's difficult for us to program with the first-timer in mind. But exercises such as the one I described help. One of the big findings from that exercise was that half the men on our team answered the "What do you wish you knew?" question with, "How long is this going to last?" As a result, we've asked our weekend hosts to include the following in their opening remarks: "We are going to be here for about an hour."

We choose all of our pre-service music with a first-time, unchurched person in mind. We include a mixture of familiar secular and not-so-familiar worship tunes as people enter the worship center. Like many churches we run recurring information slides on the screens, including a screen with the biblical text or texts for the day to allow people new to Bible study to go ahead and look them up. And as mentioned in chapter nine, about ten minutes prior to the start of the service, we begin the 10Before.

There are things that must be communicated to a local church. But they are usually so insider-focused they create a potential disconnect for guests. So we put all the insider information in the 10Before and play it just before the service officially begins. Do the folks who get there late or even right on time miss it? Yes. But I bet you already know who those folks are, don't you? They are the first-timers, the people who think that if church starts at 11:00 a.m., you show up at 11:00 a.m.

TEMPLATE ELEMENT #2: OPENER

The second potential segment in the engage portion of our template is titled *opener*. An opener is usually a song or an interactive game designed to engage the audience. We employ openers about once every four to six weeks.

In our world, it is a major win if we can get everyone in the audience to smile or laugh within the first three minutes of the service. The opener is usually designed to create a sense of enjoyment. There are people who show up at all of our churches who have never laughed *in* church. They've laughed *at* it plenty of times. But they've never enjoyed themselves in a church service. We work hard to create those moments of surprise when, for the first time or the first time in a long time, a man or a woman discovers what it's like to feel good in church. An opening song generally ties into the theme of the message or series. We often choose an opener to introduce a topic. But we do not use an opener to make a point. A good opener will create a feeling. At this point in the service, secular and familiar is better than sacred and unfamiliar. Beatles tunes win the day every time. To date, our best opener was our iBand (which you can find on YouTube under North Point's iBand). Everything about it was perfect insofar as openers go. It was unique. It was cool. It involved electronic gadgets. No one had ever seen anything like it. Everyone knew the songs. The execution was flawless. There were smiles all over the auditorium. Teenagers loved it. Middle-aged men loved it. Women loved it because their boyfriends and husbands loved it.

From time to time we get negative feedback about using secular tunes in church. I understand the concern. No, those songs don't "glorify God." Yes, the artists who sing some of those songs are pagans. But none of that bothers us. Our goal isn't to create an environment that is "set apart from the world." We are up to something way more significant than that. We want to change the world.

Template Element #3: Welcome

On weekends that include openers, the next thing that happens is the *welcome* by our host. On weekends when there is not an opener, we begin with the welcome. This is not announcement time. We call it a welcome because that's what you do when people arrive at your home. You welcome them. We don't expect guests in our homes to let themselves in while we converse with our families. Nor do we meet people at the door and begin dispensing random information. When guests arrive at our door, we give them our undivided attention. We do whatever we can to make them feel ... drumroll please ... *at home*. We want them to feel *comfortable*. In our world, the welcome is all about the new folks, not the home folks. Staying with the "visitor at the door" motif for just a moment, I've been to way too many churches where I had to let myself in the door, find a place to sit, and then listen to the church family talk to each other.

So we treat the guests in our church the way we would in our homes. After warmly welcoming the crowd, we offer information about next steps for them at our church. But we only offer information that is appropriate for guests. We avoid a calendar of events that is geared toward our regular attendees. The gravitational pull of every church is toward insiders. Nowhere is this more common and more disruptive than in the slot normally given to announcements. We have abandoned the "A" word entirely.

TEMPLATE ELEMENT #4: SINGING

The *welcome* signals the end of *engage*. This is when we invite people to get *involved*. You will note that we titled this slot *singing* rather than *worship*. This is intentional. And this is an extraordinarily important distinction. Christians, and church leaders in particular, use the term *worship* loosely. Let's face it: We use the term as an adjective as much or more than we do as a noun. We have worship music, worship leaders, worship centers, and worship services. But outsiders don't use the term that way. For outsiders, *worship* is still primarily a verb. As a verb, worship always has an object. People worship their children, their careers, their boats, and occasionally, their spouses. But even for the nonreligious, the term *worship* has religious overtones. Then there are people of different faiths. For them, the term brings something very specific to mind. And you can rest assured it is a far cry from what we are doing during our weekend gatherings. So with all that as a backdrop, what do you think comes to mind for a truly unchurched person or someone of a different faith when someone walks onstage and invites everyone to stand as "we worship together"?

Let me ask it a different way. As a Christian, if you were attending a weekend gathering at a mosque, and the person upfront invited everyone to worship, what would you think? I know what I would think: *Uh-oh! Can I do this? Am I betraying my faith?* Putting unbelievers or different kinds of believers in situations where they feel forced to worship is incredibly unfair. It's offensive. It's bait-and-switch. It's insulting. But what are they going to do? Remain seated? Leave? Their only other option is to stand and pretend to be going along with something they don't understand or believe. Now we've made hypocrites out of them! Never thought about that, did you? Know why? Because our natural inclination is to create churches for churched people.

Now I realize this section is focused on the North Point template. But allow me to reach outside of our template into yours for just a moment. If you think there might be unbelievers in your weekend gathering, drop the term *worship* from your weekend vocabulary. Besides, we all know worship is broader and more encompassing than singing. If you read the New Testament carefully, you will discover that people didn't "stand" to worship anyway. Most of them "fell down."

So use the term *singing*. From an unchurched person's perspective, it looks and sounds like singing. Inviting someone to stand and sing is very different than asking someone to worship. If you want to create a church that unchurched people love to attend, you've got to think like an outsider.

Now, having said all of that, I would be quick to point out that there is something very powerful that takes place when believers sing together. It is *worshipful*. For many, it *is* worship. Truth put to music penetrates the heart like few things can. Corporate singing has evangelistic power. This is especially true when someone who hasn't been to church in a long time is suddenly confronted with a hymn that he knew from childhood. Suddenly he is back to a place where life was simpler. Hymns can take adults back to chapters of their lives that preceded the decisions they regret most. But it's not just the returners who are impacted by corporate singing. Like me, I'm sure you've seen first-timers brought to tears by songs they've never heard before — lyrics that pierced their resistance. Suddenly they are emotional and they have no idea why. So don't hear me discounting the value of worship songs or corporate worship through singing. My point is, let's call it what it is and let God use it however he sees fit!

Deal?

No?

Oh well. I tried.

Which Ones Where

Song selection and order are important in our template. Like a lot of teams, we choose and order songs based on tempo and ease of transition. We like to start *up*. We understand the dynamic of moving from celebration to reflection. But there is an additional element to song selection and order that is important to us. We plan knowing that we will be asking people who may not buy into the whole Jesus thing to participate in corporate singing. We don't want to make liars out of them any sooner than necessary. And should they choose to opt out of singing something they don't believe, we would like to help them put that off as long as possible. So we do our best to open our corporate singing sets with the least offensive lyrics possible. We try to open with songs that highlight God's glory as revealed in nature, God's love,

God's power, God's mercy, God's forgiveness, etc.—the stuff most people don't have a problem with. Then we move to the more Jesus-centric tunes. This is a subtle thing. But we think it's important. We don't always get this right. But it is front and center in the planning process. There are songs we would never include in the weekend playlist that we may choose as theme songs for a midweek night of worship and communion. Those are two different audiences and the win for those two environments is entirely different as well.

Our music sets include two or three songs, depending on whether we are baptizing that weekend. This is due both in part to our target audience as well as our time restriction. We give people permission to sing poorly. We give people permission not to sing at all if they prefer. It is important for song leaders to remember that there is a segment of our population that doesn't like to sing. Ever. They don't sing in their cars or in their showers. And they aren't going to sing at church. I remind our song leaders from time to time that they aren't doing anything wrong. Some people just don't like to sing. And that's okay. And please don't guilt people into singing. An individual's willingness or unwillingness to participate in corporate singing is not a reflection of his or her commitment to Christ or spiritual maturity. And that goes both ways. Know any church leaders who lost their ministries over moral failures? I bet they knew all the words and even raised their hands a time or two.

Template Element #5: Baptism

We baptize two or three times a month. As I mentioned earlier, we require those who want to be baptized to allow us to record a video in which they describe their faith journeys.

These three- to four-minute recordings are designed to engage the audience emotionally. And they do. It's hard to argue with someone's story. We have a sophisticated process to help people craft and record their stories. For the majority of individuals who are baptized, this will be their best opportunity to impact the largest number of people. So we do everything we can to help them make their stories as clear and as compelling as possible. Most invite family members. But it is not unusual for an individual to bring a dozen or more unchurched friends.

The placement of baptism is strategic for us. It comes right before the offering. And just so you know, we take an offering every week. The reason this is strategic is that very few things are as unsettling to unchurched people as the way a church talks about money. By following baptism with our collection, it allows us to tie life change to generosity. That is extremely important for both the unchurched guest and the regular attendee. As church leaders, we know people's financial generosity is what enables us to create inspirational and instructional weekend experiences for entire families. And we know how expensive it is to do it right. We know there is a direct correlation between the resources available to us and the impact we can make on our communities. But that relationship is not always apparent to the average church attendee. So we are quick to point out that the stories of life change they just witnessed are an overflow of their financial generosity to their local church. And that's not a sales pitch, is it? That's the God-honest truth.

This is the slot in our service where we often address unchurched people directly. We let 'em know that we built this building for them, that we hope God will do in their hearts what we've just seen evidence of in the lives of those who were baptized. We tell 'em they can come every week for free, and the reason it's free is because they are sitting around some of the most generous people in the state of Georgia—people who are so committed to helping them connect with their heavenly Father that they love giving to their local church. Then we pray and pass the buckets.

Template Element #6: Special

This is the most infrequently used element in our template. *Specials* are generally songs, sometimes interviews or video sketches, designed to create the tension the message will address. This is another point of emotional, and to some extent intellectual, engagement. Up to this point, we've done everything we know how to do to make people *comfortable*. It's at this point in our template that we switch gears. Specials are selected to make people a bit uncomfortable. Specials raise issues. They point to unsolved mysteries. They surface felt needs and unanswered questions. A good special is open-ended. A song that resolves all the tension doesn't work here. We want to stir people up, not settle them down. For that reason, we almost never use a Christian song in this slot. Christian songs resolve things. They answer questions. That's not the role of the special. Two of my favorite specials to preach after were "Storm," by Lifehouse, and "Confessions of a Broken Heart," by Lindsay Lohan. Songs like these touch the raw nerves of human experience. Everybody has gone through a protracted time of anguish wondering if it would ever end. Many women in our congregations have languished in the no-man's-land created by an absent father. When you stand up to communicate after songs of that caliber, the table is set. The tension is in the house. Everybody's looking for a lifeline. Issues raised by songs like those take us beyond religious persuasion and anti-religious bias. They serve as an on-ramp to the commonest of common ground. But a word of warning to those of you who carry the communicator mantle: If you introduce your topic with a gut-wrenching, emotionally charged song, you'd better have something of equal significance to say. Don't choose a song that raises a question you aren't prepared to answer. Don't choose a song that promises more than you can deliver.

Been there.

TEMPLATE ELEMENT #7: TITLE PACKAGE/ MESSAGE

The *title package* is a one-minute video that introduces the title and theme for a particular message series. Functionally, it is designed to be an engaging transition as we prepare the stage for the speaker. The next chapter is focused on message preparation and delivery. What's important to note here is that when I, or any of our communicators, get up to preach, we begin the process of *engage*, *involve*, and *challenge* all over again. We look for common ground with the goal of surfacing a common emotion that can serve as a springboard into the text. We try hard to get the audience nodding their heads in the same direction before we transition into the Scriptures. But once we hit the hard realities of God's Word, the nodding starts to dissipate. And that's okay.

As you can see from the "Rules of Engagement" diagram (page 208), the message is at the narrowest point in the funnel. In our approach, this is the appropriate place to directly challenge people's beliefs, assumptions, lifestyles, and anything else that runs contrary to what the Scriptures teach. This is where we run the risk of offending our audience. This is where we start losing people. And we are okay with that. The apostle Paul warned us that the gospel is a stumbling block for some and just plain foolishness for others.[53] But in the same breath, he observed that the gospel *is* the power and wisdom of God. Some will receive it while others will be put off. In Matthew 13, Jesus introduced this idea in his parable of the sower. Our churches are full of people with differing levels of receptivity. I imagine our audience represents the entire range of soils Jesus described. In the past, I've heard pastors interpret Jesus' teaching to mean that our approach to presenting the gospel is almost irrelevant. They argue that it's the nature of the soil that makes the difference. And I would agree with that last statement. But while our approach to sowing the seed of God's Word does not determine whether the seed will take root, it does determine whether an individual is open to returning the next week for another round of sowing!

Here's something I know from my own experience. Soils change. Mine certainly did. I bet yours did as well. I'm so grateful I attended a church that connected me relationally even when my heart was resistant. While a lot of seed was wasted on me, eventually my heart's soil became more receptive. And the seed took root. This is why we celebrate when unchurched people choose to return. We know it is possible to connect an individual relationally before he or she connects theologically. We know hearts change over time. We are convinced that it's a church's approach to the weekend that determines whether those with even the most unreceptive of hearts will return.

I'm convinced that our template, our approach, is what allows us to present the gospel in uncompromising terms, preach hard against sin, and tackle the most emotionally charged topics in culture, while providing an environment where unchurched people feel comfortable. One of the myths about large churches is that they are large because they compromise the gospel, water down the demands of discipleship, and skip the tough issues, all for the sake of building crowds. While that might be true in a handful of cases, that is certainly not the norm. We don't mind offending people with the gospel. We assume we will offend people with the gospel. As a preacher, it's my responsibility to offend people with the gospel. That's one reason we work so hard not to offend them in the parking lot, the hallway, at check-in, or in the early portions of our service. We want people to come back the following week for another round of offending!

TEMPLATE ELEMENT #8: CLOSER

The last element in our template is the *closer*. As you would expect, this is generally a song. Like the *special*, we use closers sparingly. We generally reserve closers for the end of a series or for messages where we feel the need to give people an opportunity to sit and reflect on what they have just heard. In some cases, we combine a closer with a call to action. On occasion, we will give attendees an opportunity to come forward as evidence of their decisions to trust Christ. These occasions are generally accompanied by music. But not always. I'm not shy about asking people who've made decisions to follow Christ to stand where they are with no heads bowed and no eyes closed while everyone looks around.

The purpose of the closer is to punctuate a message or series. This is one reason we use them sparingly. It's not always easy to find a song that is specific to a message or series. It is tempting to close every week with a song for the sake of creating a neat bookend for the experience. But we've opted not to go that route.

If we can't find a song that really punctuates the experience, we opt for a closing prayer and dismissal. Granted, it feels a bit flat at times. But it also ensures that people don't view our closers as habits and use them as excuses to beat the crowd to the parking lot. Yeah, we have those people too! The other reason we don't use a closer every week goes back to what I said earlier: not everybody loves music. So we play to that crowd as often as we can and just let 'em go. Like most churches, our choice of closers runs the gamut from reflective ballads to songs of celebration—from solos to corporate singing.

RULES FOR THE EXCEPTIONS TO THE RULES

So those are our rules. The "Rules of Engagement" is the template we live, plan, and produce by ... most of the time. But we live in the same world you do. There are weekends when the template just won't get the job done. There are a few weekends every year when following our template would actually work against us. So we make exceptions. Our rule of thumb is that while it's acceptable to depart from the template on *purpose*, it's not okay to drift from the template by *accident*. If we are going to make an exception, there needs to be a really good reason to do so. We don't depart from "The Rules" because we are bored. We don't abandon our template in order to "do something cool."

And we don't desert this approach just because we feel like "changing things up a bit." Those are all very *insider* reasons. The production staff is the only group that gets bored with the template, not the congregation. I'm sure the young lady playing Cinderella at Disney World gets bored doing the same thing day after day. But she's not paid to be creative. She's paid to be Cinderella. So she follows the Cinderella template for behavior. And it works.

Back to my point. There are weekends when a unique agenda demands we put the "Rules of Engagement" on hold. For example, Strategic Service Sunday. This is the weekend we channel all our energy and creativity toward recruiting volunteers for the following ministry season. Everything we do on a Strategic Service weekend is focused on inspiring people to serve. Once or twice a year, we dedicate an entire weekend to moving people into small groups. On those weekends, everything is about group life. The launch of a capital campaign is another occasion when we would depart from our standard approach.

As you might imagine, this creates tension on our team. Good tension. Nobody wants to offend or drive away first-timers. We want our services to be safe. But at the same time, there are times in the life of a local church when you have to focus on the family.

On the weekends when we plan to break our own rules, we announce it upfront. We say things like, "If this is your first time, we want you to know that today is going to be a bit different than usual. In fact, the person who invited you may feel like she owes you an apology by the time this service is over. The good news is that an hour from now you are going to have the inside scoop on what makes this church tick."

On Strategic Service Sunday, I am very overt about our
agenda. I often say, "We have a very specific agenda today.
We are going to use all our creative and persuasive skills to
get as many of you as we possibly can to join a Strategic
Service team." Then I address our guests: "If this is your
first time, you could not have chosen a better weekend to
attend. When you walked onto this campus, you may have
found yourself wondering, *Who are all these people and how
is it this place is so organized?* Well, you are about to find out.
And we would love for you to join us in what we believe is
the most important undertaking on the planet." Every year,
first-time guests sign up to join a volunteer team. Every
year.

There are topics that demand a different approach to the
weekend as well.

We spent several weeks promoting a weekend service devoted to the topic of pornography. As you know,
when you're planning to address an R-rated topic, families
appreciate a heads-up. So just about everyone showed up
that weekend knowing ahead of time that this was going to
be a heavier-than-average service. It didn't feel right opening
with our typical *up* corporate singing. So we scratched that
segment entirely and got right to the point sooner than we
normally would.

Next Steps

As I stated earlier, you certainly don't have to adopt our
template. But you can't afford not to develop one of your
own. Remember, your team is already following a pattern
of some kind. Or perhaps they've fallen into a rut. Either
way, they are operating under some assumptions and

they are evaluating through some kind of filter. A service programming template will make your planning simpler and your outcomes more consistent. It will keep you from drifting off purpose. It will ensure that a new service programming staff and volunteers know exactly what's expected. There will be less guessing and better execution. By clarifying expectations, a template simplifies the evaluation process. Everybody will be evaluating with the same criteria.

A template provides your more creative types with a canvas — parameters. Creative people love to create. But as we all know, creativity is never the goal of a service programming team. The goal is to leverage creativity for the sake of the *win*. If you will clarify the win for the weekend and agree on your template, your creative arts team will find it far easier to focus their creative energies.

So spend the time necessary to establish a weekend win. Then develop a template that will get you there. Make room for exceptions. But make sure the exceptions really are exceptions and not just excuses to "do something different."

chapter eleven

DOUBLE-BARREL PREACHING

Preaching. It's by far the most stressful part of my job. Compared to the pressure of message preparation and delivery, everything else is easy. People ask me all the time how I handle the pressure of running a large, multi-faceted organization. I always chuckle. I would love to take a year and *only* run a large, multi-faceted organization. Compared to the pressure and stress of standing up thirty-plus weekends a year and facing a highly educated, successful group of congregants, some of whom have been listening to me for seventeen years, the organizational part of what I do is stress-free. For that reason, if you are reading this and you carry the communication mantle for your church, we may have more in common than you originally thought. Like you, I live with the constant pressure that only those of us who do what we do fully understand.

Group hug.

But at the same time, it's an honor, isn't it? How incredible that we get to stand up and proclaim God's Word to the church. No one is more aware of our unworthiness than we are. And yet God chooses to use us. It's really an amazing thing. I hope you never get over it. I hope I don't either. I hope we never lose the wonder of knowing that words come out of our mouths, people make decisions, and the directions of their lives change. But on Saturday night, when I'm staring at my cold, flat outline wondering where in the world my *point* went ... well, you know. Sometimes it's just work. Hard work. It can feel like a weekly oral exam. When people start with the, "Don't preachers only work one day a week?" I have a good comeback. Feel free to use it. I say, "Think for a minute about the most stressful part of your job, the part that is the make-or-break for you financially. Imagine having to do that every week on a stage in front of your family, friends, strangers, and people who don't particularly like you. Imagine not having the option to call in sick or reschedule because you weren't quite ready for the presentation." End of conversation.

Now granted, there are a lot of lazy preachers out there. I've talked to guys who start preparing on Saturday. Some on Saturday night! And then there are the mainline denominational men and women who have the entire message emailed to them. They just stand up and read it. I have a friend who is a female pastor in the Episcopal Church. During her interview, they informed her that she was never to preach longer than twelve minutes. She said a gentleman, if you can call him that, came up to her before a service and asked if she could cut the message to eight minutes. It was his birthday and he needed to get to a luncheon being held in his honor. She said she smiled and said she would see what she could do, intending to ignore him entirely. She said that about halfway through her message, she looked up and saw him standing up about halfway back circling his finger in the air as a signal for her to wrap it up. Can you imagine? Hopefully, you can't. Don't tell anyone I said this, but some churches don't deserve a pastor.

DUAL AUDIENCE, SINGLE AGENDA

As you might imagine, I get a lot of questions about preaching. One I'm asked as often as any is, "How do you engage churched and unchurched people in the same message?" In other words, how do I preach to Christians and non-Christians and somehow keep both groups engaged and coming back? I love that question. I love it because it points to a false assumption that needs to be corrected — an assumption that influences the way communicators prepare and deliver their messages.

If you are going to create a church unchurched people love to attend, then unchurched people need to *love* the weekend message. Even if they don't love it, they need to engage with it to the point that they want to return the next weekend. You, or someone on your preaching staff, must learn to engage people who disagree with the premise and possibly the application of what's being taught. And that's tricky. For most preachers, it requires some unlearning. Some retooling. But it can be done. And it's not as hard as it sounds. So in this chapter I'm going to download everything I've learned over the last twenty-five years about communicating to a dual audience.

To begin with, we need to set the record straight about one thing in particular. Engaging unchurched people with the weekend message does not necessitate watering down, skipping over, or treading lightly with the text. You can. Some preachers do. But it's not necessary. In the long run, doing so is detrimental to both believers and nonbelievers. Mature Christians don't engage with or benefit from Scripture-lite sermons. Thinking nonbelievers aren't impressed with or inspired to return for Scripture-lite sermons. There's really no win for anyone. So put that notion out of your mind.

The key to successfully engaging unchurched people in a weekend message has more to do with your *approach* and your *presentation* than your *content*. Earlier I made the point that a church's approach to the weekend determines whether unchurched people will return. The same is true for the message. In our discussion on irresistible environments, we unpacked the relationship between presentation and interest. Presentation is what determines interest. Content is often secondary. As we pointed out, it's not the content of a stand-up comedian's routine that engages us. It's the presentation. So, with all of that as a backdrop, let's talk specifically about your approach to and presentation of the weekend message.

Discovery Zone

All the senior pastors I've talked to are adamant about wanting unchurched people to attend and connect with their churches. There may be exceptions out there, but I've yet to meet one. But many of these same pastors approach the communication piece of the weekend as if there aren't any unbelievers in the house. They preach as if everybody present is a believer and attends every week. Similarly, every pastor I know is concerned about the alarming number of eighteen- to twenty-five-years-olds who drop out of church, never to return. But there's no mystery as to why they drop out. I'm convinced they dropped out because nothing compelled them to stay! The church leaders who are seemingly most concerned about the dropout rate of that demographic are the very ones who create the weekend experiences that this demographic finds entirely uncompelling. To say it another way, the group responsible for connecting eighteen- to twenty-five-year-olds to local congregations are the catalysts for driving them away. That's just tragic. They didn't intend to drive them away. That was not their *purpose*. But every weekend in this country, something trumps the good intentions and lofty purposes of the average local church. And that something is not theology, intent, or budget. It's the approach and the presentation. Week after week, preachers opt for an approach that undermines their desire to connect with the dechurched and the unchurched. The approach a church chooses trumps its purpose every time. The approach a communicator chooses trumps his or her purpose every time as well. Worse, the wrong approach can neutralize a communicator's content. Like you, I've heard gospel presentations that were so confusing even I wasn't sure how an unbeliever was supposed to respond. While there was nothing wrong with the content, i.e., the gospel, the presentation was so bad it made the gospel confusing and unappealing. Regardless of what we *intend* to accomplish, how we go about it determines the outcome.

Inheritance

The challenge for many of us is that we've inherited approaches to preaching that in many cases conflict with the reason we got into this to begin with.

If you are like most preachers, your call to preach was driven by a desire to reach people with the gospel. You came into this with a burden for those outside the faith. You felt at the time that the best vehicle for you to reach outsiders was preaching.

But preaching was whatever you saw week after week in the church you grew up in.

If you didn't grow up in church, then preaching was whatever approach the preacher who finally got through to you modeled. Either way, we've all been heavily influenced by what was modeled for us. And that becomes problematic if the approach that's been modeled for us, the approach we gravitate toward, conflicts with our purpose. Our calling. Our reason for getting into this in the first place.

Here's what I know about you. You did not surrender to God's call on your life to perpetuate a specific model, style, or approach to preaching. You didn't say yes to God in order to perpetuate an approach to anything. You said yes in the hopes that God would use you to impact your generation. And if that makes your heart beat a little bit harder, then allow me to push you a bit. If you've been called to reach this generation of unchurched people, then you must adopt an approach to ministry, and communication in particular, that advances that calling.

You don't have the luxury of babysitting the previous generation's approach to doing church. There's no time for that. Besides, you've only got one life to give to invest in this glorious cause. So invest it well. Make the necessary adjustments to your approach.

MAKING THE ASK

Maybe pulling this out of a preaching context may help. You have experienced this same dynamic in your family. Remember as a kid when you wanted something from one of your parents? Over time you learned *when* to ask, *how* to ask, and *how much* to ask for. You learned to judge when "no" meant *no* and when "no" meant *if you keep arguing, you might get your way.* If you are married, you've experienced this same dynamic at a different level. Every husband has rehearsed conversations with his wife over and over in his mind when he's got a big ask to make. Why? Because smart husbands know *when* to ask and *how* to ask. And smart husbands know what to offer in return. I have two teenagers and a twenty-year-old. On countless occasions, Sandra and I have talked through how to approach one of our kids about a delicate subject. We know, like every parent with teenagers knows, being right isn't enough. Content isn't everything. It's the approach that makes all the difference. Choose the wrong approach and you create unnecessary resistance. Choose the right approach and everything goes down easier. So the good news is you already have years of experience in adapting your approach to match your goal. Now you need to apply all that learning to your public communication skills.

So the first two questions you need to wrestle to the ground are:

1. Does my approach to preaching facilitate my desire to see unchurched people attend, come back, and then come back with a friend?
2. If not, am I willing to change my approach?

If you aren't sure about the answer to the first question, just ask some folks. Specifically, ask around to see how comfortable your core leaders are inviting their unchurched friends to a weekend service. They either are or they aren't. You owe it to yourself to know. And if they aren't, you should know why. If you really want to know how first-timers and long-timers experience your preaching, you are smart enough to figure out how to collect that data. Yes, it can be painful. But it might be that jolt of reality that pushes you to adjust your approach.

My Goal

Now, before I get into the specifics of engaging unchurched people through your sermons, I want to disclose my goal and approach to the weekend. Of course, I think this is the way everybody should do it. I would, and will, argue that you should adopt this approach as well. If I didn't believe in it, I wouldn't be doing it this way. But if you don't like my weekend communication strategy, don't be content with simply dissing mine. That's easy. It doesn't take much effort to kick over a sandcastle. Just make sure you clarify *your* goal and *your* approach.

First: *my goal.* My goal on the weekend is to present the Scriptures in a way that is so helpful and compelling that *everybody* in the audience is glad to have attended and drives away with every intention to return the following weekend.

Pretty deep, huh?

I want the audience to be so happy about being there that they come back the following week. I want them to walk away intrigued by the fact that they just heard someone teach from the Bible and it was ... *helpful.* I want skeptics to doubt their disbelief. I want believers to believe deeper. I want people who don't own a Bible to leave committed to finding one. I want cultural Christians to dust theirs off and start reading them again. That's my goal. That's my *win* as a communicator.

If you've ever heard me, you know that in just about every message I push the audience to read the Bible for themselves. I'm constantly saying things like, "Can you believe that's in here? You should read your Bible." I try to remove excuses. I remind them, "You don't have to believe it's inspired to read it." I'll even taunt when necessary: "Some of you haven't opened the Bible since a college professor told you it was myth. What other advice did you take from that professor? Probably none. What if he was wrong? Hey, what if the college professor who told you that is sitting in church somewhere today feeling bad about all the young, impressionable freshmen he misled?" I say, "Don't avoid the Bible because you don't believe it all. You don't read anything because you believe it all. Infallibility is not your litmus test for reading material, is it?" I'm not above saying things like, "You should read the Bible so you will have more moral authority when you tell people you don't believe it. Don't be like the kid who says he doesn't like string beans but never tasted them. Come on! What are you afraid of?"

Now, if all that makes you wonder why any unbeliever in his right mind would ever darken the door of one of our churches, much less come back a second time, it's because there's something important you've missed along the way. Got your highlighter? *When people are convinced you want something FOR them rather than something FROM them, they are less likely to be offended when you challenge them.* Remember your favorite coach? The one who was hard on you, but got the best out of you? We will come back to that in a page or two.

Ultimately, I want people to fall in love with the Author of the Scriptures and his Son. But I don't have any control over that. So my best option is to arrange the date. I figure if I do a good job, even if they don't fall in love on the first date, there is always the possibility that something will happen on the second or third date. Heck, I meet people who've been attending our churches for several years that say they aren't *there* yet. Nothing I can do about that except to continue arranging dates. As long as they are sitting under the proclamation of the gospel, there's hope!

Now, you may have all kinds of theological problems with my goal. That's okay. Everybody's entitled to be wrong. Including me. My hope is that you will take some time to decide what you are trying to accomplish on the weekends. Why? Because if you don't clarify your goal, you'll never identify the best approach. I don't want you to spend this next season of ministry frustrated by a lack of results that stems from a self-defeating approach to ministry. I know every weekend is a bit different from the one before. But at the macro level, what are you hoping for? What are you trying to accomplish? What's your *win* as a communicator?

My Approach

Since my purpose for preaching is Bible-centric, *my approach* is as well.

Here's my weekend communication strategy. Don't tell anyone. My approach is to entice the audience to follow me into one passage of Scripture with the promise that the text is either going to answer a question they've been asking, solve a mystery they've been puzzled over, or resolve a tension they've been carrying. Once we are in the text, I do my best to let it speak for itself. I go slowly. I highlight words. I leverage the drama. I roll 'em around in the text till it gets all over them. I bring my energy *to* a text and I do my best to uncover the energy *in* the text. Once they are thoroughly embroiled with the passage, I take one carefully crafted statement that emerges from the point of the text and do everything in my power to make it stick.

Then I let 'em out on time.

That's my approach.

What's yours?

Seven Reasons Not to Make Lists

In *Communicating for a Change*,[54] I describe my overall approach to sermon preparation and communication. For our purposes here, I want to focus on seven guidelines directly related to preaching to unchurched people. Six are helpful. One is just something I needed to get off my chest.

Guideline #1: Let 'Em Know You Know They're Out There ...

... and you're happy about it.

The key to engaging unchurched people through your weekend communication is to include them. But for them to *feel* included, they've got to know you know they are out there and that you are happy about it. Did you know that people who have not been to church in a long time feel strange when they come back for the first time? They assume they are the "odd man out." Even the women. They assume everybody in your church knows each other and knows they are outsiders. In their minds, the distance between them and the person on the platform is miles, not feet. In many churches, they feel like guests who snuck into someone's home. They are not sure you are happy they are there. In fact, in some cases the reason they haven't been to church in a while is that their last churches, in some cases the churches they grew up in, were happy to see them go! So if you never reference them in your message, you may confirm all their unfounded suspicions. So reference them. And reference them as soon as possible.

Don't just address "those who are here for the first time" or say, "If you are visiting today...." That's not what I'm talking about. You've got to develop your own style. And you should never say something you don't mean or aren't comfortable saying. But here's a sample of the kinds of things we say all the time:

> "If you are here for the first time and you don't consider yourself a religious person, we are so glad you are here. Hang around here long enough and you will discover we aren't all that religious either."

> "If you don't consider yourself a Christian, or maybe you aren't sure, you could not have picked a better weekend to join us."

> "If you've got questions about faith, the Bible, Jesus, maybe even the existence of God, you need to know we built this place for you. Our goal from the beginning was to create a church unchurched people would love to attend."

> "If the only reason you are here today is because you are visiting relatives and they said they wouldn't feed you if you wouldn't attend church with 'em, my apologies. We all still have a long way to go."

> "You may be here because somebody bribed you with lunch or told you that you would meet somebody cute. Whatever the reason, we are so glad you are here."

> "If this is your first time in church or your first time in a long time, and you feel a little uncomfortable, relax. We don't

want anything *from* you. But we do want something *for* you. We want you to know the peace that comes from making peace with your heavenly Father."

"If this is your first time in church, or your first time in a long time, and you feel out of place because you think we are all good people and you are not so good, you need to know you are surrounded by people who have out-sinned you ten to one. Don't let all these pretty faces fool you."

"We may not all believe the same, but we all struggle with the same temptations, fears, insecurities, and doubts. You have more in common with us than you might imagine. And we are so glad you took a risk and came to church today."

That's enough to get you started. But remember, the earlier the better.

GUIDELINE #2: BEGIN WITH THE AUDIENCE IN MIND ...

... not your message.

As we discussed earlier, great communicators take people on journeys. Where a communicator *begins* the journey determines who will follow. If your desire is for unchurched attendees to follow, you may need to take several steps back from where you normally begin. We saw how Jesus accomplished this in his trilogy of parables addressing God's response to sinners. He didn't begin with *sinners*. He didn't even begin with God. He began with sheep. He could have begun with God or sinners. And everything he said would have been spot on! But Jesus didn't come into the world to say true things. He didn't come to be *right*. He came to explain the Father and pay for sin. So on those occasions when clarity was utmost, he backed up far enough to get his entire audience onboard. Again, where you begin determines who will follow.

This is my intent when I say my approach is to entice the audience to follow me into a passage. Before I take people to the text, I want them to be thinking, *Oh my gosh. I'm glad I came today.* I do that by creating tension. The tension in a text is usually found in the answer to one or more of the following questions:

- What question does this text answer?
- What tension does this text resolve?
- What mystery does this text solve?
- What issue does this text address?

Before I draw people's attention to a solution, I want to make sure they are emotionally engaged with the problem. If the text answers a question, I dare not go there until everyone in the audience really wants to know the answer. The mysteries, questions, and tensions we all wrestle with serve as the common ground for believers and unbelievers. If you want non-Christians to engage with you on your journey, begin at the place where all of us shrug our shoulders and say, "I don't know, but I wish someone would tell me."

This isn't hard. Actually, it's quite easy. Contrary to what you might have been told, or otherwise believe, we have far more in common with unchurched people than we have differences. We all worry about the same things. None of us feels like we have enough money. Every married couple faces similar challenges. We all wonder what happens when we die. Parents are concerned about their children's friends. We all need friends. We all face overwhelming temptations. We all have regrets we don't know what to do with. We've all been hurt. We struggle to forgive. We are plagued by guilt. Honestly, I can't think of a single uniquely "Christian" problem. There are just problems. Which means there is fertile common ground everywhere we look. That's where we must begin.

Where do you begin?

GUIDELINE #3: PICK ONE PASSAGE AND STICK WITH IT …

… everybody will be glad you did.

Since my goal in preaching is to present the Scriptures in ways that are helpful and compelling, I've got to make the Scriptures approachable. People unfamiliar with the Bible are intimidated by it. It is unlike any other "book" they've ever handled. They are told not to try to read it from beginning to end. Imagine how that sounds. They are often told to begin with John. Who? *And would you look at that? There are four sections called John. Three of 'em have numbers in front of them. Must have been a race.*

Anything we can say to make the Bible more approachable and less intimidating is a win. This is why I am such a proponent of focusing the message around one text. I realize there are topics that demand we draw people's attention to more than one passage. My advice is to make that the exception, not the rule. Jumping all over the Bible illustrates how smart you are. It rarely enhances an audience's understanding of or love for the Scriptures. And it totally confuses non-Christians. Worse, it sets a terrible precedent for how they should read the Bible. We don't want new and non-Christians looking around the Bible for the verse that says what they are hoping it says. We want them to let the Scriptures speak for themselves. Messages built around proof-texting accomplishes the opposite. And while I'm picking on you—careful with the Greek. Don't accidentally erode your audience's confidence in their English texts. Besides, you probably know just enough to be dangerous. You think it makes you look smart. And it may. But over time, it makes our English translations look unreliable. But they aren't. So, go easy on the Greek.

Pick a passage and stick with it. Five passages aren't better than one. Five passages make a series. Choose one passage and stay with it until everybody gets it. Make it so interesting that your audience wants to go home and read it again on their own. Make it so clear that when they do, they understand it, and they keep reading!

GUIDELINE #4: GIVE 'EM PERMISSION NOT TO BELIEVE...

... or obey.

The imperatives of the New Testament are addressed to Christians.

Consequently, Christians are accountable to each other for how they live. But for reasons unbeknownst to me, Christians love to judge the behavior of non-Christians.

What makes this doubly perplexing is that the apostle Paul addresses this issue directly. Here's what he says:

> What business is it of mine to judge those outside the church? Are you not to judge those inside? God will judge those outside. (1 Corinthians 5:12–13)

There you have it. But historically, the church has been way better at policing the behavior of outsiders than it has been at policing its own. That's unfortunate. And unnecessary. Few things discredit the church more in the minds of unbelievers than when it holds them accountable to a standard they never acknowledged to begin with. Nothing says *hypocrite* faster than Christians expecting non-Christians to behave like Christians when half the Christians don't act like it half the time. First-century Christians certainly didn't judge non-Christians for behaving like non-Christians. They expected Christians to behave like Christians. Again, the apostle Paul writes:

> Be wise in the way you act toward outsiders; make the most of every opportunity. Let your conversation be always full of *grace*, seasoned with *salt*, so that you may know how to answer everyone. (Colossians 4:5–6, emphasis added)

Like you, I've heard way too many messages addressed *at* nonbelievers that were full of salt seasoned with grace. That's part of the reason so many unchurched people are just that: unchurched. I think we would be wise to extend Paul's advice to our preaching. When addressing unbelievers, it should be all grace with just a pinch of salt. To do that, we must distinguish between what the biblical authors expected of believers and what is expected of nonbelievers. In short, give non-Christians an out.

I'm very intentional about this when I preach. I make statements like, "If you aren't a Christian, you are off the hook today." Or, "If you aren't a follower of Jesus, then you are not accountable for what we are about to read. You get a pass."

I'll even go so far as to say, "Today's text may make you glad you aren't a Christian! You may put it off indefinitely after today." On most weekends, non-Christians are not your target audience. They are welcome guests. Just as we don't expect guests in our homes to clear the table after dinner and serve the coffee, so there are things we shouldn't expect nonbelievers to do while visiting our churches. And we need to tell 'em. And if you do, if you let them off the hook, you might be surprised at the response.

My experience is that *when you give non-Christians an out, they respond by leaning in.* Especially if you *invite* them rather than *expect* them. There's a big difference between being expected to *do* something and being invited to *try* something. We naturally push back when pushed. But we don't generally push back on an invitation. So I always invite our nonbelieving friends to try living like Christians, to apply the principles we've discussed, to adopt the new way of thinking that the Scriptures present. And I usually give them a time frame. A week or a day.

Maybe an example would help.

In the opening installment of our series *The New Rules for Love, Sex, and Dating*, I asked the singles in our audience: "Are you the person the person you are looking for is looking for?" I taught through 1 Corinthians 13, discussing the various terms Paul uses to define love. Then I closed by reading verse 11:

> When I was a child, I talked like a child, I thought like a child,
> I reasoned like a child. When I became a man, I put the ways
> of childhood behind me.

I reminded them that childhood stories always END with *and they lived happily ever after*, that children's stories END when the prince and princess finally get together. The assumption being that once the prince and princess meet, the rest is easy! "That's how children think," I said. "Some of you still think that way." From there, I proceeded to challenge the Christian singles in our churches to put away their childish views of love, sex, and dating and to grow up. I told them that the time had come for them to begin focusing on what they were *becoming* rather than whom they were *hunting*. Catchy, huh? I went on to say that meeting the right person without first becoming the right person is a recipe for an unhappily-ever-after ending.

Ahhh, but that's true for everybody, isn't it? So I addressed the non-Christians in the audience: "You may not be a particularly religious person. Certainly not a Christ follower. But you know in your heart that what you've heard tonight is true. You've had enough relationships go bad to see *the right person myth* for what it really is. A myth. You've met the right person. Several times! So during this series, I want to invite you to wrestle with this question as well: *Are you the person the person you are looking for is looking for?* If not, we want to help you become that person. And, more importantly, we believe you have a heavenly Father who wants to help as well."

This brings me back to the statement I made earlier that I promised we would return to: *When people are convinced you want something FOR them rather than something FROM them, they are less likely to be offended when you challenge them.* And you know what? I really do want something FOR the singles in my city—the Christians *and* the non-Christians. And we've positioned our church to help both.

If you tell me I have to, I assume you want something from me. If you offer me an opportunity to, I'll be more inclined to believe you have my best interests at heart. Inviting unchurched people to take small steps is the same as inviting them to take first steps. We've all seen God honor first steps. We've seen God honor childlike faith. Learn to create space in your preaching for those who are unsure, skeptical, disbelieving. Give them an out. But then offer them an invitation.

GUIDELINE #5: AVOID "THE BIBLE SAYS"...

... because it doesn't.

Okay, this next point is a minefield. So I'll try to tiptoe carefully.

Technically it is incorrect to say, "The Bible says ..." or "The Bible teaches...." The *Bible* doesn't really say or teach anything. I'll explain what I mean in a moment. But not only is it technically incorrect, that phrase creates an unnecessary obstacle to faith, i.e., belief in the infallibility or inerrancy, whatever term you prefer, of the Scriptures. I believe the Scriptures are God-breathed.[55] You believe it. But most people don't. Most people assume the Bible was written by men and is, therefore, full of errors. You can't really blame them for thinking that. Just read your local newspaper. If you expect the unbelievers in your congregation to overcome that obstacle BEFORE they place their faith in Christ ... well, good luck. It's not going to happen. Not for sincerely secular people anyway. And it doesn't need to happen. People don't have to believe the Scriptures are God-breathed to become followers of Christ.

Wait ... don't light that torch just yet. Think about it.

There was no Bible as we know it for the first three hundred years of Christianity. People were becoming followers of Christ before the Gospels were even written. Remember our journey through Acts 15 a few chapters back? Do you remember anything about Gentiles having to accept the Jewish scriptures? Me neither. Not only were the first-century Gentiles not required to accept the Old Testament as infallible, they weren't even required to read it. They got a pass on following its teachings. Remember, as well, that the apostle Paul became a Christ-follower before *any* of the

New Testament was written. So, let's be honest. There's some wiggle room. And if you are serious about creating an environment free of unnecessary obstacles to faith, you may need to make some adjustments in the way you refer to the Scriptures. I'm not suggesting you change your view, just your ... approach. So here are a few suggestions about how to talk about the text in ways that don't place unnecessary obstacles in the way of someone who is coming to church for the first time or someone who is honestly wrestling with who Jesus is.

It's Not a Book

Most people, including most Christians, don't understand what the Bible actually is. Making a few adjustments in the way you reference the Bible, as well as specific texts, will help everybody in your congregation gain greater understanding of and appreciation for our Scriptures. If you are consistent with your terminology, over time you will help skeptics deconstruct their resistance. Their resistance is usually based on false assumptions that are often reinforced by the way Christians talk about the Scriptures. By making a few minor adjustments, you will help everybody in your church gain a better understanding of just how amazing the Bible really is. After all, if people are going to reject the message of Christianity, let's make sure they are rejecting the actual message and not some poor caricature.

To begin with, don't refer to the Bible as a *book*. That's an injustice. It's not a book. It's way better than a book. As you know, but they don't, the Bible is a collection of ancient manuscripts written over a period of about fifteen hundred years by over forty authors that tells one story. This is why it's technically incorrect to say, "The Bible says...." Specific authors in the Bible say things. When we say, "The Bible says," we treat it like a mere book. But books have authors. Ask average Christians who the author of the Bible is and they will say "God." Tell average skeptics that and they will laugh. As they should. Let's be honest. God did not *write the Bible* in the way people write books. So while that kind of terminology works for the already convinced, it's an obstacle for those who aren't. The good news is we know who wrote most of the texts collected in our Bibles. We should take every opportunity to point that out. The stunning thing about the Bible is not that God wrote it. What's stunning is what we mentioned earlier: The texts that make up the Bible were written by over forty men over a period of about fifteen hundred years, and yet they tell one story. That's amazing! And unlike the claim of divine authorship, it's indisputable. Don't believe me? Read it.

In some ways the Bible *is* a miracle. We should develop terminology that refers to it as such. I'm sure you get as miffed as I do when you hear people dismiss the Bible as full of contradictions, unreliable, myth, etc., etc. Honestly, a large part of culture's confusion is the church's fault. We've not taught people what the Bible actually is. For the most part, what we've communicated is, "Hey! It's God's Word! Stop arguing and obey it!" As a result, we've created a straw man that is difficult, if not impossible, to defend. I would like to be part of the generation that changes that. I would like for you to join me. We can change the conversation about the Bible if we change our terminology. So, don't talk about it like it is a divinely inspired book. It's not. It is a collection of divinely inspired manuscripts.

Cite Authors, Not "The Bible"

When we say, "The Bible says," we actually mean a specific author or two. Cite the authors. It carries more weight and reinforces the fact that the Bible is a collection of writings from many authors. For example: which would you consider a more substantial argument for the resurrection of our Savior from a skeptic's perspective?

> *Exhibit A:* The Bible says that Jesus rose from the dead after being in the tomb for three days.

> *Exhibit B:* Matthew, an ex-tax collector who became one of Jesus' followers, writes that Jesus rose from the dead and he claimed to have seen him. Not only that, Luke, a doctor who interviewed eyewitnesses, came to the conclusion that Jesus rose from the dead. He was so convinced he gave up his practice and became a church planter. Mark, a friend of the apostle Peter, believed Jesus rose from the dead based on Peter's account. Peter, the man who denied even knowing Jesus, claimed to have seen the resurrected Christ. Later he was crucified, not for what he believed, but for what he said he saw: a resurrected Jesus. James, the brother of Jesus, believed his own brother rose from the dead. The apostle Paul, based in part on his time with eyewitnesses, concluded that Jesus, in fact, rose from the dead.

And on and on I could go. You see my point. One argument rests on an assumption about a "book" that's not a book. The other argument rests on a multitude of eyewitness accounts. All of which are contained in the Scriptures. We shouldn't expect rational people to believe Jesus rose from the dead because "the Bible says so." That's not much of an argument. But I love to challenge people to consider the historical authenticity of the resurrection based on the testimony of Matthew, Peter, John, James, Luke, the apostle Paul, and a dozen other lesser-known people referenced throughout the New Testament.

Our culture needs to understand that the foundation of the Christian faith is not an infallible Bible. The foundation of our faith is a single event in history attested to by individuals who lived and wrote during the days when this event transpired. For the sake of convenience, their writings were gathered up and published in what we refer to as the New Testament, a phrase that was first used at the end of the second century. The best thing we can do for unbelievers in our congregations is to continually drive them back to *the* prevalent issue for anyone at their stage in the journey: *Who was Jesus?* And close behind is this question: *What are you going to do with the overwhelming evidence that he rose from the dead?* The way you reference the Scriptures is a constant apologetic for their reliability and trustworthiness.

Don't Assume They Know

Our culture is biblically illiterate. I bet you knew that. The Christians in your church may not be. But society in general is. Which means you have a decision to make. If you want to engage secular people with your preaching, you've got to quit assuming your audience knows anything about the Bible. We invited a couple into our small group several years ago who had never been to our church. We knew them through our son's baseball team. They knew I was a preacher and that was it. They both went to the Catholic Church when they were children, but both of their families dropped out before either of them entered middle school. The first night our group gathered, the leader thought it would be fun to divide us into groups of three and have us compete in a Bible knowledge quiz. Big mistake. Seriously, they knew nothing. They were both successful in the healthcare field. Jay eventually went on to run one of the largest hospital conglomerates in our state. The first question had something to do with David and Goliath. Jay turned to me and said, "Andy, I'm embarrassed to tell you this. But I didn't know that was in the Bible. I thought it was a figure of speech. You know, like when a small company goes toe-to-toe with a large company in the same retail or technology space." So what do you think a guy like my friend Jay thinks when he sits through one of your sermons? Stupid? Like an outsider? Somebody who doesn't know the secret handshake?

Bob, one of my best friends, was not a believer when we first met. Like Jay, he knew virtually nothing about the Bible. But whereas Jay had respect for this strange book he had never read, Bob didn't even have that going for him. For him, the Bible was just one of several religious books written by men in order to control people. After we had known each other for a couple of years, he started coming to church off and on. One night during these formative years, he called me: "Hey Andy, I just finished watching a program on the History Channel about Joseph." That was encouraging. Then he said, "But it was so confusing. They got through the entire thing and never mentioned Mary or Jesus or any of that. The whole thing was about his brothers." Hmmm.

So, the last time you preached a message on the story of Joseph and his coat of many colors, did you think to tell your congregation that there were two famous Josephs in the Bible? If not, people like my friend Bob would have left wondering why Jesus was born in a stable when his father was the prime minister of Egypt!

Don't assume. Always start on the bottom rung of the ladder. Bring people along with you. Define *epistle*. When you reference the book of Mark, make sure you tell your audience that Mark wrote one of the four accounts of Jesus' life. Keep the cookies on the bottom shelf. That's not shallow. That's how you ensure that everybody in your audience can follow you on the journey.

GUIDELINE #6: ACKNOWLEDGE THE ODD ...

... it would be odd not to.

The Bible says some really strange things, doesn't it? Actually, *it* doesn't. Some of the *biblical writers* make some really strange statements and tell some really strange stories, don't they? Those of us raised in church just go with it: a floating axhead; wild animals showing up in pairs to board a ship; a man's shadow passes over a stranger and he is healed of a disease; a sea parts in the middle and a nation walks across on dry ground. Dry ground? Seriously? For you and me, it's just another day in church. We've heard those stories so many times, we immediately go in search of applications and transferable principles. Meanwhile, there are people in our churches thinking, *Huh? Do I have to believe that stuff actually happened to be a Christian?* We do ourselves and the unbelievers in our congregations a disservice when we forget to pause and consider how weird some of what's in the Bible must sound to someone who wasn't raised in church.

When you get to those unusual verses and narratives, acknowledge them as just that: unusual. Hard to believe. As a general rule, *say what you suspect unbelievers are thinking.* When you do, it gives you credibility. And it gives them space. It says you are a rational being like they are, that you didn't check your brain at the door and you don't expect them to either. The other thing it communicates is that it's permissible to read the Bible critically. It's okay to *read* it before they *believe* it.

Natural vs. Supernatural

Most unbelievers assume there's a conflict between science and religion. Anything you can do to affirm their skeptical, inquisitive nature is a plus. The last thing you want to do is appear critical of people who don't "just take it by faith and believe!" After all, we want the smart people in our world to be on a constant search for natural causes. You wouldn't go back to a doctor who looked at an MRI of your kidney and said, "Well, it looks like God has allowed a spot to develop. Why don't you go home and pray; then come back in a couple of weeks and we'll do another MRI to see if anything has changed." Nope. You want a doctor who understands the natural world of cause and effect. You want a doctor whose knowledge of the natural functions of the human body allows her to make an educated guess as to what caused the spot. You want a doctor who knows how to find out exactly what it is. Most importantly, you want a doctor who knows how to get rid of it. You want a doctor who understands natural causes and solutions. If he is a Christian doctor, all the better. But you don't really want a Christian answer. You want an answer answer. So, if that's what you and I expect at the doctor's office, why should we expect people to abandon that same way of thinking when they walk into our churches?

There is no actual conflict or contradiction between Christian faith and science. Science continues to discover how God put everything together and how he holds it together. If I disassemble the laptop I'm working on and have one of my smart IT friends come over and explain exactly how it works, I wouldn't conclude that there's no laptop maker. On the contrary. I would probably be more impressed than ever. We need not discourage those who seek natural causes and solutions. For some, that's the path that will eventually lead them to their Creator.

My doctor is also one of my best friends. He's not a Christian. But it's not from a lack of conversation. In some respects he's a better "Christian" than a lot of the Christians I know. He closes his practice every Thursday to volunteer at a local hospice. He holds dying people's hands, does what he can to make them comfortable, and speaks to the concerns and expectations of family members. Basically, he's a pastor on Thursdays. But don't tell him.

When I meet with him to go over the results of my annual physical, the teacher in him comes out. On one occasion, he was drawing an elaborate picture of how different drugs interact with specific enzymes and how a particular blood test can predict the impact of certain interactions. He was lost in his explanation. I was following about half of what he was saying when he stopped suddenly. Then with a big grin on his face, he said, "I don't know how anyone doesn't believe in God. Do you?" I laughed out loud. Here's a guy who has a hard time believing the miracles recorded in the New Testament, but who finds the fingerprint of God all over the human anatomy. His observation of how God put us together fuels his faith. His search for natural causes has led him to the Creator. All that to say, we need not fear those who go in search of natural causes. Ultimately, that path leads directly to the Creator. So have no fear. More importantly, carve out room in your preaching for those who just can't accept the things that are ... difficult to accept.

When dealing with miracles, Satan, hell, and even certain aspects of heaven, acknowledge that these are difficult things for the modern mind to accept. Here's one of my scripts. Feel free to plagiarize or adapt:

> For those of us raised in church, it's easy to believe these things took place. But if you are new to Bible study, I can understand why you may have questions or even doubts. You may be interested to know that some of Jesus' own followers had a difficult time believing some of this stuff. You've probably heard the phrase 'Doubting Thomas.' Thomas was one of Jesus' followers who didn't believe Jesus rose from the dead. Thus the nickname. Apparently Jesus' own brother, James, didn't believe for a long time either. So you are in good company. No pressure.

As stated earlier, the primary claim an unbeliever must come to terms with has nothing to do with the long list of miracles scattered throughout the Old and New Testaments. The primary issue is what a person believes about Jesus. So I'm always looking for opportunities to shift the discussion in that direction. Anytime I'm teaching a passage that unbelievers may object to as unbelievable, I take a minute to affirm their doubts and then offer a simple rationale as to why they may want to reconsider. My simple rationale is this: Jesus believed this incident actually took place. Every time I mention Adam and Eve, I say something along the lines of:

> I'll tell you why I believe Adam and Eve were actual people. Jesus did. I'm a simple man. If somebody predicts his own death and resurrection and then pulls it off, I'm with him. I don't really care what he says, I'm with the guy who rose from the dead. I would like to do that someday myself. And he said those who believe, even though they die, they will live. So I go with what Jesus said.

I apply that same logic every opportunity I get. By doing so, I accomplish three things. I'm pointing unbelievers back to *the* issue. Secondly, I'm providing believers with an insight that strengthens their faith. Lastly, I'm giving attendees an argument/apologetic they can use in conversations with their skeptical friends. Salting our preaching with similar statements allows us to admit the difficulties we all have with certain passages, while at the same time providing a way forward for those who are genuinely wrestling with matters of faith.

GUIDELINE #7: DON'T GO MYSTICAL ...

... unless you want a new car.

If you are serious about your weekend service serving as a bridge for those who are returning to faith or exploring faith for the first time, stay away from the mystical. Even if you are in a highly charismatic church, stay away from the mystical. You don't live that way. Nonbelievers don't live that way. So don't preach that way. Mystical just puts distance between you and your audience.

Now, on the other hand, if you are into positioning yourself as "God's man" or "God's anointed mouthpiece" or other such nonsense, then mystical is the way to go. Mystical communicates that you have an inside track; you are closer to God than the people in the audience could ever hope to be. Mystical creates ... mystery! And with mystery comes fear! And that puts *you* in the driver's seat. Once you get your people thinking you are something special, they will treat you special. Throw in a little prosperity theology and in no time you will be driving in style, dressing in style, and the people close to you will never question your decisions. How could they? You are God's man. It'll be awesome.

Now, your spouse and kids will know you are a poser and a phony. But eventually your spouse will get so accustomed to the fortune and fame, he or she won't say anything. Your kids, on the other hand, well, they'll be a mess. But you'll have the resources necessary to ensure they get the best treatment options available. Wear contacts. Avoid reading glasses. Get yourself an entourage, an Escalade, and some armor-bearers, and you will be good to go. Oh, one other thing. Stay away from the Gospels. Things didn't go well for those guys. Stick with the Old Testament. The Gospels could be hazardous to your charade!

Soon, at a Theater Near You

If you found this chapter to be particularly disruptive and disturbing, I can understand that. I just hope that once you've finished your imaginary conversation with me, you will stop and ponder exactly what about it bothered you so much. I don't know what you are hoping to accomplish through your preaching, but I hope *you* do. I don't know what your approach to preaching looks like, but I hope you will stop and define it. Most importantly, I hope the approach you take weekend after weekend is perfectly designed to help you get done whatever it is you are trying to do. And if not, I hope you have the necessary courage and humility to make some changes.

Obviously, I think we should all preach with unchurched people in mind. I'm convinced that we should let their presence shape our approach. I think Jesus' brother would agree. I think he would suggest that we not do anything in our preaching that would make it difficult for those who are turning to God. But, that's just me. You may have no desire to tweak your communication style so as to be more appealing to the unchurched and biblically illiterate in your community. That's okay. There are a whole bunch of us out here committed to doing exactly that. And eventually we will get around to planting a church in your community. And if you are like most church leaders, you'll have a bad attitude. And we won't care. We think that trilogy of parables regarding lost things reflects the heart of God. And we believe Jesus came to seek and to save that which was lost. We believe the church is the body of Christ and that the body of Christ should be about the activity of Christ. Funny thing, I bet you believe all that as well. So what are you going to do about it? What you've been doing? Seriously?

Mad yet?

Okay, maybe we should end with something we can agree on. Currently, I've got two kids in college and one who is about to finish high school. All three of them love the local church. If by some freak of chance they should end up living in your town and attending your church, please don't ruin it for 'em. Please don't hide behind your tradition and your "this is how we do it here" habits and preach brown-and-serve messages to my kids. Please don't steal their passion for the church because you are too lazy to learn. Too complacent to try something new. Too scared of the people who sign your paycheck.

Okay, so my kids probably won't attend your church. But somebody's kids are attending your church. If you have kids, *they* are attending your church. Every Sunday you are either instilling a deeper love and appreciation for the church or you are doing what most pastors do and providing them with one more reason not to attend when they no longer have to. That's a big deal. I don't want you to preach like me, but I do want you to be part of the solution. I want the fact that twentysomethings are leaving the church and never looking back to bother you. A lot. It bothers me. I think it bothers our heavenly Father. Do you?

So if we can't agree about the importance of preaching to unchurched people, surely we can find some common ground around our passion to recapture the attention and imagination of a generation of kids that is growing up in church but that can't wait to leave. *What's stopping you from making the necessary adjustments in your preaching to capture that segment of our population?* There's really only one answer to that question.

It's the third word in the question:

You.

BECOMING
DEEP
AND
WIDE

Transitioning a
Local Church

I hope our time together has sparked an idea or two. Ideally, I would love for you to join us in our campaign to create more churches unchurched people love to attend. Either way, you're probably scheming and dreaming. But schemes and dreams eventually necessitate change. And as you know, initiating and implementing change in a local church is ... well, a lot of terms come to mind: arduous, thorny, frustrating, suicidal. No doubt you could add a few descriptors of your own.

In spite of that, church leaders attempt it all the time. I did. I bet you have as well. The fact that you've hung with me this long means you're probably good for another round or two. Assuming that's the case, in this final section I'm going to tell you everything I've learned about implementing change in a local church. More specifically, I want to teach you what I've learned about creating a ministry culture that embraces rather than resists change.

As you know from my story, I didn't transition a church from one model to another. When I started the second campus for my father, the facility forced us to amend our model. Circumstances caused us to adopt a different approach to just about everything. Granted, nobody on my team complained. We loved the rawness of our poorly lit, climate-control-challenged, ramshackle warehouse environment. Our physical environment gave us the permission we needed to adopt a different approach to ministry. But that's different than transitioning an established church that has no intention of changing buildings or locations.

Where I can speak with some authority is in the area of transitioning *people*. I've had a great deal of experience helping church people adopt a different way of thinking about local church ministry. Like many start-ups, North Point began with a core that had come from traditional churches. As much as they appreciated our *vision*, there was lingering skepticism regarding our *approach*. It took some convincing. Along the way, I learned some important lessons about leading people through change. And yes, much of what I learned I learned the hard way.

chapter twelve

COMING TO BLOWS WITH THE STATUS QUO

Every innovation has an expiration date. At some point, *new* isn't *new* anymore, regardless of what the package says. Eventually, new ideas feel like yesterday's news. Bread is not the only thing that gets stale over time. Every new and innovative approach to ministry has an expiration date as well. Every single one. Nothing is irresistible or relevant forever. That should unnerve you a bit. Like me, you've visited (or perhaps worked for) churches where it appears as if they haven't seen a new idea in decades. Oddly enough, those are often the churches that are most resistant to change. Go figure.

Like me, your initial reaction to all this is, "Not on my watch. That'll never happen at my church." To which I would say, "Really? What makes you so sure?" Has it occurred to you that once upon a time the ideas and approaches to ministry that seem so stale now were actually fresh and innovative? Everything that is currently in place was originally considered a good idea. Otherwise, it would have never been implemented to begin with. Everything that is currently in place was adopted as an improvement over an outdated approach that was at one time a revolutionary idea. And so it goes. Everything that is currently in place began as a challenge to the status quo in a previous generation. People fought for those paint colors, that furniture, the architectural design of that ... ugly building. Yeah, it's hard to imagine. But it's true. What's ugly now was beautiful then. What feels irrelevant now was cutting edge once upon a time.

Speaking of once upon a time, once upon a time the only musical instruments considered appropriate for church were the piano and the organ. Bet you knew that. Then some radical music directors and pastors began experimenting with orchestras. Imagine that, orchestras in the sanctuary. My dad was one of those unwashed heathens. I was on the second row the first Sunday our music director stepped up on his kitchen step stool, raised his fiberglass wand, and brought the orchestra to life. It was magical. Powerful. Mostly, it was loud. While most people loved the addition of the orchestra, there was a faction that came unglued over the idea of bringing drums into the sanctuary. Not a kit, mind you. Timpani drums. Remember those? Drums were "worldly." Bet you didn't know that. Apparently, my dad didn't either. Drums in the sanctuary were evidence that we were becoming worldly. So a few weeks after the orchestra's debut, my dad preached a sermon on why it was okay to use drums in worship.

It wasn't too long afterward that he preached an entire message on why it was okay to clap in church. Seriously. Clapping was such a big deal that for a year or so our church actually had a clapping policy. Clapping was allowed during the Sunday evening service but not on Sunday morning. Instead of clapping, men were allowed to growl *Amen* when something good happened. I can still remember men growling *Amen* during the sermon on clapping.

Then somewhere along the way, big choirs and orchestras started feeling like yesterday's news. Depending upon your age, you may have never attended a church with an orchestra. You assumed electric guitars had always been part of the Sunday morning experience. Not so. Many a pastor lost his job and his religion over introducing Satan's instrument to weekend worship. While drums were worldly, electric guitars were of the devil. Then came drama. Followed by interpretive dance. You get the point. New ideas are generally considered bad ideas. Then they become normative. Then, eventually, they are yesterday's news. Nothing is new or innovative forever. Your best idea, the one that other churches emulate and take credit for, will eventually go the way of handbells and bus ministries. It's naive and arrogant to think otherwise. Perhaps the one exception is preaching from a stool beside a plasma TV.

We are foolish to assume our ideas are transgenerational. We are equally foolish to assume that we will intuitively be able to sniff out the need for change in our own organizations. If it were that easy, everybody would have made the proper transitions at the proper time. Truth is, the clock is ticking on our good ideas. It's ticking backward. And it's ticking faster than we think.

RESISTING THE RESISTANCE MOVEMENT

The resistance to change experienced by leaders in every discipline may be best summarized by James M. Kouzes and Barry Z. Posner when they write: "Any system will unconsciously conspire to maintain the status quo and prevent change."[56]

While leaders are often quick to blame people for their stubborn unwillingness to change, Kouzes and Posner rightly point out that the problem is much deeper and more complex than inflexibility or stubbornness. It's a systems problem. Every local church is a complex collection of systems. Every church has its way of doing things. And for the most part, it works. Consequently, change is rarely perceived as a solution. In most cases, change feels like an interruption. An expensive interruption to something that's fine the way it is. An interruption with no guarantee at the end. Only promises and wishful thinking. So, your church system will "unconsciously conspire to maintain the status quo and prevent change." The *way things are done* at your church is so deeply ingrained that you will meet resistance at every turn. And in spite of what you might be tempted to think, it's not anyone's fault.

Think about it this way: The facilities on your church campus are designed around *the way things are done*. The budget is organized around *the way things are done*. Staff has been hired and trained to implement *the way things are done*. Most everybody in attendance has come to expect the current *way things are done*. If you are in a church facility with dozens of adult Sunday school classrooms, it's going to be a bit difficult to convince people to embrace a model that doesn't require that kind of facility. The facility is conspiring against you! If your church's income is consumed entirely by the current model, it's going to be difficult to introduce anything new. The first question you'll be asked is, "How do you plan to pay for that?" If your staff's job security is tied to the preservation of *the way things are done*, they are going to oppose you at every turn. And if the people in your church aren't particularly bothered by *the way things are done*, they have no incentive to join you on your grand adventure. So yeah, just about everything in your current "system" is conspiring against you. No wonder most pastors, preachers, and teachers are content to tweak the model they inherited rather than introduce something new. It's too hard. Too expensive. Too disruptive. Too risky.

BACK IN THE DAY

When we launched North Point in 1995, our approach was a significant paradigm shift for churchgoers in our city as well as our part of the country. The Southeast is the buckle of the Bible Belt. It's one of the most churched regions in our nation. In 1995, nobody in Atlanta was clamoring for a new church or a new kind of church. Church was church. Either you went or you didn't. And if you wanted to go, it was easy to find one. And for those who didn't attend, they knew what to expect on those rare occasions when it was unavoidable.

Just about everything we did was a challenge to the status quo. And I'm not just referring to music style. We built a facility that didn't look like a church. We introduced home groups to a culture that had grown up with Sunday school. We didn't have deacons. We allowed women to serve communion. Heck, we allowed women to do just about everything. Our staffing structure was different. We built margin into our budget. We didn't do men's or women's ministry. No new members classes. We branded and named everything. We fast-tracked people into leadership.

Contrary to what some think, we didn't launch North Point on the back of a gang of twentysomethings who didn't know better and who were looking for something new. I was thirty-eight. Our original staff members were all in their late thirties. I was the youngest person on our board. Everybody else was over fifty. Bunch of old people. I don't remember them being dissatisfied with the *model* they left when they came to be a part of North Point. In fact, if I had introduced the model I had grown up with, I'm confident most would have followed along. Many would have followed along more willingly. Familiar is ... familiar. It's comfortable. You know how to behave and what to do and what to expect. Problem was, the model we had come from was perfectly designed for people like us. Church people. So the status quo had to go.

Easier said than done.

But it can be done.

Here's how to do it.

There, Not Here

The sentence following this sentence is so important I decided to write a sentence before *the sentence* to ensure you didn't miss the point of the next sentence. *The catalyst for introducing and facilitating change in the local church is a God-honoring, mouthwatering, unambiguously clear vision.* You may be tired of hearing about and reading about vision. Especially from me. But after twenty-five years of church leadership, I'm more convinced than ever that shared vision is the key to bringing about change. And once initial changes have been made, vision is the key to maintaining organizational focus and momentum. Shared vision is critical to getting your church on the right track and keeping it there.[57] While there's much that could be said about vision, most germane to our discussion is the fact that *vision is the place to begin every discussion pertaining to change.* Start the discussion anywhere else and you will experience resistance.

When I hear church leaders complaining that their people won't change, I always say, "Before we talk about your 'people,' let's talk about your vision. Tell me in one sentence where you're taking your church. Describe the future. Paint me a word picture." *In 100 percent of the cases, the leaders who can't get their people to change can't articulate their visions either.* So where do you suppose they began their conversations about change with the people who don't want to change? They began with the things that needed to change. And what did they experience? Resistance.

The most ineffective way to begin a conversation about change is to talk about what needs to change. You should never begin a conversation about change by addressing where you are now. You should always begin with where you want to be. When you begin a conversation about change by discussing what needs to change, you generally begin with something that someone is emotionally invested in. That's a recipe for failure. Or termination. During my first two years of college, I knew I needed to *change* my study habits. Actually, I didn't need to change them; I needed to have some. Anyway. Nothing *changed* until I decided to go to graduate school. Once I got a clear picture of a preferred future, my behavior changed. That's what vision does. It allows me to see where I am in relation to where I need to be. Reminding me of where I am and then telling me I need to change is neither compelling nor inspiring. But pointing

me toward a preferred future and helping me discover what
I need to do now in order to get there ... that's different.
So the best place to begin any conversation about change is
the future. What could be. What should be. Perhaps what
must be!

As a leader, your responsibility is to make the people in
your church discontent with where they are by painting a
compelling picture of where they could be. It wasn't until
our core embraced the vision of a church unchurched
people loved to attend that they were willing to let go of
their comfortable, we've-always-done-it-that-way notions
of how to do church. When they held their emotionally
charged biases about church up against a description of our
preferred future, they eventually realized that the two were
incompatible.

Something *had* to change.

They didn't really choose to change as much as they
chose to pursue something different. Our old ways of doing
things weren't wrong; they just weren't compatible with the
future we had chosen. Our core eventually realized their
preconceived notions about church would not facilitate our
vision. If you make people discontent with where they are,
they are likely to loosen their grip on their current way of
doing things. But if you try to pry their fingers off, get your
resume ready.

CHANGE ISN'T A VISION

So, what's your vision for your church? In a sentence
or two, what do want the future to look like? Feel like?
For the record, *change* is not a vision. Nor is *relevant* or
contemporary. If the primary thing bothering you about

your church is that you lack the *cool factor* and therefore young families don't stick, you've got some work to do. If your sudden compulsion to change is fueled by your board's observation that people are leaving your church to attend the contemporary church down the street, that's not enough. If your burden isn't any deeper than a desire to update and upgrade so people won't leave, you're better off continuing to babysit the previous generation's model. No need stirring things up for the contented flock you're currently leading. Perhaps you should pray that God would bring a leader along who is actually consumed by a genuine burden for people who are far from God. If you're lucky, maybe he or she will let you stick around and watch what happens when a leader who is naive enough to believe that Jesus is still building his church stands up and casts a vision so compelling that it ignites the imaginations of people who were secretly longing to give their lives to something bigger than themselves.

That wasn't very nice, was it?

So come on, what would you like to see God do in your local expression of the *ekklesia* of Jesus? Does anything bother you other than your attendance? Your style of music? Your level of excellence? You know from previous chapters that I believe those things are important. But if you want to implement meaningful change in your local church, you need a burden from God that keeps you up at night. To borrow a phrase from Bill Hybels, you need an intoxicating dose of "holy discontent." You want to see change? Ask God to start with you. Ask him to burden you with something worth risking your career for. And no, that's not hyperbole. That's the nature of a God-ordained vision. It's not simply something that could be. It's something you are convinced *must* be. When that's clear, and when you think you're ready to begin talking about it in terms people can understand and get behind, then and only then are you ready to start talking about what needs to change.

KEEPING IT ON THE RAILS

In addition to vision being the starting point for any discussion about change, vision fuels organizational focus and momentum going forward. Here's why. There is an inexorable link between an organization's vision and its appetite for improvement. Vision exposes what has yet to be accomplished. In this way, vision has the power to create a healthy sense of organizational discontent. A leader who continually keeps the vision out in front of his or her staff creates a thirst for improvement which, in turn, produces an appetite for change. In this way, vision contributes to developing a culture that is comfortable with change. Vision-centric churches expect change. Change is a means to an end. Change is critical to making what could and should be a reality. Bottom line, there is no way to overestimate the importance of a clear and compelling vision if you sense things need to change.

From day one we've been a bit paranoid about drifting from our vision. We are not immune. Vision is not very adhesive. It takes constant effort to ensure that it sticks. In some ways, our numeric success works against us. If we begin to drift, we will still be big. We may even be full. But *big* and *full* are not what we set out to do. *Big* and *full* could easily become a distraction. Maintaining *big* and *full* could accidentally become our mission. It certainly is for a lot of churches. So we are constantly looking for ways to keep our simple vision front and center at every level in the organization.

So once more, what's your church's vision?

What are you hoping to accomplish?

What could be and should be in your community?

Until you know, there's no point trying to change anything.

chapter thirteen

MISSION
AND MODEL

Chances are, if you stand up next weekend and present a new vision for your church, you probably won't feel much resistance. In fact, you might find that people are more engaged than usual. New ideas always pique people's interest. For those who've been praying for something new to happen, your new vision may feel like an answer to prayer. If you lead an evangelical church and your vision includes reaching unreached people, you might even get an *Amen* or two. If you're real good, you might even get a smattering of applause. As long as you keep it biblical and intangible, you'll be fine. But once Nelly McCloud finds out that your new vision requires her to give up her Sunday school classroom ... well, that's when the fun begins, doesn't it?

How did I know?

When I was twenty-six years old, I convinced the deacons at my dad's church to let me host a citywide evangelistic event for teenagers. They were on the edge of their seats as I explained my plans. I shared my goal to get our guest preacher into local high schools for assemblies. They loved my idea of asking other churches in the area to bring kids from their student ministries to our one-night event. Everybody in the room thought the event was a great idea ... until they experienced it.

Unfortunately for them, by the time the event began, it was too late to stop it. Fortunately for me, by the time the event began, it was too late to stop it. And fortunately for me, I was the pastor's son. They stood around the back of the sanctuary while two thousand somewhat rowdy teenagers were entertained by *not the choir and orchestra.* What they were envisioning after my most excellent vision cast was a far cry from what was actually taking place. As they described it later, "It was irreverent and unruly." They were disturbed by what they saw taking place "on the very spot where God's Word is preached each Sunday." As one gentleman put it, "That's not who we are."

I was speechless. I looked at the gentleman who made that comment and asked, "Did you stay till the end? Did you hear the message? Did you see the close to two hundred kids who came forward to pray with a counselor and give their lives to Christ?" I'll never forget his response. "You could have done it without that music." That was it. No one expressed gratitude for all the hard work. Nobody seemed to be moved by the response at the end. I was devastated. But it was not an isolated incident. And it serves to illustrate a dynamic that every vision-laden church leader has experienced at some point along the way. Namely: *New ideas are good ideas as long as they don't require anyone to actually do anything new.*

Model vs. Mission

The changes people resist are changes associated with the way ministry is *done*, the model the church has adopted. The model defines the church and thus, more than anything, determines the status quo. *This is how we do it here. This is who we are.* Over time, churches fall in love with their models. But models are meant to be a means to an end. Models are created to support the mission of the church. Once upon a time, every existing church model supported the mission of the church. But then a generation fell in love with the model at the expense of the mission. Truth is, for most churches, sustaining the current model *is* the mission of the church. Staff is trained with that particular model in mind. People come to expect the programs associated with a particular model. Budgets are established around the model.

It's a bit like that old couch your parents keep carting around from house to house every time they move. They originally purchased that couch because they needed a place to sit. They picked it out based on the size and decor of a particular room. In its original setting, it was perfect. Over time, however, it was more than just a place to sit. It became part of the family. Eventually it became associated with memories. There was a story associated with every stain. Babies were nursed on that couch. Heck, babies may have been . . . never mind. Point is, they became emotionally attached. To a piece of furniture! And when it came time to move, in spite of the fact that it didn't really fit with the new house and the new decor, they put it on a truck and took it with 'em. And a few years later, they packed it up and moved it again. And now it's faded and torn. There's nothing attractive about it. But they just can't part with it.

What started out as a solution to a problem—namely, *Where are we going to sit?*—became a mascot. And there's nothing wrong with that. No harm done. You know that it will eventually end up out on the street or at Goodwill. By golly, if they want to keep that eyesore of a couch, God bless 'em.

But bring that same dynamic into organizational life and it's devastating. This explains in part why participation in mainline denominations continues to decline. They fell in love with the model to the neglect of the mission. Eventually, a generation came along that said, "I'm not sitting on your couches." Then they left to go sit somewhere else. And how did denominational leaders respond? They started advertising campaigns! *Hey guys, come on back! No, we haven't replaced our couches. But we have a new ad campaign!* They don't understand why the next generation doesn't want to return to the very thing they left. They can't understand why twenty- to thirty-year-olds won't come back and sit on their ugly, outdated couches. They don't get why "young people" can't appreciate the stories associated with all the stains. Then, when somebody starts a church with new couches, couches chosen with the next generation in mind, they're critical! When a model is no longer an actual means, or the best means, to an end, the model must be adjusted or abandoned. If not, well, look around.

Ministry models that don't support the mission of the church eventually impede the mission or become the mission. Did I mention that after my successful student evangelistic crusade I was told never to schedule an event like that again? This was a church that had an altar call after every sermon. This was a church with a mission statement taken directly from Matthew 28. As much as I love the church I grew up in, it was married to a model, not its mission.

One of the primary reasons churches are empty is because church leaders love their models more than they love people. Writing to business leaders, author Seth Godin addresses a parallel tension in the marketplace when he writes: "Don't fall in love with a tactic and defend it forever. Instead, decide once and for all if you're in a market or not."[58] I'm afraid too many church leaders are in love with their tactics, their approaches to doing church. Jesus called us to be in a market. One of the reasons our church grew as fast as it did was, to pivot off Seth's quote, every other church in Atlanta was competing for the church-people market. We decided to get into the unchurched people market. That's a much larger market, and we had no competition at the time. Our challenge is to make sure we stay in that market. To do that, we dare not fall in love with our way of doing things.

DIRTY LITTLE SECRET

Before we leave this topic, there's one more embarrassing American church reality I should point out. The actual mission of many churches is *Pay the Bills*. No, you won't find that written anywhere. But let's be honest, most local churches don't feel any urgency about anything until the money starts running out. Then suddenly they are concerned about "reaching people." That's when they start talking about how to attract young couples. A church can go for years and baptize nobody but children and no one is concerned. A church can go for a decade without a single profession of faith and nobody calls a special meeting. But miss budget for three or four months running? Suddenly everybody's concerned. They're talking about change. But not because they've had an encounter with God. Oh no. It was their encounter with an Excel spreadsheet that drove 'em to their knees. Then, to add divine insult to injury, once the financial crisis passes, everything goes back to the way it was. The tragic truth is, most churches in the United States won't change until finances force them to.

Jesus and Model Makers

Jesus was confronted with this same dynamic. The Pharisees loved their model. Of course, they claimed it was Moses' model. But by the time the first century rolled around, so much had been added and adapted that the current system was a mere shadow of what God originally intended. The issue over which Jesus found himself in continual conflict was the Sabbath. Silly Jesus, he kept healing on the Sabbath! He should have known better. Never mind that it was okay to pull your goat out of a well on the Sabbath. But heal a creature made in God's image? That was off-limits.

At the end of yet another *what's appropriate Sabbath behavior* debate, Jesus made the following observation: "The Sabbath was made for people, not people for the Sabbath."[59] The Pharisees had it all turned around. They thought the model was the priority. Jesus said, no, *people* are the priority. The Sabbath, along with the entire law, was given for the benefit of the nation of Israel. God never intended for the Jews to serve the law. His intent was for them to serve him. The law was a means to that end. God intended for the Jews to love their neighbors.[60] The law was a means to that end as well. Jesus died at the hands of men who were convinced they were doing the will of God, men who were committed to protecting and defending the law. Tragically, they protected and defended it to the exclusion of its purpose.

I'm guessing I don't need to make much application here. Both modern as well as ancient church history is filled with tragic examples of what happens when church people fall in love with a model or an approach to church and lose sight of why the church was instituted to begin with. The church I grew up in has a terrible civil rights history. There was a season when black people were actually asked to leave the sanctuary. I know a woman who was among the white people who gathered in the lobby one Sunday morning staring into the sanctuary where one lone black woman sat waiting for the service to begin. They weren't sure what "to do." Can you imagine? Maybe you don't have to. Perhaps you have your own story.

Granted, those are extreme examples. But I don't want you to underestimate how powerful and insidious this dynamic can be. It's this dynamic that's currently keeping thousands of churches in a holding pattern. They can't advance. They can't reclaim their mission. They're bound to a model that no longer serves their original purpose. And if you are in one of *those churches*, you know the severe frustration of watching it become less and less appealing while insiders turn their backs on the market and curse our irreligious culture. If you are in one of *those churches*, this quote from Jim Collins might make you wonder if he's been looking over your shoulder:

> When institutions fail to distinguish between current practices and the enduring principles of their success, and mistakenly fossilize around their practices, they've set themselves up for decline.[61]

How did he know? I doubt seriously that you need any help contextualizing Jim's insight. But for the sake of keeping us here for a moment, I'll restate it in our terms:

When a *church* fails to distinguish between its current *model* and the *mission* to which it has been called and mistakenly fossilizes around its *model*, that church sets itself up for decline.

Maybe you should print that on a card for each of your elders or board members, pass it out next time you meet, and discuss it for an hour or so.

Maybe not.

Even if you are not in one of *those churches*, you are in a church that runs the risk of being so in love with a model that it accidentally abandons its mission. All of us live and lead on the edge of that potential. It's the nature of what we do. So allow me to be very direct. And rest assured I'm not pointing fingers. This is something we talk about all the time around North Point.

Marry your mission.

Date your model.

Fall in love with your vision.

Stay mildly infatuated with your approach.

No Exception

Whenever I challenge church leaders to *date their models* and *marry their missions*, I find myself taking a personal inventory. What am I most committed to ... really? What is our team most passionate about ... really? Perpetuating the model our team created or creating churches unchurched people love to attend? The day may arrive when our current model conflicts with our stated mission. When that day arrives, we will be dangerously comfortable with *the way we do it around here.*

So we talk about this dynamic all the time. We do not want to spend one day babysitting a model that is no longer working. We don't want to become guardians of a previous generation's approach to ministry even if *we* are the previous generation that created it. We know that eventually all our new and innovative ideas will become institutionalized. Many of them already have. Eventually, they will no longer reflect *the best way* to do ministry. They will simply be *our way.* When that day comes, it will be our turn to decide: Do we want to be guardians of a model or do we want to be a church unchurched people love to attend?

David McDaniel, director of Strategic Partner Churches, is our multi-site video venue expert. I was in a Q&A with David when the question was asked, "How long can a church survive on video preaching? Is there a plan to transition your churches to live preaching?" The gentleman asking the question was looking for a time frame, which was perfectly understandable. I'll never forget David's answer. He said, "When we sense that video teaching is no longer an effective means of *leading people into a growing relationship with Jesus Christ* in that particular church, we will transition to a live communicator."

Right answer.

It was the right answer because David prioritized mission over method. When video preaching no longer serves the mission of our church, it's got to go. It'll just be another ugly old couch that somebody will have to carry out to the street.

However, I'm sure I could find room for a projector or two in my basement.

CONNECTING DOTS

In church world, resistance to change occurs primarily around any attempt to modify or eliminate programming. As you know, programming is where churches get trapped in an era and languish until the money runs out. So at some point, you will be forced to address changes to your church programming. For the remainder of this chapter, I'm going to provide you with terminology and a single catalytic question to facilitate your messaging.

Programming is not an island unto itself. So to begin our discussion and to arm you to begin your discussion, let's take a look at four components of church ministry and specifically how they relate.

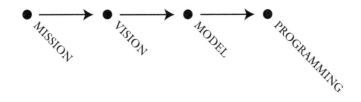

There are dozens of ways to define and explain mission and vision. We've already discussed both briefly. For our purposes, think of **Mission** as the nonnegotiable imperatives related to *the church*, the church at large. For us, it's making disciples. Or in our terminology: *leading people into a growing relationship with Jesus Christ*. Your tribe may view the mission of the church in different or broader terms.

Consider **Vision** as your local church's or perhaps parachurch's contribution to the overarching mission of *the* *church*. Organizations such as Compassion International, Fellowship of Christian Athletes, and Samaritan's Purse all contribute to the mission of *the church*. But not in the same way, not to the same target audience, and not in the same manner as a local church. Seminaries and publishers contribute as well. But their vision is different than a local church. Our contribution to the mission of *the church* is to create churches unchurched people love to attend. I'm pretty sure you know that by now.

A church **Model** is essentially the framework a church or denomination chooses or creates to advance its specific vision. The model is the organizational principle or theme under which programming operates. A model is broader than a specific program. A model encompasses all the programs in a church. Every church has a model, but not every church knows what its model is. Many churches have unknowingly embraced the *More Is Better* model. That's the model where you keep adding programs in hopes that something will work. Other churches run the *What's the Big Church Down the Street Doing?* model, which needs no explanation. Way too many churches run the *Flavor of the Week* model. That's the one where the pastor goes to a conference, hears about a new fad that's working in another part of the country, and then comes home and bolts it onto everything else the church is already doing. There's the *Worship* model, where the lion's share of resources and energy is dedicated to the weekend gatherings. Each mainline church has its own model, the advantage being that when people relocate they can find a church similar to the church they left behind. From the beginning, we embraced a *Groups* model. Everything we do is designed to funnel people into small groups.

And that brings us at last to programming.

Programming is chosen or created to facilitate a specific model, which in turn facilitates a church's vision. Or at least that's how it's supposed to work. All programming was originally created as a means to an end. The problem, as we've seen, is that over time leaders forget the end because they've fallen in love with the means. But if you will lead your influencers to adopt the perspective I'm about to explain, you will make it easier for them to break off their love affair with a specific approach to ministry.

The best way to think about programming, and perhaps the best context for discussing programming with your leaders, is to think of each program as the answer to a question beginning with the phrase, *"What is the best way to* _____*?"* Just about all church programming was originally introduced to address a *what is the best way* question. This is an extraordinarily important concept to keep front and center as you develop your strategy for change.

Approaching programming from this angle is one of the best ways to ensure alignment between *vision* and *activity*. Why? Because questions, unlike mission statements or values propositions, demand a response. Questions have the potential to stir emotion. Questions expose the weaknesses and gaps in any ministry model or approach to programming. Engage your leaders in a conversation around a list of *what's the best way* questions and there is a high likelihood that they will see the weaknesses and strengths in your current programming without you having to point them out.

For example, our *Groups* model demands that we constantly wrestle with questions such as:

- What is the best way to assimilate adults into small groups?
- What is the best way to find and train group leaders?
- What is the best way to assimilate children and teenagers into groups?
- What is the best way to introduce newcomers to group life?
- What is the best way to introduce seekers and returners to group life?

We evaluate programming on the basis of how well it serves our goal to involve members and attendees in group life. A program must be a group, prepare people for group life, or serve as an *easy*, *obvious*, and *strategic* step into a group.

Then there are the broader questions that every church must address.

Questions such as:

- What is the best way to introduce children to the gospel?
- What's the best way to provide teenagers with a biblical worldview?
- What is the best way to equip couples to build healthy marriages?
- What is the best way to involve attendees in the community?
- What is the best way to motivate and train parents to take responsibility for the spiritual development of their children?
- What is the best way to prepare engaged couples for marriage?
- What is the best way to recruit and train volunteers?

- What is the best way to introduce attendees to their global responsibility?

Once church leaders are able to see each program in your church as an answer to a specific *what's the best way* question, it will be easier for them to loosen their grip on the way things have always been done. Why? Because though the questions are transgenerational, the answers are not. The questions remain the same; the answers *change*. Exposing the conflict between these critical questions and your current programming is a powerful way of preparing people for change.

INSTITUTIONALIZING THE ANSWERS

Every church gravitates toward institutionalizing its answers to these questions. Programming that is originally introduced as a culturally relevant answer to a timeless question eventually defines a church. It becomes part of *this is who we are.* Explaining this dynamic to your leaders and providing them with a helpful context in which to wrestle with these issues will go a long way in helping them think outside your current programming box. Insisting that your leaders and influencers continue to address questions such as these will ensure that your church resists the gravitational pull toward institutionalizing your answers.

It is natural to assume that what worked in the past will always work. But, of course, that way of thinking is lethal. And the longer it goes unchallenged, the more difficult it is to identify and eradicate.

As Richard J. Harrington and Anthony K. Tjan write,

The assumptions a team has held the longest or the most deeply are the likeliest to be its undoing. Some beliefs have come to appear so obvious that they are off limits for debate.[62]

Did you catch that last sentence? Nothing in our menu of programming should ever be off limits for debate. Why? As we said earlier, "Every innovation has an expiration date. At some point *new* isn't *new* anymore." Along with a clearly stated vision, helping your team understand the dynamic relationship between mission, vision, model, and programming is critical to introducing change. These relationships serve as the context for your discussions. Your goal, of course, should be to create a church culture that is so vision-centric that there is more anxiety about losing focus than making changes. But being a vision-centric organization requires more than a vision. And that *more* has lost me *more* fans among pastors, preachers, and teachers than anything else.

So I saved it for last.

chapter fourteen

LED TO LEAD

If you've been in church work for five years or more, I seriously doubt that anything in the previous chapter came as a shock or surprise. I think most church leaders would agree with my premise. I've never met a church leader who felt called to babysit a model that worked well twenty years ago but ceases to make an impact today. Nobody wants to work in a church that clings to an approach that doesn't actually further its mission or vision. Most church leaders are intuitive enough to know when something is working and when it's not. And that leads us to the question that begs to be asked: Why haven't we already done something about this?

Why aren't more pastors more intolerant of what doesn't work? Why do so many churches lack vision? Why don't the Great Commandment and the Great Commission inform every programming decision we make and every dollar we spend? Why do churches wait until there is a financial crisis to begin talking about change?

Third person is great, isn't it?

Why do *you* allow stagnant programming and outdated models to define your church? Why do *you* wait until there is a financial problem before suggesting change? Is somebody in your church reading this chapter and wondering why you don't step up and do something?

Many dynamics contribute to this generational epidemic. I want to draw your attention to what I'm convinced is the primary culprit. If you find yourself arguing with me during the next several paragraphs, I get it. Whenever I teach this material, I get pushback. All I ask is that you pay close attention to exactly what bothers you about what I'm suggesting. Because while you are arguing with me in your head, another group has to pause every few sentences to do cartwheels around the room. While you're thinking, *I can't believe he's saying that!* the other group is thinking, *Finally, somebody's saying it!*

So here we go.

The primary reason churches cling to outdated models and programs is that they lack leadership. For an organization to remain vision-centric, it must be led by a vision-centric leader or leaders. Problem is, church boards rarely recruit and hire leaders. They recruit and hire pastors, preachers, and teachers. Then they expect those pastors, preachers, and teachers to lead. But pastors, preachers, and teachers are trained and gifted in … you guessed it … pastoring, preaching, and teaching. In most churches, the man or woman who carries the preaching responsibility is expected to carry the mantle of leadership as well. This is true whether he or she is gifted and trained to lead or not.

I attended a highly respected seminary for four years. Do you know how many leadership classes my school required me to take? I bet you do. None. Not a one. And my degree was *the* degree designed for those who felt called to lead a local church. Worse than the fact that leadership wasn't taught was the implicit message: *Leadership isn't important.*

If you know the Bible, you know all you need to know to lead a local church. But knowing the Bible does not a leader make. Several years after I graduated, the seminary added a leadership track. And I applauded that move. But here's the challenge: Teaching leaders leadership will result in better leaders. Teaching leadership to pastors, preachers, and teachers results in pastors, preachers, and teachers who've taken a leadership course. A leadership course may make them better, but it won't make them leaders.

Pastors, preachers, and teachers who are not gifted in the area of leadership default to *management*. Best-case scenario, they take what's handed to them and nurture it, protect it, defend it, and in some cases, improve it. Worst-case scenario, they focus on pastoring, preaching, and teaching, and delegate key leadership decisions to committees. They are reticent to move outside the lines they were hired into. It's neither intuitive nor comfortable for them to abandon the approach they inherited in order to lead out in a new direction. Consequently, they end up married to the model they were hired into.

HOLD ON THERE!

The pushback I generally receive when I teach on this subject goes something like this: "The New Testament writers use the terms *pastor*, *shepherd*, *elder*, and *overseer* to describe those giving oversight to the church. There is little mention of the term *leader* or *leadership* in the New Testament." In addition, I'm often reminded of the problems and abuses associated with point leadership.

Here, it is important to remember something I stated earlier: If you want to know what people mean by what they say, watch what they do. Actions not only speak louder than words, they interpret an individual's words. If we want to know what our first-century role models meant by what they said, we should pay close attention to what they did. In the arena of church, Jesus and the apostle Paul are the ones to keep an eye on.

Paul, via Luke, instructed the elders in Ephesus to:

> Keep watch over yourselves and all the *flock* of which the Holy Spirit has made you overseers. Be *shepherds* of the church of God, which he bought with his own blood. (Acts 20:28, emphasis added)

If you want to know what Paul meant by functioning as a shepherd of the church of God, follow him through the book of Acts and take note of what he *did*. Is there anything about the apostle Paul's approach to ministry that reminds you of our twenty-first century version of pastor/shepherd? When you read Paul's epistles, what comes to mind? The average pastor? Perhaps we are guilty of defining Paul's terminology by our twentieth- and twenty-first century approaches to ministry instead of holding it up against what he actually did.

Once after I taught on this subject, a pastor in the audience raised his hand and asked, "Andy, if God wanted the church led by leaders the way you define *leadership*, why did Jesus choose uneducated fishermen, tax collectors, and blue-collar types to lead the early church? Why didn't he choose educated and sophisticated types like the Pharisees?"

Good question.

I smiled and said, "Actually, he *did* choose a Pharisee. And that Pharisee did the lion's share of the work. In exchange, he got to write most of the New Testament."

Ever think about that?

Best I can tell, here's what happened. After Jesus ascended into heaven, the Father said, "Those are some really nice fellows you chose. But they aren't going to get much done. They certainly aren't going to 'go into all the world.' More than likely, they're going to hang around Jerusalem and teach whoever's interested. So I need you to go back and find somebody who has the ability to lead and equip men and women who will lead and equip other men and women. Otherwise, this thing isn't going to survive the first century. We need somebody with pedigree. Somebody people will take seriously. We need someone who's not afraid to take big risks."

So, Jesus came back and tracked down the most educated, politically connected, pedigreed, zealous, won't-take-no-for-an-answer Pharisee in the country. And, if that wasn't enough, he was a Roman citizen! Then he paired him up with a doctor, not an uneducated fisherman, and together they visited every primary port city along the Mediterranean rim. In their wake, they left a string of small *ekklesias* made up of both Gentile and Jewish believers. These became the nucleus of the church.

That's some serious *shepherding*.

It's so strange. When it comes to leadership in the church, we are often quick to dismiss the importance of things like education and gifting. Evangelicals, in particular, like to talk about "calling" and "anointing." Did you ever stop to think about the fact that the apostle Paul had all the things we assure people they don't need in order to be used by God? We say silly things like, "It's not your ability that matters; it's your availability!" Really? You wouldn't choose a surgeon based on that criteria, would you? "Hey you! Can you spare a few minutes to remove an appendix?"

Yes, God uses the uneducated to confound the wise. But that doesn't make ignorance a virtue. Yes, in the moment that you need to know what to say, the Spirit of God can bring to mind the right words. But that's not an argument against preparation. Is it?

To hold up the exceptions as the rule is not only foolish, it's unbiblical. Can God use anybody he chooses to use? Of course. But when we are considering our roles, we would do well to lean into the Scriptures that address the rules, not the exceptions to the rules. And Paul couldn't have been any clearer. Here's his take on who should do what:

> We have different gifts, according to the grace given to each of us. If your gift is prophesying, then prophesy in accordance with your faith; if it is serving, then serve; if it is teaching, then teach; if it is to encourage, then give encouragement; if it is giving, then give generously; if it is to lead,[63] do it diligently; if it is to show mercy, do it cheerfully. (Romans 12:6–8)

The short version of all that: *In the church, do what God gifted you to do.* In the church, don't spend a lot of time and energy trying to do something God has not gifted you to do. You won't be any good at it. If you have been gifted to lead, lead! Diligently. With earnestness! Paul believed the church needed to be led. He should know. And did you catch what he said about *calling* and *anointing*? Yeah, I didn't see it either.

Guess we should go with gifting.

Paul was a leader. Paul was a leader before he became a Christ follower. Ability matters. Giftedness matters. Jesus chose a gifted leader to lead the church outside the predictable, and for a while, comfortable, world of Judaism.

THE GOOD SHEPHERD

If you want to know what Jesus meant by what Jesus said, pay attention to what Jesus did. If you want to know what Jesus meant when he talked about being the good shepherd, just follow him through the Gospels. Fasten your seat belt. One day Jesus invited a man to join him, and the gentleman replied, "Lord, first let me go and bury my father."[64] Remember the good shepherd's response? Wasn't very pastoral as we typically define *pastoral*, was it?

Jesus said to him, "Let the dead bury their own dead, but you go and proclaim the kingdom of God."[65]

Then another gentleman, who apparently wasn't paying attention to the conversation, commented, "I will follow you, Lord; but first let me go back and say goodbye to my family."[66] Jesus, the good shepherd, replied, "No one who puts a hand to the plow and looks back is fit for service in the kingdom of God."[67] Translated: *You aren't fit to be my follower.* Clearly, Jesus needed some additional pastoral training. Or, perhaps, we have misinterpreted what it means to pastor the church. If the Gospels are a reliable record of what Jesus said and did, I'm tempted to conclude that the good shepherd was a great leader. He was not content to reorganize and improve what was; he introduced something new and set leaders in place to complete what he started.

TAKING INVENTORY

Now what I'm about to say is hard. But I'm convinced it's true. If no one is following you, if you are uncomfortable asking people to follow you, if the only people following you are people you secretly wish would follow somebody else, you may not be the one to introduce and implement change in your local congregation. Change requires vision. Sustained vision requires leadership. Leadership is a gift. Can you become a better leader? Yep. We can all get better at just about everything. But that's not really relevant to our discussion. Change requires vision. Sustained vision requires leadership. Leadership is a gift. If you have it, Paul would tell you to *lead diligently*. If you don't, discover the gifts God has blessed you with and lean into them with all your heart. Find a staff position that allows you to operate from your strengths. That's the biblical model. Churches and church leaders who organize and operate around that premise do well. Those who don't, don't.

So, as you contemplate the changes you feel need to be made in your current context, first determine whether or not you are the one to lead the charge. Take a personal inventory. An honest inventory. My hunch is you've been doing just that throughout this chapter. If you've been arguing with me in your head and writing objections in the margin, you may not be the one. If you are more comfortable problem solving than vision casting, you're going to have a difficult time of it. If the thought of scheduling a meeting with your key influencers to evaluate your model and programming makes your stomach churn, don't. If you are conflict- or risk-adverse, there's no need to start a process that you probably won't finish. You are better off managing what's been handed to you and praying that God will raise up a leader who will challenge the status quo and introduce change. Your observations about what needs to change may be spot on. You just may not be the one to drive the process.

Our Way

This discussion reminds me of a conversation I had with a pastor in our community. His church was looking for a student pastor. He began the conversation complaining about the previous person in that position. He was frustrated with his ex-employee's inability to get any traction with high school students in our community. I asked him to describe his church's approach to student ministry. When I suggested the problem might be a *what* rather than a *who*, I felt resistance. I suggested his church rethink their student ministry model before hiring another student pastor. Further, I recommended he sit down with one of our student ministry directors in order to get some suggestions on how his church could tweak or restructure its model to make it more conducive to student culture.

In so many words he said, *There's no point in having a discussion on how we approach student ministry. This is the way we do it in the _____ church.* He didn't argue that his approach was the best approach. That wasn't the issue. It was apparent he didn't have the energy or interest necessary for rethinking their approach. It was too complicated. In his denomination, program changes required going before a committee and making a case. He just wasn't up for it. Too much red tape. He wanted someone who would make *their* approach work the best it could. What I heard was, *Preserving our model is more important than reaching students in our community.* I was polite but direct. "Why should I recommend anyone I respect to join a church staff that is married to a model that even the staff knows isn't the best approach?" He knew. But he wasn't about to try to *lead* his church in a different direction. He was content to *manage* what he had inherited.

Fortunately, there are exceptions.

Lots of 'em.

If you are feeling relieved, like maybe you aren't crazy after all, you're probably one of them.

Perhaps the best thing about the current explosion in church planting is that it's attracting more leaders into the field of church leadership. Leaders don't mind waking up every day to their own problems. They have little patience babysitting problems left over from a previous generation. Church planting provides leaders with opportunities to create their own challenges. Church planting provides leaders with opportunities to lead. But not everybody gets to create his own problems. Most of us are called to dive in and fix someone else's. If that's you, the best way to create leverage as a leader is to begin asking tactical questions. People will hate you for it.

A Culture of Questions

Asking the right questions (and asking them over and over) will ensure that the vision of your church remains paramount while your programming remains subservient. So as we close this chapter, I am going to leave you with seven questions that cause managers to run for the hills and leaders to charge into the fray. These are questions our team circles back around to year after year at just about every level of our organization. They provoke us. They irritate us. They force us to address things that it would be easier to just ignore. But in the end, they make us better. Feel free to rephrase them, improve upon them, and then introduce them as your own. Or introduce them as they are and blame me for the ensuing chaos.

1. **Do we have a transferable mission or vision statement?**
   • Do our members and attendees know why we exist?

- By what standard do we measure our success as a church ... really?
- Which of these three drive the majority of our decisions: reaching people, keeping people, or paying the bills?

2. **What have we fallen in love with that's not as effective as it used to be?**
   - What do we love doing that's not really working?
   - What's off limits for discussion?
   - Do we have any "old couches" that need to be thrown out?

3. **Where are we manufacturing energy?**
   - What are we promoting that we secretly wish we didn't have to attend?
   - What would we love to quit doing but continue to do because we fear the consequences of change?
   - What are we doing programmatically that we would never dream of inviting a friend to attend?

4. **If we all got kicked off the staff and the board, and an outside group (a group of leaders who were fearlessly committed to the mission of this church) took our place, what changes would they introduce?**[68]
   - What's the first thing they would do?
   - Who would they replace?
   - What would they refuse to fund?

5. **What do we measure?**
   - Is there a natural relationship between what we measure and our mission?

- Are there things we should be measuring that would give us a more accurate read of how well we are accomplishing our mission?
- What are we afraid to measure?

6. **What do we celebrate?**
   - Is there a natural relationship between what we celebrate and our mission?
   - Are there things we should be celebrating that would help reinforce our mission?
   - Do we celebrate anything that reinforces a behavior that shouldn't be reinforced?

7. **If our church suddenly ceased to exist, would our community miss us?**
   - If so, why?
   - What value do we bring to our community?
   - How do people outside our church view our church?

So there you have it: discussion questions for your next seven staff meetings. Any of those make you a bit uneasy? They make me uneasy. They make me uneasy because they force me to take an honest look at current reality. Those questions keep me from lying to myself. They force me to lead openhanded. They remind me that there is no autopilot and no cruise control for those who have signed on to lead a local church. Those seven questions take me back to something I wrote years ago that I am apt to forget: *Write your vision in ink; everything else should be penciled in. Plans change. Vision remains the same.*

So, church leader, let's be the generation that asks the hard questions and answers them honestly. Let's be the generation that models for the next generation what it looks like to marry a God-honoring mission while staying mildly infatuated with our methods and models. I love what my friend Craig Groeschel says: "To reach people no one else is reaching, we must do things no one else is doing." Sounds good. But know this: You will never manage, oversee, or shepherd your congregation into that mindset. You will have to *lead* them there. And the fact that you've stuck with me this far is a good indication that you are the one to do just that!

conclusion

WHAT IF?

It's Sunday afternoon. I'm exhausted. Every weekend communicator knows the feeling. It was a good day. We baptized at all of our Atlanta-area churches. Baptism is always emotional for me. The stories are inspiring. Hearing our congregation cheer for individuals going public with their faith is compelling. And then there's that look Sandra gives me. It's a look that communicates something she's only verbalized once. Now her eyes say it all.

This nonverbal exchange began years ago following a particularly moving baptism story. Barry was in his thirties. He'd struggled through the complexity of growing up without a father. He quit attending church as a teenager, when his mother could no longer force him to go. He embraced just about every vice imaginable. Married early. Had a couple of kids. Was on the verge of destroying his family when someone in their neighborhood invited them to attend North Point. He wasn't the least bit interested. But his wife was. So she attended. And she loved it. And their two kids loved it. It was the children who eventually convinced Barry to give our church a try. Even then, he insisted they come in separate cars in case he decided to leave early. As it turned out, he arrived late. He didn't try to find his wife. He was there to put a check in a box. So he went directly to our worship center in search of a back-row seat as close to the door as possible. But what Barry didn't know was that we were expecting him.

No, nobody called to tell us he was coming. We are a church for unchurched people. We assume guys like Barry are showing up every week. Heck, we designed the place for the Barrys of the world. We're on the lookout for them. So when one of our Host team members saw a lone gentleman who looked a bit lost, uncomfortable, and sportin' an attitude that said, *Don't talk to me; I don't really want to be here*, he did what our Host team does best. He introduced himself and ushered Barry down to the second row. We save about fifty seats down front for folks like Barry. We learned a long time ago that the people who show up early to get the best seats are the people who need them least. So we save seats for the latecomers. As I referenced earlier, it's not fair to the people who arrive early for us to save seats for people who arrive late. But the people in our churches who've embraced our vision are glad we save seats for the people who need 'em most.

The Sunday Barry attended, we were in the middle of a series entitled *Fight Club*. We were talking about the importance of fighting for the relationships that are most precious. As Barry explained in his baptism video, "It was as if a light switch turned on inside of me." So a random decision to attend church in order to get his wife and kids off his back turned out to be a divine appointment. Six months later, Barry and his wife were baptized. Just as Barry was coming up out of the water and our congregation began to cheer, Sandra turned to me with tears in her eyes and whispered, "What if we had never left?"

There's so much packed into that question. What if we had never left the security of an established church with a future full of possibilities? What if we hadn't said yes to the prompting we both felt at the Silver Spoon Café after leaving a neurologist's office all those years ago? What if we had simply taken the first good job offer that came along? What if we had taken the easier path of creating a church similar to the churches we'd grown up in? What if, what if, what if? It's an unspeakable question because it immediately brings to mind all we would have missed if we had chosen to stay rather than leave. But more importantly, it makes us wonder what the thousands of men, women, and children who have connected or reconnected with their heavenly Father through our churches might have missed. Would anyone have invited Barry's family to church? Would there have been a church to invite him to? No one knows the answer to those questions. But having been part of the group that decided we were going to do everything in our power to create a church for people like Barry, we can't help but wonder. So today, during baptism, when Jake, a tenth grader from Alpharetta High School, described how his faith in God and the guys in his small group gave him the strength he needed to get through the suicide of a dear friend, Sandra gave me that look again. What if?

BRIANNA

Something else happened today. A seven-year-old girl named Brianna showed up in UpStreet, our Sunday kids' ministry, on the verge of tears. Brooke, her small group leader, noticed something was wrong and asked if she could help.

Brianna began attending UpStreet about four months ago at the invitation of a friend. Now her mother is attending North Point as well. In fact, she usually sits with Sandra and me on the front row during the eleven o'clock service. Brianna's father is a functional alcoholic. He's gone for weeks at a time. When he does come home, he's detached and at times verbally abusive. Both Brianna's mom and dad want out of the marriage. It's only a question of who's going to file first.

Brianna was upset this morning because once again her dad had broken his promise to pick her up and take her somewhere special. And par for the course, he didn't call to explain. And she knows that the next time she sees him, he won't even bring it up. This was the story that spilled out of little Brianna to Brooke, her group leader.

Brooke has her own story. Actually, it's an identical story. She hasn't heard from her father in over a year. Brooke is sixteen years old. She's part of our student volunteer program that recruits and trains high school students to lead small groups for elementary-aged and middle school students. Brianna has told her mom on several occasions that Brooke is the coolest person she's ever met.

So, a few minutes ago, as I was sitting here trying to figure out how to wrap up our time together, Sandra walked in and told me what I just shared with you regarding the exchange between Brooke and Brianna this morning. Then she told me to get a tissue before she would tell me the rest of the story.

After small group this morning, Brooke made a point to talk with Brianna's mom. She gave both of them her cell number and encouraged them to use it. On the way home from church, seven-year-old Brianna texted Brooke from her mom's phone and thanked her for listening. Within seconds, Brooke texted her back. Brooke, the sixteen-year-old high school student who's probably just a few steps ahead of Brianna in her own journey with Christ. Brooke, who doesn't know any better than to think she has what it takes to lead a small group. Brooke, who has her own set of issues to work through. Brooke, who was given an opportunity to serve in a significant way and took it. Here's her text:

> Hi sweetheart! You are more than welcome. I know how hard it is, but I PROMISE you that God is the best father ever and he's never going to cancel plans or not have time for you, okay? You are such an awesome girl and you need to keep on being that way because there are so many people who love you.

Sandra was right. I needed a tissue. A couple, actually. Dang, I love my church.

YOUR MOVE

So, do you want to do this or not?

Do you want to create or be part of a team that creates a church unchurched people love to attend? Are you ready to try some things? Possibly fail at some things? Is there part of you that desires to step away from the familiar and predictable to embrace something new?

Are you really content to spend the rest of your life doing church the way you've always done it? The way your tradition expects you to do it? Do you really want to continue designing services and programming for churched people? Do you want to spend another season of ministry doing things that make unbelievers unnecessarily uncomfortable because it's comfortable for you? I know your current approach is easier, cheaper, and not nearly as messy as what I'm suggesting. My hope is that our time together has awakened, or reawakened, something in you that's willing to take on something *harder, expensive,* and *messy.* Something you can't manage. Something that forces you to pray as you've never prayed before.

Speaking of prayer, what does your church pray for? What does the staff pray for? What do your elders or deacons pray for? God's blessing? The presence of God? A pouring out of the Holy Spirit? Safety? As far as the "presence of God" and "a pouring out of the Holy Spirit," you're a bit behind. Both of those were covered on the day of Pentecost.[69] Regarding God's presence, Jesus promised to be *with* those who were *making disciples,* not *gathering for worship.* So besides *you,* and what *you* and *your* congregation want God to do for *you,* what does your church pray for?

Now, I hesitate to even bring this up. Do you remember what the first-century church prayed for? You know, the one that operated under the threat of extinction for the first decade or two? They should have prayed for protection. Like American Christians do. I told the people in my church to quit praying for protection. It's embarrassing. Especially when people from other countries visit. Protection from what?

The first church prayer meeting we know anything about took place right after Peter and John were released from jail with instructions to stop speaking in that "name"—or else! They gathered with the leaders of the church, reported what happened, and had a prayer meeting. According to Luke, they only asked God for two things. Not protection. Or a blessing. Or an outpouring of the Holy Spirit. I'll let you read it for yourself.

"Now, Lord, consider their threats and enable your servants to speak your word with great *boldness.*" (Acts 4:29, emphasis added)

Seriously? Boldness. Peter and John still smelled like jail and they are asking God for more boldness. Boldness is what got 'em thrown in jail to begin with. They should have prayed for *discernment.* But that wasn't all they asked for.

"Stretch out your hand to heal and perform signs and wonders through the name of your holy servant Jesus." (v. 30)

In other words, do stuff that draws the attention of unbelieving people in our direction so we can point them in your direction. They prayed for healing, but not their own. They asked God to do something powerful through them, but not for their sake. They were totally focused on those outside the walls of their gathering place. That was a lesson they learned on opening day. Remember opening day for the first-century church? Luke tells us that on opening day all the Jesus followers were gathered together in one place when suddenly the Spirit descended on them. Remember what happened next? Bible study? Nope. Worship service? Nope. Prayer meeting? Nope. They were doing all of those things *before* the Holy Spirit arrived. Hmmm. Once he showed up, *the church left the building.* With the events of opening day still fresh on their minds, a night or two in jail wasn't going to deter them. So they prayed for boldness. They were not about to stay put. They were not about to keep the good news in the building.

So back to my original question. What does your church pray for? If your church isn't praying for boldness, I can tell you why. You don't need it. How do I know you don't need it? Because we pray for what we need. Parking spots. Patience with our kids. A job. But boldness? Who needs it?

But the minute you decide to get back in the business the church was commissioned for in the first place, you will pray for boldness. Not because you are supposed to. You'll pray for boldness because you'll need it. If you decide to get into the unchurched people market, if you decide to take James' advice and remove every obstacle that's in the way of those who are turning to God, you'll need every ounce of boldness you can get. You will have to cast a bold vision. You will need to make bold changes. You will wrestle with questions that require bold answers. Your new direction will require bold leadership. Categories will get scrambled. Consistency will go out the window. You'll save seats for late arrivers. You'll let people out on time. You'll begin evaluating everything through the eyes and ears of the unchurched. Things will get a bit crazy. And you'll love it. You will never be content with anything less.

Still not convinced?

Well, there's always this.

THE PARABLE OF THE CREDIT CARD

Suppose you had seven credit cards in your purse or wallet and you lost one. Wouldn't you leave the six and go search for the missing one until you found it? I lost a credit card recently and never once pulled out the one I hadn't lost to obsess over it. I felt no urgency about my un-lost credit card. I didn't call a single person to say that I still had my American Express Card. But I did start calling around to see if anyone had seen my lost MasterCard. When you lose something important, you obsess over it; you get preoccupied with it. It's pretty much all you think about. Remember the last time you couldn't find your phone? Remember the embarrassing, ashamed-to-admit-it, I'm-such-an-American panic that started to filter past your common sense? You took no comfort in all the other un-lost electronic gadgets lying around your house, did you? You were on a mission. Why? You lost something important.

What does your church obsess over?

What is your church preoccupied with?

Churches for churched people obsess over the most frivolous, inconsequential things. It's why you dread your board meetings, your elder meetings, and your committee meetings. You rarely talk about anything important. You're managing found people. I know you care about un-found people in your heart. But do you care in your schedule, your programming, your preaching style, or your budget? Do you know how much difference the care you feel in your heart makes in the life of someone far from God? *None.* No difference. Your dad loved you in his heart. But it was the love in his schedule that made the difference, wasn't it? Do you really want to spend the rest of your ministry years feeling something you don't do anything about?

I hope not.

You know what I did when I finally retrieved my lost credit card? I called my wife and said, "Rejoice with me: I have found my lost credit card." I don't have to tell you how Jesus wrapped up each of his three parables about lost things. We've covered that already. You know what he said. You've taught it! In fact, you're thinking about using this credit card illustration in a message right now, aren't you?

Jesus said there is more rejoicing in heaven over newly found people than people who haven't been lost for a long time. Would you like to know why there's not all that much rejoicing in your church? It's a church full of found people.

Come on, do you really want to spend your life managing what *was* lost to the neglect of what's *still* lost?

So, regarding my credit card illustration. You have my permission to use it. But under one bold condition. At the end of the message, you have to tell your church that starting immediately, you're going to evaluate everything your church does and every dollar it spends with the one lost person in mind rather than the found ninety-nine. Then you have to sit down with your influencers and create a transition plan. If you aren't willing to do that, then you'll have to get your own illustration.

I've been in church all my life. So I know that even if you aren't willing to reorganize your church around the Great Commission, you'll still see some people come to faith. Parents will insist that their children be baptized. Your sanctuary will continue to be full on Easter. But that's not what you got into this for, is it? Remember when you said yes to God? Remember when he interrupted your life and called you as a teenager, college student, or marketplace leader? You had dreams. You wanted to make a difference. Perhaps it's time to let go of what you are currently doing and embrace what you were originally called to do. And as for the excuse that just popped into your mind, ignore it for now. Just dream a little. It won't cost you a thing. Think back to the time when you wrestled with God over whether ministry was your future. Remember that?

MY WISH

If I could make a wish for your church that I knew would come true, I would wish that the loudest, rowdiest, most emotionally charged celebrations in your gatherings would be in response to people going public with their faith through baptism. I want you to be able to turn to your spouse or to someone on your team who's shared the journey with you and say, "What if?" What if we had refused to act boldly? What if we had refused to change? What if we had refused to lead? What if we hadn't allowed God to break our hearts? What if we had resisted his prompting? What if we had ignored his whisper?

Look what we would have missed.

Look what *they* might have missed!

So come on.

Let's link arms with the bold leaders at the Jerusalem Council. Let's decide not do anything that makes it unnecessarily difficult for those who are turning to God.[70]

Let's go deep.

But let's be wide.

Let's be so wide that the whole world knows the church isn't for church people.

It's for people, people.

It's for everybody!

appendix a

NORTH POINT
SURVEY CARDS
AND
RESULTS SAMPLE

CONTEXT

On January 22, 2012, we surveyed worship service attendees at four of our five local churches: Browns Bridge Community Church, Buckhead Church, North Point Community Church, and Watermarke Church. Attendees self-selected as either "New Guests" (attended five times or less) or "Regular Attendees" (everyone else). Replicas of the surveys appear on pages 320–321 and key results and detailed data follow thereafter.

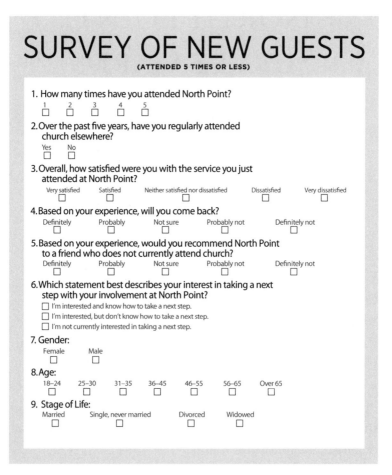

SURVEY OF NEW GUESTS
(ATTENDED 5 TIMES OR LESS)

1. How many times have you attended North Point?

   1 ☐ 2 ☐ 3 ☐ 4 ☐ 5 ☐

2. Over the past five years, have you regularly attended church elsewhere?

   Yes ☐ No ☐

3. Overall, how satisfied were you with the service you just attended at North Point?

   Very satisfied ☐ Satisfied ☐ Neither satisfied nor dissatisfied ☐ Dissatisfied ☐ Very dissatisfied ☐

4. Based on your experience, will you come back?

   Definitely ☐ Probably ☐ Not sure ☐ Probably not ☐ Definitely not ☐

5. Based on your experience, would you recommend North Point to a friend who does not currently attend church?

   Definitely ☐ Probably ☐ Not sure ☐ Probably not ☐ Definitely not ☐

6. Which statement best describes your interest in taking a next step with your involvement at North Point?

   ☐ I'm interested and know how to take a next step.
   ☐ I'm interested, but don't know how to take a next step.
   ☐ I'm not currently interested in taking a next step.

7. Gender:

   Female ☐ Male ☐

8. Age:

   18–24 ☐ 25–30 ☐ 31–35 ☐ 36–45 ☐ 46–55 ☐ 56–65 ☐ Over 65 ☐

9. Stage of Life:

   Married ☐ Single, never married ☐ Divorced ☐ Widowed ☐

SURVEY OF REGULAR ATTENDEES
(ATTENDED MORE THAN 5 TIMES)

1. How long have you been attending North Point?

Less than 1 year   1 to 3 years   3 to 5 years   Over 5 years
☐   ☐   ☐   ☐

2. During the five years prior to attending North Point, did you regularly attend church elsewhere?

Yes   No
☐   ☐

3. Which of the following next steps have you taken?
- ☐ Starting Point Orientation
- ☐ NEXT
- ☐ Fusion
- ☐ Access Group
- ☐ Community Group
- ☐ Strategic Service
- ☐ Other

4. Over the past 12 months, how many times have you invited someone to North Point who does not attend church anywhere else?

0   1   2   3   4+
☐   ☐   ☐   ☐   ☐

5. Gender:

Female   Male
☐   ☐

6. Age:

18–24   25–30   31–35   36–45   46–55   56–65   Over 65
☐   ☐   ☐   ☐   ☐   ☐   ☐

7. Stage of Life:

Married   Single, never married   Divorced   Widowed
☐   ☐   ☐   ☐

Key Points

- On any given week, roughly 10 percent of our attendees are new to North Point Ministries.
- New guests are 98 percent satisfied or very satisfied—an extremely high number.
- Roughly 40 percent of our attendees each week are unchurched. (We define *unchurched* as not having regularly attended church during the five years prior to attending a North Point Ministries church.)
- With more than 50 percent of its attendees age 35 or younger, Buckhead Church's demographics are significantly younger than the other participating churches. At the other North Point Ministries churches surveyed, only 25 percent of attendees were 35 years old or younger.
- The percentage of our attendees who are divorced or single (never married) is trending up. Nineteen (19) percent of new guests are divorced (vs. 11 percent of regular attendees); 39 percent of new guests are single, never married (vs. 22 percent of regular attendees).
- Three out of four new guests are interested in taking a next step. However, of those three, one does not yet know how to take that step.
- Eighty (80) percent of our regular attendees have taken a next step.

RESPONSE RATE AND PROJECTIONS
Actual Surveys Filled Out

	All
Regular Attendees	5,610
New Guests	550

Projections for Sunday 1/22

	All
Total Attendance	22,412
Regular Attendees	20,396
New Guests	2,016
New Guest %	9%

Notes:
- There was a 27 percent response rate across all North Point Ministries churches.
- The 11:00 a.m. service at Buckhead Church was the service with the highest projection of new guests attending: 443. (Though responses by service time were only available for Buckhead Church and Browns Bridge Community Church, we were able to estimate numbers by service time for our other churches as well.)

DATA

Churched vs. Unchurched (Regular Attendees and New Guests)

During the five years prior to attending a North Point Ministries church, did you regularly attend church elsewhere?

	All
Yes	62%
No	38%

Notes:
- The percentage of unchurched attendees is nearly 40 percent.
- Unchurched percentage is the same for regular attendees and new guests.
- The Buckhead Church 6:00 p.m. service had the highest percentage of unchurched attendees: 47 percent. (Though responses by service time were only available for Buckhead Church and Browns Bridge Community Church, we were able to estimate numbers by service time for our other churches as well.)

Interest in Next Steps (New Guests Only)

Which statement best describes your interest in taking a next step with your involvement at North Point?

	All
I'm interested and know how.	47%
I'm interested but don't know how.	26%
I'm not currently interested.	26%

Note:
- Sixty-four (64) percent of those attending for the very first time are interested in taking a next step.

Overall Satisfaction (New Guests Only)

Overall, how satisfied were you with the service you just attended?

	All
Very Satisfied	74%
Satisfied	24%
Very Satisfied + Satisfied	98%

Notes:
- These satisfaction numbers are extremely high.
- The percentage of very satisfied attendees drops from 82 percent for the 9:00 a.m. services to 71 percent for the 11:00 a.m. services.

Inviting Others (Regular Attendees Only)

Over the past 12 months, how many times have you invited someone who does not attend church anywhere else?

	All
0	17%
1–2	44%
3+	39%

Notes:
- More than 80 percent of our regular attendees have invited at least one person to church over the past year.
- The differences across churches are negligible, other than Watermarke Church, which has the highest percentage (48 percent) of attendees who have invited three or more people.

Taking a Next Step (Regular Attendees Only)

Which of the following next steps have you taken? (We provided the following options for our regular attendees to choose from: Starting Point Orientation, NEXT, Fusion, Access Groups, Community Groups, and Strategic Service [volunteering in Sunday environments].)

	All
Percentage who have taken a next step	80%

Notes:

- The 6:00 p.m. service at Buckhead Church has the most attendees who indicated that they have taken a next step: 86 percent.
- The 11:00 a.m. service at Browns Bridge Community Church was the service with the most attendees reporting that they have not taken a next step.

appendix b

Starting Point Ministry Description

We knew that if we were going to build a church that unchurched people loved to attend, we had to be ready if they actually showed up. Part of being ready was creating a safe environment for them to explore their questions about faith and God. *Starting Point* is that environment.

Almost every church has something for new people. Most of them are for people who are new to *that* church, not necessarily new to church. But we knew that we wanted to be ready for people who didn't know what to expect. Or better yet, for people who were afraid of what they expected.

The mission of our church is to lead people into a growing relationship with Jesus Christ. The mission of Starting Point is to lead people into a growing relationship with Jesus Christ by creating a conversational environment where they can explore faith and experience community.

All who come expect to explore their faith, but many are surprised by their first tastes of community. Of course, long-term relationships will not fully form during Starting Point. But in light of the discussions that take place and the common bond that participants share, this experience often moves them to take a next step into a Community Group.

The common bond we refer to is the participant's relationship, or lack of relationship, with church and faith. We target three different types of people:

- *Seekers*: those who are curious about God, Jesus, the Bible, or Christianity
- *Starters*: those who are new to a relationship with Jesus Christ
- *Returners*: those who have some church experience, but have been away for a while

You'll notice that "New to North Point" isn't a category. For those churched people who are new to our church, we have an environment called NEXT. There we explain what we're all about and how we may differ from their previous church experiences. You can find out more about *Next* at *www.insidenorthpoint.org/next/*.

We wanted Starting Point to be more about taking a next step toward God and less about a next step within our church. So obviously, Starting Point isn't for everyone. Even all unchurched people. Some people may be so unreceptive to Christianity that they cannot engage in meaningful discussions of faith without compromising the environment. Or, they may be unwilling to commit to the preparation and attendance requirements.

While there is some required preparation for the group member, we have tried to keep the emphasis on conversation and away from teaching. This isn't an apologetics course or a class on Christian theology. Naturally, those elements may take place from time to time, but at its core, Starting Point is a conversational environment.

For more in-depth information on Starting Point, please go to *www.insidenorthpoint.org/groups/starting-point/*.

MEASURABLE MINISTRY WINS

We have clarified the win for each of our ministry areas, from children through adult. In addition to the primary win for the ministry, we have defined several measurable wins for each area.

Waumba Land – Our ministry for preschool-aged children

Primary Win:
To make a first impression of the heavenly Father in such a way it makes a lasting impression on the heart of a child

Measurable Wins:
1. Kids attend.
2. New kids connect.
3. Parents partner with us.
4. Volunteer leaders are retained.

UpStreet – Our ministry for elementary-aged children

Primary Win:
To guide children to put their faith in Jesus and to teach them who God is and how he wants them to live

Measurable Wins:
   1. Kids attend.
   2. Parents partner with us.
   3. Kids take a next step.
   4. Volunteer leaders are retained.

KidStuf – Our foyer environment for elementary-aged children and their parents

Primary Win:

To effectively inspire and equip parents in the spiritual development of their children by applying the *Big Idea* at home

Measurable Wins:
   1. Kids and parents attend.
   2. Parents partner with us by using the Take-Out.
   3. Families invite friends.

Transit – Our ministry for middle school students

Primary Win:

To effectively inspire and equip middle school students to develop a faith of their own

Measurable Wins:
   1. Students attend Transit.
   2. Students attend a special event (camp, retreat, etc.).
   3. Students take a next step.
   4. Volunteer leaders are retained.

InsideOut – Our ministry for high school students

Primary Win:

To effectively inspire and equip high school students to develop a faith of their own

Measurable Wins:
1. Students attend InsideOut.
2. Students attend a special event.
3. Students take a next step.
4. Students volunteer in personal ministry.
5. Volunteer leaders are retained.

Service Programming – Our division responsible for creating adult worship environments

Primary Win:

To create worship experiences that make people want to come back and take a next step

Measurable Wins:
1. People come back.
2. People take a next step.
3. People invite others.

North Point Online – Our online worship environment

Primary Win:

To provide an alternative worship environment for the churched and an engaging first step for the unchurched

Measurable Wins:
1. People tune in for the experience.
2. People are raving fans of the experience.
3. People invite others to tune in for the experience.

GroupLife – Our small group ministry for adults

Primary Win:

To create small group environments where people connect relationally and grow spiritually

Measurable Wins:
1. People participate.
2. Disconnected people are connected.
3. Leaders replace themselves.
4. Leaders are retained.

Starting Point – Our small group ministry for unchurched and unbelieving adults

Primary Win:
To create a conversational environment where people can explore faith and experience community

Measurable Wins:
1. People attend an orientation.
2. People participate in a group.
3. Participants take a next step.
4. Leaders replace themselves.

Singles – Our ministry for single adults

Primary Win:
To lead single adults into a growing relationship with Jesus Christ

Measurable Wins:
1. People attend a gathering, a series, or a special event.
2. Gathering participants take a next step.
3. Volunteer leaders are retained.

MarriedLife – Our ministry for married adults

Primary Win:
To help married couples experience the individual growth necessary for healthy marriages

Measurable Wins:
1. Couples intentionally invest in their marriages.
2. Couples leverage the *Great Date* resources.
3. Couples invite others to a MarriedLife event.
4. Couples are satisfied with their MarriedLife experience.

Care Network – Our pastoral care ministry

Primary Win:

To help people grow as individuals and to provide assistance in times of need

Measurable Wins:
1. People find the care support they need.
2. People complete their programs.
3. People take a next step.
4. Care leaders are retained.
5. Care receivers return as care leaders.

NORTH POINT'S MISSION, STRATEGY, AND BELIEFS

OUR MISSION

... to lead people into a growing relationship with Jesus Christ.

OUR STRATEGY

... to create churches where people are encouraged and equipped to pursue intimacy with God, community with insiders, and influence with outsiders.

WHAT WE BELIEVE

About the Scriptures—We believe the entire Bible is the inspired Word of God and that men were moved by the Spirit of God to write the very words of Scripture. Therefore, we believe the Bible is without error.

About God—We believe in one God who exists in three distinct persons: Father, Son, and Holy Spirit. We believe that Jesus Christ is the second member of the Trinity (the Son of God) who became flesh to reveal God to humanity and to become the Savior of the lost world.

About Humanity—We believe that all people were created in the image of God to have fellowship with him but became alienated in that relationship through sinful disobedience. As a result, people are incapable of regaining a right relationship with God through their own efforts.

About Salvation—We believe that the blood of Jesus Christ, shed on the cross, provides the sole basis for the forgiveness of sin. Therefore, God freely offers salvation to those who place their faith in the death and resurrection of Christ as sufficient payment for their sin.

About the Christian Life—We believe all Christians should live for Christ and not for themselves. By obedience to the Word of God and daily yielding to the Spirit of God, every believer should mature and be conformed to the image of Christ.

About the Church—We believe that the church is the body of Christ, of which Jesus Christ is the head. The members of the church are those who have trusted by faith the finished work of Christ. The purpose of the church is to glorify God by loving him and by making him known to the lost world.

appendix e

NORTH POINT COMMUNITY CHURCH CHARTER MEMBERS

Brian "Keith" Adams
Christopher Adams
Cynthia Adams
David Adams
Jenni Adams
Jeremy Adams
Karen Adams
Roy "Tony" Adams
Peter Addona
Ciara Alley
Matt Alley
Tiffany Alley
Jennifer Allison
Patsy Allison
Wally Allison
Melanie Amos
Ginger Arias
Mitch Arias
Edsel Arnold
Julie Arnold
Matthew Arnold
Leon Askew

Cristy Atchley
Darrin Austin
Glenda Avery
Mike Avery
Bethany Bailey
Boyd Bailey
Douglas Bailey
Marianne Bailey
Rachel Bailey
Rebekah Bailey
Rita Bailey
Amy Balogh
Mary Bane
Warren Bane
Jan Baranak
Lawrence "Buck"
     Barber
George Barnes
H. "Carey" Barnes
Laura Barnes
Linda Barnes
Sheila Barnes

Hubert "Hugh"
     Barnhardt
Lou Barnhardt
Beth Batten
Tim Batten
Claude "Dan" Beeco
Cheryl Bell
David Bell
James "Frank" Bell
Maribeth Bell
Angela Bemiss
Kevin Bemiss
Jean "Beth" Bennett
Marielena Bernal
Sabrina Berry
Jeffrey Bertsch
Pamela Bertsch
Charles Bethel
Leanne Blakeslee
Cheryl Blanchard
Christian Borthayre
Michelle Borthayre

Anne Marie Boshoff
Donovan Boshoff
Eric Boshoff
Shelby Bose
Thomas Bose
Ann Botta
Vince Botta
Thomas Bound
Doris Bowen
Howard Bowen
Scott Bowen
James Braden
Victoria Braden
Gary Brazier
Deborah Bright
David "Ron" Brooks
Janelle Brooks
Eric Brown
Rodney Brown
Sharon Brown
Bruce Browning
Rita Browning
Alyson Brownlee
Betty Bryant
Bob Bryant
Brandi Bryant
Tim Bryant
Anna Bugg
Brenda Bugg
Katie Bugg
Randy Bugg
Cheryl Buhre
Richard Buhre
Bobby Burgner
Carrey Burgner
Elizabeth "Genie"
   Burnett
Jeffrey Burns
Deborah Burzotta
Jim Burzotta
Meredith "Becki"
   Byars

Terry Byars
Lisa Byrd
Jennifer Calbert
Jonathan Calbert
Laura Calbert
David Campbell
Miriam Campbell
Regi Campbell
Ken Cantrell
Lisa Cantrell
Pat Carithers
Thomas Carson
April Carter
David Carter
James Carter
Lillian Carter
Ron Cash
Chuck Catledge
Kaye Catledge
Kimberley Chapple
Robert Chapple
Nancy Charles
Andy Christiansen
Nikki Christiansen
David Christman
Meredith Cimmino
Amy Clark
Ashley Clark
Ben Clark
George Clark
Houston Clark
Houston
   "McClendon"
   Clark
Paula Clark
Randy Clark
Sherry Clark
William "Chadwick"
   Clark
George Clary
Phyllis Clary
Charles "Curt" Clause

Bunnie Claxton
Russell Claxton
Richard Clay
Kathleen Coder
Ron Coder
Kimberly Coe
Stuart Coe
Karen Cole
Mary Katherine Cole
Todd Cole
David Collins
Don Collins
Stacy Collins
Carol Colton
Lynn Conner
Michael Conner
Greg Cook
Jessica Cook
Amanda "Amy"
   Cooley
Tish Coppolino
Danielle Counts
Reynold Counts
Bob Cox
Lisa Cox
Mary Ann Cox
Michael Cox
Amy Craig
Dwayne Craig
Becky Crandall
Mike Crandall
Peter Crawford
Roxanne Crawford
Craig Cromwell
Melissa Cromwell
Carole "Missy"
   Crosson
Susan Csire
Carol Curtis
Jill Curtis
Leonard Curtis
Maurice Davis

Jeffrey Deaton
Sherry DeLoach
William DeLoach
Shirley Deupree
Dianne DeVore
Howard DeVore
Landon Donoho
Lanny Donoho
Peggy Donoho
Cynda Douglas
John "Fraser" Douglas
Justin Douglas
Ray Douglas
Diane Dover
Greg Dover
Erin Dudley
Robert Eagar
David Edwards
Julie Edwards
David Egan
Stuart Elder
Brenda Eller
Daniel Eller
Debbie Evans
Bill Fair
Rebecca Fancher
Timothy Fancher
Mike Faulkner
Rick Faulkner
Wayne Faulkner
Brad Fields
Deborah Fields
Sammy Fields
Haynes Finney
James Finney
Leah Finney
Vicki Finney
Lisa Foreman
Mark Foreman
Julia Francesconi
Kathi Francesconi
Michael Francesconi

Tom Francesconi
Eleanor Francine
Mary Francine
Morris Francine
Timothy Francine
Cathy French
David French
Babs Fry
Ron Fry
Suzanne Galloway
Dana Garrard
Rochelle Garrard
Ron Garrard
Gina Gay
Roger Gay
B. "Keith" Gentry
Vickie George
Louie Giglio
Shelley Giglio
Gina Gilmore
Thomas "Dewayne"
 Gilmore
Rebecca Givens
Michael Gladden
Laura Gondolfo
Jeff Goode
Patricia Gordon
Diane Grant
Keith Grant
Charles Gray
James Gray
Regina Grice
Stewart "Randy" Grice
Bonnie Griffith
Leslie Griffith
Matt Griffith
Gillian Grimsley
Amy Grisham
Thomas "Powell"
 Grisham
Betsy Griswold
Daryl Griswold

Elizabeth Guerrero
Lisa "Lynn" Hall
C. "Andrew" Harbour
Helen "Lisa"
 Hardeman
Jana Harmon
Stephen Harmon
Bradley Harris
James Harris
Judy Harris
Kathy Harris
Margaret Harris
Kerry Hawkins
Dianne Haygood
J. "Cliff" Haygood
Sandy Henderson
Carmen Hendricks
Robert Henry
Cindy Herceg
Richard Herceg
Jesse "Darren"
 Herringdine
Barry Hilliard
Bee Bee Hilliard
Elizabeth Hinson
John "Brady"
 Holcomb
Allison Holley
Rob Holley
Pamela Holliday
Rick Holliday
Anne Holtzclaw
Shawn Holtzclaw
Carole Hooks
Larry Hooks
Joe Houston
Lori Houston
Christopher Ingraham
Kimberly Ingraham
Lynn Jackson
Tom Jackson
Carolynn James

Holly James
Jesse James
Patti James
Renee James
Scott James
Carrie Johnson
Heidi Johnson
Jill Johnson
Kory Johnson
Norma Johnson
Susan Johnston
William Johnston
Debbie Joiner
Hannah Joiner
Jimmy Joiner
LaShelle Joiner
Reggie Joiner
Reggie Paul Joiner
Bill Jones
Caitlin Jones
Carla Jones
David Jones
Helen Jones
Holly Jones
Jared Jones
Jean Jones
Leslie Jones
Natalie Jones
Ronald "Lane" Jones
Shelton Jones
Traci Jones
Mark Jordan
Michelle Jordan
Lauren Karasek
Cathy Kelley
Jennifer Kelley
Robert Kelley
Lynne Kelly
Debbie Kennedy
Tammy Kennedy
Bill Kidd
Erika Kidd

Gloria Kim
Debbie Knight
Don Knight
James Knight
Penny Knight
Curtis Knorr
Nancy Knorr
Camille Lacy
Mary Ann Lacy
Melanie Lacy
Rusty Lacy
Karen Lauder
Bill Laux
Bryan LaVigne
Cheryal "Sherry"
    LaVigne
Adam Lawsky
Jenny Lawsky
Joseph Lawsky
Patrick Lechtenbergert
Connie LeHeup
Herb Lewis
Jodi Lewis
Joseph "Jody" Lewis
Kenton Lietzau
Amanda Lightfoot
Della Lightfoot
Erin Lightfoot
Gail Lightfoot
Gale Lightfoot
Gary Lightfoot
Lauren Lightfoot
Leigh Lightfoot
Rebecca Lightfoot
Jerry Lindaman
Katherine Lindaman
Mitchell Linnabary
Stephanie Linnabary
Doug Liptak
Laura Liptak
Barry Luff
Donna Luff

David Lundy
Donald Lundy
Douglas Lundy
Linda Ann Lundy
Peggy Lundy
Robert Lynch
Wendy Lynch
Carolyn Lyon
Jim Lyon
Mary Lyon
Gayle Mahon
Kevin Mahon
Leo Mallard
Lori Mallard
Becky Martin
Paul Martin
Jeff Mason
Karen Mason
Laura Mason
Thomas Mason
Catherine "Ashley"
    Mast
David Mast
Michael Masters
Melinda Mayton
Andrea McArthur
Dana McArthur
Jane McCall
Marcia McClure
Robb McClure
Caroline McCravy
Bob McDonald
Sabrina McDonald
Sheri McHugh
Jim McKeithen
Donna McMurry
Tom McMurry
Casandra McPeters
Marla McVinnie
Chris McWilliams
Jacqueline
    McWilliams

James "Thomas" McWilliams
Jeff McWilliams
Lee Ann Meadows
Donna Mechler
Elizabeth Mechler
Paul Mechler
Paul Mergenhagen
Kelly Merritt
Scott Merritt
Lynne Middleton
Mark Middleton
Beverly Miller
Charles Miller
Heather Miller
Sharlene Miller
Lori Milliman
Janet Milton
Renita Morgan
Mary Ann Nay
Robert Nay
Barbara "Babs" Neidlinger
Beth Neidlinger
Darryl Neidlinger
William Neidlinger
Cheryl Nelson
Eric Nelson
David Newcomb
Amanda Newton
Cindy Newton
Mark Newton
Jennifer Nichols
John "Pat" O'Quinn
Leah O'Quinn
Brian Odom
Howard Odom
Karen Odom
Sharon Odom
Susan Odom
T.C. Ong
Benjamin Ortlip

Lisa Ortlip
Harold Osmon
Kathleen Osmon
Stephen Ostrander
Mike Overstreet
Robert Pardee
Cynthia Parker
Paula Parker
Terry Parker
Susan Parris
Nancy Pashman
Rick Pashman
Rachel Payne
Steve Payne
Dario Perla
Ginger Peterson
Paul Peterson
Andrea Petkau
Gerald Petkau
Christy Pierce
Jim Pierce
Andrew Pinckney
Fred Pinckney
Rebecca Pinckney
Steven Pinckney
Jan Piner
Mark Pinson
Jan Pix
Montague "Monte" Pix
Kim Poe
William "Monty" Poe
Cathy Powel
Geoff Powel
Jenny Powell
Joyce Powell
Jim Power
Adam Pozek
Julie Pozek
Steven Prescott
Paul Preston
James Price

Judi Quigley
Pat Quigley
Jacqueline Quinn
Thomas Quinn
Gina Ragsdale
Kevin Ragsdale
Christy Rahn
Robbie Rahn
Raymond Ramirez
Brian Ray
Chelsea Recicar
Deborah Reed
Jim Reinoehl
Louise Reinoehl
Colleen Reiter
Charlie Renfroe
Patty Renfroe
Dean Rice
Sharon Rice
Stefanie Roberts
Beth Ann Robinson
Cliff Robinson
Jacob Robinson
James Robinson
Leslie Robinson
Jan Rock
Robin "Rob" Rodgers
Katherine Roe
Julie Roller
Cyndi Rollins
J. "Kevin" Ross
Jaqueline Ross
Kathy Ross
Paul Ryden
Vicky Ryden
Nina Samples
Kimberly Scales
Vincent Scales
Alexander Schroer
Bethany Schroer
David Schroer
Debbie Schroer

Katy Schroer
Louis "Steve" Schroer
Rebekah Schroer
Tom Schroth
Al Scott
Dennis Scott
Elaine Scott
Jackie Scott
James Scott
Lois Scott
Beth Shaffner
Dick Shaffner
Stacey Sharpe
Wanda Sheets
Elizabeth Sherrill
Kristen Shipley
Randy Shipman
Christie Shipton
Andrea Shupert
Emily Shupert
Lauren Shupert
Richard Shupert
Liz Simpson
Nace Simpson
Don Simril
Gail Simril
Donald Smith
Harriett Smith
Jane Smith
Merrit Smith
Ronald "Rick" Smith
Troy Smurawa
Sheila Sommavilla
Elizabeth Spence
Randy Spence
Angela Spivey
Duane Spriggs
Barry St. Clair
Carol St. Clair
Jonathan "Jay" St.
    Clair
Katie St. Clair

Jill Stafford
Bobbi Jo Stanfill
Steven Stanfill
Charles "Andy"
    Stanley
Sandra Stanley
Kayron Stevens
Aaron Stoddard
Anne Stoddard
David Stoddard
Sarah Stoddard
Scott Storey
Margaret "Margo"
    Strasinger
Abbie Strickland
Bob Strickland
Gayle Strickland
Robert Strickland
Brent Stromwall
LeAnne Stromwall
Kim Strube
Ted Strube
Marcia Stuber
Paul Stuber
Jackie Stull
Jacob Stull
James Stull
John Stull
Katie Sulpy
Margie Sulpy
Megan Sulpy
Steven Sulpy
Aimee Suter
Joe Swafford
Laura Lynn Swafford
Melissa Swann
Lawrence Swicegood
Patricia Swicegood
Mary "Libby"
    Tappan
Jim Tart
Maria Tart

Phyllis Tatgenhorst
Richard Tatgenhorst
Robert Taylor
Carolyn Teeter
Jody Teeter
Karen Thomas
Keith Thomas
Amy Todd
Russell Todd
Elizabeth "Libby"
    Trest
Felicia Tucker
Brenda Tuminello
John Tuminello
J. "Tim" Turner
Elizabeth Underwood
James Underwood
James "Jim"
    Underwood
Kathryn Underwood
Kay Underwood
Walter Upton
Cara Van Norden
Carol Vann
Bill Vescovo
Kim Vescovo
Kathryn Vieh
John Vogt
Nancy Vogt
Jane Waddel
Gordon Wadsworth
Janet Wadsworth
Barbara Wagner
Scott Walker
Susan Walker
Lauren Walters
Mike Walters
Regina Walters
Trent Walters
Cheryl Watford
Mike Watford
Desiree Watkins

Gretchen Weigele
Daniel Wiggins
Sheila Wiggins
Lindsey Wilkins
Robert Wilkins
Sarah Wilkins
Camilla Williams
David "Michael"
    Williams
John Williams
James Williamson
Wendi Williamson
Bill Willits
Terry Willits

Stephen Wise
Tutu Wise
Bryana Witt
Janice Witt
Lindsay Witt
Chris Wooten
Stanley Word
Angela Wright
Diane Wright
Beverly Wylie
Jerry Wylie
James "Walker"
    Yarbrough
Luann Yarbrough

Joe Yeager
Pam Yeager
Debbie Yoshimura
Tracy "Ty" Yoshimura
Jason Young
Jenny Young
Julie Young
Ken Young
Brock Zauderer
James Zauderer
Karen Zauderer
Christian Ziegler

NOTES

Introduction

1. The Malcolm Baldrige National Quality Award recognizes U.S. organizations in the business, health care, education, and nonprofit sectors for performance excellence.

Chapter 1: Not All That Deep

2. Andy Stanley, *Louder Than Words* (Portland, Ore.: Multnomah, 2004).

Chapter 2: Family Matters

3. Gene Edwards, *The Tale of Three Kings* (Carol Stream, Ill.: Tyndale, 1992).

Section 2: Introduction

4. You probably wouldn't return to or refer a doctor who, after examining you, informed you that God made you sick. You want a doctor who can diagnose the *natural* cause of your illness and prescribe a remedy. We expect that even of Christian doctors.

Chapter 3: Words Matter

5. Matthew 16:13; Mark 8:27; Luke 9:18.
6. Matthew 16:16.
7. Matthew 16:17–18 NIV 1984, emphasis added.
8. Walter Bauer, *A Greek-English Lexicon of the New Testament and Other Early Christian Literature*, 2nd ed. (Chicago: University of Chicago Press, 1957, 1979), 240–241.
9. *www.aotfb.com/ekklesia/church.html*

10. Bruce L. Shelley, *Church History in Plain Language*, updated 2nd ed. (Dallas: Word Publishing, 1995), 268.
11. Geoffrey W. Bromiley, *The International Standard Bible Encyclopedia, Revised,* vol. 2 (Grand Rapids: Wm. B. Eerdmans, 1988, 2002), 85.

Chapter 4: Just As I Ain't
12. 1 Corinthians 6:9–11.
13. Charlotte Elliott, "Just As I Am," 1835.
14. See John 8:10–11.
15. John 5:3.
16. Matthew 21:23–27.

Chapter 5: Defying Gravity
17. Acts 11:26.
18. Acts 15:5.
19. Acts 15:9–10.
20. Acts 15:11, emphasis added.
21. Go to *www.vimeo.com/northpointmedia* to see a sample of our baptism videos along with other Sunday morning video samples.
22. See Appendix B for a description of our Starting Point ministry.
23. Gungor, "Beautiful Things." Copyright © 2009 *worshiptogether.com* Songs (ASCAP) (adm. at *EMICMGPublishing.com*). All rights reserved. Used by permission.

Chapter 6: My Big Discovery
24. In Matthew 8, Jesus is *amazed* at the faith of the Roman centurion. Matthew writes, "When Jesus heard this, he was *amazed* and said to those following him, 'I tell you the truth, I have not found anyone in Israel with such great faith'" (v. 11, emphasis added). In Mark 6, Jesus is *amazed* at his hometown's lack of faith (v. 6).
25. I created a message series by this title and I preached through all five catalysts. To view the messages free online, go to *http://www.fivethingsgoduses.com*.

Chapter 7: Playing My Part
26. Μακάριος can be translated "favored," "blessed," "fortunate," "happy." Walter Bauer, *A Greek-English Lexicon of the New Testament and Other Early Christian Literature*, 2nd ed. (Chicago: University of Chicago Press, 1957, 1979), 486.
27. Matthew 6:5–13.
28. Matthew 6:1–18.
28. John 6:6.

Chapter 8: From Out of Nowhere

30. Andy Stanley and Bill Willits, *Creating Community: Five Keys to Building a Small Group Culture* (Portland, Ore.: Multnomah, 2004).
31. Walter Isaacson, *Steve Jobs* (New York: Simon and Schuster, 2011), 15.
32. James 1:17.
33. 1 Corinthians 10:26.
34. Romans 8:28.
35. Ecclesiastes 4:10.
36. Matthew 11:3.
37. Matthew 11:4–5.
38. Matthew 11:6.
39. Hallie weighed four pounds, fifteen ounces at birth and was able to leave the hospital, but sadly died five days later in her mother's arms.

Chapter 9: Creating Irresistible Environments

40. The exception would be if you are new to your current post and are waiting to earn the right to make changes.
41. The last sentence is quoted from the chorus of "The River" by Garth Brooks.
42. Matthew 7:28–29.
43. John 8:32.
44. Romans 12:2.
45. James 2:26.
46. James 2:20.
47. Matthew 7:24, emphasis added.
48. Andy Stanley, Stuart Hall, and Louie Giglio, *The Seven Checkpoints for Student Leaders* (Brentwood, Tenn.: Howard Books, rev. ed., 2011).
49. *www.northpoint.org/theopraxis*
50. *www.bibletraining.com*

Chapter 10: Rules of Engagement

51. Andy Stanley, Lane Jones, and Reggie Joiner, *The Seven Practices of Effective Ministry* (Portland, Ore.: Multnomah, 2004).
52. Chip and Dan Heath, *Made to Stick* (New York: Random House, 2007).
53. 1 Corinthians 1:23–24.

Chapter 11: Double-Barrel Preaching

54. Andy Stanley, *Communicating for a Change: Seven Keys to Irresistible Communication* (Portland, Ore.: Multnomah Books, lst ed., 2006).
55. 2 Timothy 3:16.

Chapter 12: Coming to Blows with the Status Quo

56. James M. Kouzes and Barry Z. Posner, *The Leadership Challenge* (San Francisco: Jossey-Bass, 4th ed., 2008), 48.

57. In my book *Making Vision Stick* (Grand Rapids: Zondervan, 2007), I give a detailed description of the critical components of effective vision casting.

Chapter 13: Mission and Model

58. Seth Godin, *The Dip* (New York: Portfolio, 2007), 51.

59. Author paraphrase of Mark 2:27.

60. Leviticus 19:18.

61. Jim Collins, *How the Mighty Fall* (Boulder, Colo.: Jim Collins, 2009), 36.

62. Richard J. Harrington and Anthony K. Tjan, "Transforming Strategy One Customer at a Time," *Harvard Business Review*, March 2008.

Chapter 14: Led to Lead

63. Προϊστάμεος, from προϊστημι, means "rule, direct, be at the head (of)," in other words, to exercise a position of leadership. Walter Bauer, *A Greek-English Lexicon of the New Testament and Other Early Christian Literature*, 2nd ed. (Chicago: University of Chicago Press, 1957, 1979), 707.

64. Luke 9:59.

65. Luke 9:60.

66. Luke 9:61.

67. Luke 9:62.

68. I borrowed and contextualized this question from Andy Grove. His version is, "If we got kicked out and the board brought in a new CEO, what do you think he would he do?" Then he asked, "Why shouldn't you and I walk out the door, come back, and do it ourselves?" See Andrew S. Grove, *Only the Paranoid Survive* (New York: Crown Business, paperback ed., 1999), 89.

69. Acts 2.

70. Acts 15:19.

Other Books by Andy Stanley

Creating Community

Communicating for a Change

Making Vision Stick

Seven Checkpoints

Seven Practices of Effective Ministry

Share Your Thoughts

With the Author: Your comments will be forwarded to the author when you send them to *zauthor@zondervan.com*.

With Zondervan: Submit your review of this book by writing to *zreview@zondervan.com*.

Free Online Resources at

www.zondervan.com

Zondervan AuthorTracker: Be notified whenever your favorite authors publish new books, go on tour, or post an update about what's happening in their lives at www.zondervan.com/authortracker.

Daily Bible Verses and Devotions: Enrich your life with daily Bible verses or devotions that help you start every morning focused on God. Visit www.zondervan.com/newsletters.

Free Email Publications: Sign up for newsletters on Christian living, academic resources, church ministry, fiction, children's resources, and more. Visit www.zondervan.com/newsletters.

Zondervan Bible Search: Find and compare Bible passages in a variety of translations at www.zondervanbiblesearch.com.

Other Benefits: Register to receive online benefits like coupons and special offers, or to participate in research.

ZONDERVAN®